Severe Domestic Squalor

Severe Domestic Squalor

John Snowdon

Clinical Professor in the Discipline of Psychiatry, Sydney Medical School, and Old Age Psychiatrist for Sydney Local Health District, Sydney, Australia.

Graeme Halliday

Senior Specialist in Psychiatry, Sydney Local Health District, Sydney, Australia.

Sube Banerjee

Professor of Mental Health and Ageing, Section of Mental Health and Ageing, Health Service and Population Research Department, The Institute of Psychiatry, King's College London, UK.

CAMBRIDGE
UNIVERSITY PRESS

CAMBRIDGE UNIVERSITY PRESS
Cambridge, New York, Melbourne, Madrid, Cape Town,
Singapore, São Paulo, Delhi, Mexico City

Cambridge University Press
The Edinburgh Building, Cambridge CB2 8RU, UK

Published in the United States of America by Cambridge University Press, New York

www.cambridge.org
Information on this title: www.cambridge.org/9781107012721

First published 2012

Printed and bound in the United Kingdom by the MPG Books Group

A catalogue record for this publication is available from the British Library

Library of Congress Cataloguing in Publication data

Severe domestic squalor / [edited by] John Snowdon, Graeme Halliday, Sube Banerjee.
pages cm
Includes bibliographical references and index.
ISBN 978-1-107-01272-1
1. Obsessi ... don, John. II. Halliday, Graeme. III. Banerjee, Sube.
RC533.S
616.85'2
2012014616

ISBN 978-

Cambridge ... bility for the persistence or
accuracy o ... internet websites referred to
in this pub ... that any content on such
websites is, ... priate.

Every effort ... book to provide accurate and up-to-date information which is in ... nd practice at the time of publication. Although case histories are drawn from actual cases, every effort has been made to disguise the identities of the individuals involved. Nevertheless, the authors, editors and publishers can make no warranties that the information contained herein is totally free from error, not least because clinical standards are constantly changing through research and regulation. The authors, editors and publishers therefore disclaim all liability for direct or consequential damages resulting from the use of material contained in this book. Readers are strongly advised to pay careful attention to information provided by the manufacturer of any drugs or equipment that they plan to use.

Contents

Contributors

Charles Chan
Registrar and Research Assistant, Concord Hospital and the University of Sydney, Concord Hospital, Sydney, Australia.

David Mataix-Cols
Professor of Clinical Psychobiology, Departments of Psychosis Studies and Psychology, King's College and the Institute of Psychiatry, London, England.

Christopher Ryan
Consultation-Liaison Psychiatrist, Westmead Hospital; and in the Discipline of Psychiatry and the Centre for Values, Ethics and the Law in Medicine, University of Sydney, Sydney, Australia.

Michele Slatter
Adjunct Associate Professor at CHURP, the Centre for Housing, Urban and Regional Planning at the University of Adelaide, Adelaide, South Australia.

Foreword

Some memories are stronger than others. For example, ask a colleague to remember a patient with dementia or depression. They will think for a moment and describe someone. But ask a colleague to remember visiting a patient who lived in squalor and notice their facial expression and how vividly they recall the experience. They remember not only the person but the sights and smells. These are the most memorable people we see.

Snowdon, Halliday and Banerjee have given us an exceptionally thoughtful and well researched book on domestic squalor. They have reasoned through every element starting with the term squalor itself, and explain how hoarding and self-neglect, while related to squalor, are different. Their extensive experience is evident as they discuss intervention techniques and the difficulties in not only getting the individual to accept assistance, but coordinating efforts among the multiple agencies that typically become involved. The chapters on animal hoarding, legal aspects of squalor (with the wonderful title 'Law and mess'), and the ethics of intervening are the most useful I have seen on these infrequently addressed topics.

The authors have admirably achieved their stated goal of bringing together all of the major elements in this conundrum. They are persuasive in their arguments about why this is an important topic and where research needs to go. But after reading the book I found that my thoughts turned to a different question. Why do geriatric psychiatrists choose to make this a serious focus of attention?

It is easy to understand why newspapers and television are interested in squalor – the stories are sensational and grab one's attention. But why do we geriatric psychiatrists choose to involve ourselves with these deplorable situations where success is such a relative term? Surely we have all we can handle with improving the recognition and treatment of dementia, and improving outcomes in late life depression. In thinking about the question, I came up with two reasons.

First, I think geriatric psychiatrists tend to find people more interesting than diseases. We are less likely to dwell on the deplorable conditions than to wonder who would live this way and why. Our curiosity leads us to try and determine if there are characteristics they share or diagnoses that predispose. We wonder about their stories and our interest about them as individuals trumps the discomfort we experience in seeing how they live.

Second, I think we are more energised by cognitive than technological problem solving. We have the human response of revulsion to severe domestic squalor but this is quickly set aside in favour of wanting to relieve the miserable conditions in front of our eyes. We are not satisfied just to understand, we want to make things better. And we particularly love to find solutions that rely more on our own cognitive processes than the results of a scan. Digesting lots of information, then finding precisely the one or two places where our efforts can best be directed to get a good result, gives us a feeling of satisfaction.

To reflect just a bit, these two reasons – qualities in fact – are what I liked and admired about geriatric psychiatrists as I was considering what path to take after finishing my training. Reading this book not only taught me about domestic squalor, it reminded me why I went into this field.

Burton V. Reifler, MD, MPH
Kate Mills Snider Professor of Geriatric Psychiatry
Wake Forest School of Medicine

Preface

Why in the world would one wish to publish a book on squalor? Who could possibly be interested and why would they be moved to read about such a subject? As our reader you may be better able to answer these questions than we are as authors. As authors this is an area that fascinates us. Squalor transcends definition and categorisation. As doctors, we came to squalor through those living in domestic squalor where risks were high and the question of whether the squalor was a function of treatable mental disorder was paramount. But the minute you start looking, you start realising that the world is full of squalor. Media of all types – print, radio, television and the internet – are full of the stories of those that live in severe domestic squalor. It seems that we are fascinated by squalor. Yet we know so little about it. This book seeks to change that, bringing together the evidence base on severe domestic squalor and making it available to the lay reader, the researcher and the health or social care practitioner presented with a human conundrum based on squalor.

To do this we will draw on scientific papers in medical and other journals to provide some of the relevant information, and reports and guidelines give some ideas on how best to intervene. We know of three books that describe psychological approaches to dealing with hoarding and clutter, but these give little guidance about intervention strategies other than on techniques for 'de-cluttering' and by recommending cognitive re-structuring. We hope that this book will be of positive help in dealing with the issues raised as a whole.

Considerable attention is currently being given to the concept of 'hoarding disorder' and how to deal with it, and there are proposals to make it into a formal psychiatric disorder by including this term in the newest version of the American Psychiatric Association's *Diagnostic and Statistical Manual (DSM)*, DSM-5. The DSM is a comprehensive list of all mental disorders and the criteria that need to be met to make a particular diagnosis. It forms the basis for what is and what is not reimbursed by US health maintenance organisations.

We have written this book for people who care about or care for individuals who, for whatever reason, have been unable to properly look after their dwellings. These living environments may appear very disorganised. We have attempted to examine some of the reasons why some people live in conditions so unclean that most fellow citizens would consider them unacceptable. Why do they live like this?

Our belief is that how best to intervene depends to a large part on the answer to this fundamental question.

Our book is intended to provide ideas and understanding to the general public and to service providers around the world, working in agencies that have to work out how to intervene in cases of squalor. These include community health staff, mental health professionals, doctors, environmental health staff in municipal council offices, community service providers (for example, home care agencies), government housing inspectors, drug and alcohol counsellors, non-governmental agencies that aim to counter homelessness and neglect, animal welfare agencies, guardianship and protective offices, police, fire officers, legal services, heavy cleaning services – and others. Regulations, laws and job titles may differ between countries but the work that needs to be done is likely to be similar. The book is also designed to promote discussion, debate and further enquiry. This is one of those areas where what we don't know outweighs what we do know.

We would not have been able to even start to address these issues without the help of those who contributed special chapters to this book. We are profoundly in debt to Charles Chan, David Mataix-Cols, Christopher Ryan and Michele Slatter. The detailed consideration of the complex specialist themes of animals, hoarding, ethics and law are responsible for much of the value of this book. We are very grateful for the creative and constructive approaches they all took in contributing to this book.

Some may criticise us for perpetuating the use of 'squalor' as a term to describe the living conditions under discussion here. We accept that the word is strong, confronting and value laden, and we have considered alternatives. However, there is no other word available that would convey our messages adequately to the practitioners, politicians and policy makers who could help ensure action to deal with the problems. At the heart of all severe domestic squalor is the human story that has led to the situation evolving. The fundamental aim must be to assess and meet these human needs where at all possible. What is needed is understanding, resources, coordination and a determination to help people unable sufficiently to help themselves.

We include a colour plate section between pages 150 and 151. The plates show photographs of various squalor situations to illustrate some of the problems that are discussed throughout the book.

John Snowdon
Graeme Halliday
Sube Banerjee

1

Definition and description of severe domestic squalor

The way we live

Some people live in very messy dwellings. But a relatively small percentage of the world's population lives in conditions that nearly everyone in their local community, and in their cultural group, would consider unacceptable. One of the first questions we are posed with is 'whose squalor is it anyway?' These are people and circumstances that the community can start to feel concern about. The worry may be for the health and safety of the neighbour who lives in exceedingly unclean, odorous and physically precarious domestic circumstances. Other observers might find such conditions to be repulsive, offensive and intolerable, but might be thinking primarily about the effects on themselves and the majority of the community, rather than of the people residing in those conditions.

The way individuals live, and the habits and cultural expectations they acquire, vary between population groups and over time. They differ between people of different backgrounds, upbringing, education, culture and beliefs. Factors differentiating countries and regions, be they rich or poor, hot or cold, urban or rural, mountainous or flat, all may affect living habits. How people live their lives is determined partly by personality and perceptions, but also by other characteristics and factors. The views of men and women, old and young, hunters and gatherers, may diverge. What is acceptable to one person may not be acceptable to another. What is acceptable to a university student may not be acceptable to their parents. On such subjects there will be a range of opinions, even among people of similar background. The 'average' view may well differ between communities.

Accumulation of dirt, refuse, degraded material and vermin can result in living conditions within a dwelling being unhealthy, unsafe and potentially harmful. If the filth and degradation are so foul that they are likely to have unacceptably deleterious effects on the people living there or nearby, we believe 'severe domestic squalor' is an appropriate descriptive term. The term does not describe the people; it refers to the living conditions.

Before we attempt to justify our use of the word 'squalor', we might consider a news item in the *British Medical Journal*: 'Half of the world lives in "medieval" squalor' (Hope, 1997). The headline was prompted by a 1997 report from the United Nations Children's Fund, which stated that half the world's population has no access to hygienic sanitation and would not progress beyond 'medieval' living conditions until this basic need is met. It stated that almost three billion people could not (in 1997) safely dispose of their bodily waste, thus resulting in spread of disease that was paralysing whole communities. The report blamed a lack of political will in countries facing this debilitation, plus a need to repay foreign debt, with a resultant decrease in investment in improving sanitation. There was reference to one country where annual spending per capita on water and sewerage had fallen from £27.78 to £2.47 in a six-year period.

Even now, in spite of advances in sanitation, there are places where horrifying squalor (defined by the Oxford Dictionary as 'a state of being extremely dirty and unpleasant, especially as a result of poverty or neglect') can be observed. Naming them might help provoke political action to improve living conditions, but might also be considered as insulting to those who live there. Even if aware of squalor in their midst, some inhabitants of those countries might ask why we single them out for disparaging comment. However, the squalor inherent in the megacities even of one of the rapidly developing BRIC economies was communicated around the world in the film *Slumdog Millionaire*. The film showed rich people living in pleasant and healthy surroundings, and destitute fellow-countrymen living in unhygienic, unhealthy, dispiriting conditions. The film asked what is being done about it.

We have observed squalor around the world, in developed as well as developing nations, the extent varying within and between countries. One of us, while travelling to a city along a major highway, saw filth in open drains, and truck-high banks of garbage (discarded clothing, water bottles, packaging and disposable material of all kinds) along the sides of the road for many kilometres. A home visit in the city with an old age psychiatry team to see a client with mild dementia necessitated a walk along rubbish-strewn roads, across streams and rivers that were blocked by garbage. There was a smell, of course. The floors of the client's house were clean but there were flies everywhere: they had flown in from the garbage heaps.

How can it be? What had those responsible for the administration of that city and care of that highway done about the squalor? Ten years previously, a government report relating to waste management in that province read 'The uncontrolled disposal of liquid waste into open gutters, open spaces, along roads, etc., poses serious health hazards. Bodies of stagnant water produce bad odours.' Successive governments since then had not been able to gain control of relevant systems. Those with power, money and influence had failed to effect a change. Was it an issue of priority of resource? Was it corruption or incompetence? Were the garbage workers being paid enough? More garbage was being thrown on the streets than was being collected by them. Why had the cycle not been reversed?

The squalor observed in this present century is not new. Indeed, it was because of neglectful attitudes of nineteenth century politicians and administrators that Charles Dickens, Balzac and others drew sharp and disturbing word pictures to provoke the consciences of their readers. Dickens, in *Oliver Twist* wrote of:

> rooms so small, so filthy, so confined, that the air would seem too tainted even for the dirt and squalor which they shelter . . . and dirt-besmeared walls and decaying foundations, every repulsive lineament of poverty, every loathsome indication of filth, rot and garbage: all these ornament the banks of Folly Ditch.

At a similar time, in 88-year-old Sydney, a Sewage and Health Board report described visits to crowded and unwholesome localities:

> Peering down narrow passageways opening off the busy thoroughfares of the City's business centre, committeemen found tenement blocks squeezed among crazily patterned canyons formed by the blank walls and paling fences of surrounding buildings, where the trapped air was fouled by the stench from uncollected house rubbish and accumulations of slops, and the sewage from defective closets and drains. Inside such dwellings the heat seemed intolerable, the rooms small and wretchedly furnished, the windows insufficient in number and so inadequately designed as to open only partially, if at all. In many a backyard, an out-of-repair and evilly smelling closet stood only feet away from living quarters. (Mayne, 1982)

Something was done about the slums of London. On the whole, English streets are now clean. Slums have been cleared away in Sydney, too. In both cities, there are people who discard litter carelessly – and one can wonder if they would do the same in their own homes and gardens; they may do and so may be at risk of living in squalor – but city care has improved since the 1870s. Governments enacted laws and gazetted regulations to improve hygiene and living conditions. They have ordered appropriate protection for those unable to look after themselves. Major advances in health care and technology have reduced much of the unpleasantness that was described in those nineteenth century novels and reports. But standards of care and provision vary, and that is part of the reason why squalor is much more pervasive in some jurisdictions than others. Another reason is that governments and administrators vary in their ability and determination to provide help, support and care for those who do not have the physical resources or capability to look after themselves properly.

Much of the above discussion relates to squalor outside dwellings, in public places and on streets. We believe there will be almost universal agreement that the word 'squalor' is meaningful and appropriate in describing conditions such as those portrayed in *Slumdog Millionaire*. Those in a position to act and get rid of the squalor should be strongly and persistently criticised if they fail to do so. Using the word 'mess' does not have the same impact. Getting messy can be fun. Living in

Box 1.1 Observations on squalor.

(1) Horrific squalor can be seen in open areas of cities across the world.
(2) This squalor has been recognised and has been deemed unacceptable by responsible people within those populations and by outsiders, but it is still there. Attempts at action have failed.
(3) Equivalent squalor can been seen in dwellings across the world.
(4) This squalor has been drawn to the attention of authorities and services, and action has been taken in many cases.
(5) Attempts to deal with this squalor have commonly proved unsuccessful and ineffective.
(6) There is good reason for the community and administrators to seek improved ways of intervening in such cases, as part of their duty of care to individuals and their communities.
(7) Use of the word 'squalor' is confronting, and some critics regard it as a pejorative and degrading term. We believe that it is the right word to use in describing living conditions, not people, and that the strength of the word is consonant with the strength of response needed.

squalor is not enjoyed, even if the occupants commonly seem not to recognise the unpleasantness.

Similarly, we contend that 'squalor' is the most appropriate word to use if we want to describe the sort of unclean living conditions that, across countries and cultures, are regarded as unacceptable (Box 1.1). If the dirt and filth and (in many cases) clutter are not absolutely unacceptable, maybe we might call it 'mess' or 'mild squalor' or even 'disorganised living'. Thresholds for what is acceptable vary, but if the condition of a particular dwelling is putting people at significant risk, then there is a need for action to deal with it. This state of uncleanliness is what we propose to call 'severe domestic squalor'.

In cases of severe squalor, caring and responsible members of a community will generally feel impelled to make sure that something is done. In milder cases, we, as good neighbours or even as people who just happen to come across someone who seems to need some help or support, may, as responsible individuals, want to take some action. The least we would do is ensure that appropriate persons are aware of the need for monitoring.

A central focus of this book will be a consideration of how and when to intervene in cases of severe domestic squalor – squalor in the home as opposed to squalor in the streets and open places. To do this we need to try to understand what factors result in a person living in squalor. We will describe varying situations of squalor. We will start with descriptions to illustrate what we recognise as severe domestic squalor.

Descriptions of severe domestic squalor

The following examples will illustrate what is meant by 'severe domestic squalor':

- Cooney and Hamid (1995) referred to 'a dilapidated, filthy house. The home is cluttered with rubbish and infested with vermin. Excrement and decomposing food are strewn around the floors, and the stench emanating is unbearable to all but the occupant, who is blissfully unconcerned by the situation.'
- An Australian local newspaper (name and date withheld in order to preserve anonymity – though the paper itself published the name of the woman concerned) wrote: 'It could take up to 6 months for [named] Council to rid a [suburb name] apartment of rats, mice and cockroaches while it awaits a court order... The council subsequently called in cleaners but suspended work at the unit, citing escalating costs (almost $17,000) and saying work had reached the stage where baiting, fumigation, replacement, renovation and painting, rather than cleaning, was needed... A council official said Mrs [name] had repeatedly refused to leave... and said it was up to [named] aged care assessment team to persuade [her] to leave temporarily... The council issued a plea to the [named] aged care assessment team to act, after cleaners threatened to walk off the job because Mrs [name]'s health had reached "crisis" stage.'

The problems posed by this case, and the frustrations of neighbours in the block of units, were shown in a national television programme. The appalling [our word] state of the unit, with a mish-mash of rubbish, discarded plastic bottles, rotting food and attendant vermin in all rooms (but especially the kitchen) must surely have aroused feelings of nausea in many of the watching millions, even without being able to smell it. The television segment showed forensic cleaners, wearing face-masks, and the lady herself. The journalist asked her how long it had been like this and she said 'Three days'. Yet the aged care assessment team reportedly declared that action could not be taken under the Mental Health Act to have her conveyed to hospital to assess whether treatment and intervention were thought to be needed. The team did not consider that she had a mental disorder as defined by the Act.

This account not only demonstrates that failure to keep domestic environments reasonably clean and clear of rubbish leads to hazards and unpleasantness for the community, and risks to occupants, but also makes clear the failure, in this case, of community and caring services to take appropriate and coordinated action within a reasonable time. Such ineffective intervention is common across continents. We know of numerous situations where there has been a lack of coordinated response to referral of such cases, varying in severity but all meriting support, help or intervention.

- A national tabloid newspaper commented on four children watching television in a 'government-owned house amid the rancid smell of dog faeces and rotting food... Urine and faeces lay on the shower floor... and a pot roast in the oven was full of mould and decay'.

- A team of forensic cleaning professionals (Clean Queens) talked of a place they had been asked to clean: 'The smell on entering the flat is over-powering. There's cat mess in trays on the floor and stains on the mattress, which looks like it hasn't seen a sheet in months. The living room is crammed with random objects... and mouldy coffee cups. Clothes cover the bedroom floor and spill from the disused washing machine.' But the Clean Queens noted that it was 'actually not too bad. With a lot of squalors, you've got cockroaches, fleas, mites and worse.'
- Fry (2000) mentioned two occupants of an unremarkable house in suburbia. Whenever they 'had no further use for what they were holding in their hands, they dropped it on the floor. There was no space in any room in the house where one could put a foot on the floor without encountering some flotsam – discarded clothing, food scraps, cartons, bottles, magazines, newspapers.'
- Cole *et al.* (1992) visited an upstairs flat that was uncarpeted and dirty, with sparse, shoddy furnishings. Clothes and manuscripts were strewn about, together with empty sherry bottles. The kitchen contained little food, but a pile of empty tins and dirty pans in the sink. There was human and feline excrement throughout the flat. In the bedroom were found several trays of cat litter and three very well-kempt cats.'
- Fry (2000) also described a house where the approach to two arm-chairs was 'via a narrow corridor between compacted rubbish which was greater than knee-high at the sides of the corridor and consisted mainly of paper, food scraps, cartons and empty bottles. The corridor forked before the final approach to the arm-chairs... The electricity was disconnected. The other rooms in the house were similarly full of rubbish.'
- French clinicians (Esposito *et al.*, 2003) described the home of two siblings: 'At the entrance, the flat was grossly dirty and untidy, with an unbearable stench. Rubbish had been hoarded to the extent that most of their living space was taken up with full cardboard boxes, bins and heaps of magazines. Miss and Mr M denied the precariousness and the insanitariness of their living conditions and vehemently refused any assistance.'
- A report from a Canadian 'Task Force on Senile Squalor' (Pelletier and Pollett, 2000) described an apartment where 'the living area had a pathway from the hallway to the single bed between boxes and clothes piled to the ceiling... The kitchen counter and floor were covered with appliances, food cans, used coffee filters, dirty dishes and pipe smoking paraphernalia. The refrigerator was stuffed with small white plastic bags. There was a pile of crushed food cans behind the stove piled from the floor to the top of the stove. The bathroom had an assortment of gallon bottles of chemicals. The fixtures and floor were coated with filth. The apartment had that distinctive odour of filth that was noticeable in the apartment building hallway.'
- Another newspaper described 'an overgrown backyard full of cardboard boxes, old tyres and discarded furniture. Cats perch on every surface; kittens roll about among the rusted drums and long grass. Inside, behind closed curtains,

the rooms are piled high with papers, cups, plates and bottles. Broken toys, old clothes and shopping bags spill across kitchen benches and floor, smothering the stove and filling the sink, neither of which has been used in years. The stench of cat faeces, urine and food scraps fills the house.'

- Fish (2008), writing in the *New York Law Journal*, referred to the opinion of Judge Anthony J. Cutrona in the matter of a couple who lived in Brooklyn: 'Evidence was presented to this court that [named] suffers from Collier (sic) Brothers Syndrome, in other words, he is a hoarder. Their apartment at [address given], Brooklyn, was stacked floor to ceiling with magazines, newspapers, garbage, old mail (from the Post Office) etc. There was severe insect infestation. Moreover, there were two dogs in the apartment who were allowed to defecate and urinate in the house. In sum, the apartment was an unsanitary, unhealthy, disgusting mess. The description of the apartment was confirmed by several photographs taken by the court evaluator.' A witness had observed mice all over the apartment as they skittered over the heaps of old newspaper and other assorted trash – 'there were mounds of mouse feces everywhere and every square inch of the apartment was infested with cockroaches'.
- The *Washington Post* reported that 'Last month, in San Jose, California, police entered the home of 70-year-old [name withheld] after neighbors complained her house gave off a disgusting odor. The house was brimming with more than 25 tons of rotting garbage, infested with maggots, mice and rats. Charged with violating state laws on storing refuse, [name withheld] argued that most of the heap was books and clothing she was saving.'
- In a book describing 'true stories of tackling extreme clutter', Paxton (2011) described 'a classic, stereotypical hoarder who had clearly given up years ago. Living in a three-bedroom, double-wide trailer home in rural Idaho with too many dogs to count, she had been without electricity or running water for years. The floors were damp with brown muck. Decomposing trash was piled up to five feet high, through which narrow walkways gave limited access to each room. In the kitchen, flies swarmed the windows... All of the appliances and cabinets were smeared with unidentifiable black and orange gunk. Dust and cobwebs covered the walls and hung from the ceiling. The bathrooms were just as bad... The smell was overwhelming – a mix of urine, rotting food, and dog feces.'
- Randy Frost, in a book titled *Stuff* (Frost and Steketee, 2010, pp. 169–71), described a dwelling that was later compulsorily cleaned: 'The apartment was dark... No floor was visible, only a layer of dirty papers, food wrappers, and urine-stained rags... From the edge of the door, the massive pile of junk rose precipitously to the ceiling, like a giant sea wave. It could have been landfill: papers, boxes, shopping carts, paper bags, dirty clothing, lamps – anything that could be easily collected from the street or fished out of a dumpster. It was one solid wall of trash twenty feet deep, all the way to the back of the apartment. There must have been windows on the far wall, but they were darkened by the broken fans, boxes, and clothing covering them. Inside the condo the sweet,

pungent odor of insects and rotting food enveloped us... I could feel the cockroaches surrounding me as I stepped in. The walls were coated with their brown dung, and occasionally one dropped from the ceiling onto the piles of debris below. I walked further in to get a better look at the kitchen, or what I thought was the kitchen. It was impossible to tell, since everything was covered with bags. Food, mostly old and rotting, empty but unwashed tuna cans, and colourful coupons adorned the room. There was a path into the kitchen, though it was atop six inches of trash on the floor... All four adults living in the five-room condo had become so habituated to the squalor that they barely noticed it anymore.'

- Frost and Steketee (2010) provided descriptions of a number of other people who 'hoard', resulting in varying degrees of difficulty in cleaning, but none as severe as Frost's case described above.
- An American television series (called *Hoarders*) showed a person who had a compulsion to purchase items she did not need, and that she then felt unable to let go. Inability to clean, because of the piles of hoarded material, resulted in squalor. Her two children were removed by authorities because of the hazardous and insanitary conditions. To get the children back she was required to clean up her house and get psychological help.

We, ourselves, have visited literally hundreds of dwellings following referral of the occupants, the referrers having described them as living in very unclean conditions. A few are now presented in order to enhance awareness of the range of 'types' of squalor situation that clinicians may encounter.

- We called, with police, to see if anyone was residing at a house surrounded by an overgrown garden, where rats were seen often, and from which fleas came across to the adjoining property and bit the legs of children playing there. The occupant appeared only after police had forced a way into the house. The ceiling in the living room was falling in and all walls were filthy. The house was almost bare of furniture, and was very dusty. Piles and scatterings of newspapers were observed. A brown liquid filled the bath. (Plates 2.1, 2.2)
- We visited a professional man's house, which was in a smart suburb. The furniture was basic and greasy looking. The bed-clothing was stained, and vomit, faeces and urine were seen on the floors of the bathroom, toilet, hallways and other rooms. There was a profusion of maggots in the refrigerator. Cigarette ends, ash, dirt and empty cardboard wine casks littered the living room floor. Neither floors, walls, windows nor ceilings had been cleaned for years.
- Access was given on one occasion (but never willingly again) to a house and garden that exemplified very severe squalor. The garden was several inches deep in dried-up dog faeces. Access to sinks was restricted, and all surfaces and floors were very dirty and covered with an assortment of disorganised unusable objects, some electrical. Articles were piled up to near the ceiling in one room. Wires hung loose. The house was dilapidated. The owner's car (apart from the driving seat) was full of more items, and he drove off in it, daily, leaving large dogs to guard his home.

- There were a number of houses that we never entered because they were 'stuffed' with objects and materials. There was certainly no room for anyone to get inside and clean. One house (worth several million dollars if cleared and structurally sound again) contained a multitude of toys collected from the streets – as well as other objects. Items were piled up on top of the toilet (in an outside hut or 'dunny') and had to be removed when the occupant or his guest wanted to use it. His wardrobe was hung up on a washing line that extended the length of his garden. He slept under an umbrella by the back door. Rats were seen running along a fence. He was referred to us by his neighbour after the weight of piles of accrued possessions weighed down the fence on one side of the garden. (Plate 5.1)
- We visited the dwelling of a woman whose sleeping hollow was a depressed area on top of a pile of items, the uppermost being clothing. We could not safely climb over the pile to inspect the bathroom. Her windows (seen from outside) were very dirty, but we cannot comment on the cleanliness of her floors, surfaces or walls because they were mainly hidden from view. (Eventually this lady was evicted. She then went to live under a bridge across a park, and there accrued items, many of them toys, which formed a bank stretching about eight metres along a wall. Council clean-up trucks used to take away a large fraction of her possessions once a fortnight.)

Defining and understanding 'severe domestic squalor' and 'hoarding'

Squalor varies. Some of the people mentioned above could not get into their homes because they were packed with items. Others lived in relatively bare premises, which were still very unclean. The extent of the accumulation of rubbish and/or valued items differs between cases, and observing what and how much has been accumulated will give an indication of factors relevant to why their living conditions have been brought to attention.

The term 'syllogomania' was coined by Clark *et al.* (1975) to mean accumulation of useless rubbish (they referred to it as 'hoarding of rubbish'). 'Hoarding' refers to the purposeful collection and storage of articles or material. Rubbish has been defined as meaning refuse, waste, litter, garbage or trash (*Oxford Thesaurus*; Urdang, 1991). Do some people purposefully collect and store rubbish, refuse, garbage, trash? Accumulating it in order to have enough to make it worthwhile discarding it is understandable. It might even be purposeful to some extent, though once the pile has grown big it would seem that occupants have neglected to discard rather than purposefully collected what is in the pile. If some people purposively collect and store waste products such as excreta, then their beliefs should be questioned, and the possibility of mental disorder should be considered. We will discuss the role of mental disorder in squalor later in the book.

However, what is clear is that there is variation in views about which articles or goods should be regarded as waste and garbage, and which a legitimate focus for preservation or collection. This will depend on individual attitudes and capacity for lateral and creative thinking. For example, cardboard rolls discarded after using up the encircling sheets of toilet paper might be regarded by some as waste, but others might regard it as wasteful to throw away items that could be used in artistic endeavours or collected for recycling. Out-of-date newspapers can be seen as potentially interesting and useful – but to whom, and when? Whether 'rubbish' and 'hoarding' are appropriate words to use in particular cases will depend on observers' views concerning whether accumulated articles should have been thrown away (i.e. that they are garbage, waste or trash) and whether accumulation of such trash was indeed purposeful. Amassing of trash and garbage (discarded food wrappings and the like) in a purposeful rather than neglectful way would surely be unusual and raise questions about mental disorder.

We believe that it could be useful to reserve the term 'syllogomania' so that it refers specifically to the accumulation in a dwelling of rubbish or garbage/waste, as a result of not discarding it – the accumulation occurring whether or not the occupants perceive such rubbish as having value, or whether or not they state a reason for retaining it. We accept that sometimes the accumulation of garbage can be viewed as purposeful (and thus that it is hoarding), but usually it is not. 'Hoarding' describes the purposeful accumulation and retention of items that are perceived by occupants as having a value or purpose (and thus, usually, as not being rubbish). There will still be an overlap in usage of these two terms: one person's valued possession may be perceived by others as garbage or rubbish. For example, retention of numerous empty cocoa containers may be viewed by some as retention of rubbish, and by others as retention of potentially useful and therefore valued containers.

Visitors to the trailer home described by Paxton (see above), in which a woman was surrounded by decomposing trash piled up to five feet high, might well have had feelings of revulsion. She was living in what we would regard as severe squalor. The trash and filth had accumulated. We would surmise that this was largely passive accumulation rather than active hoarding – even if (as Paxton intimates) she also had cravings to collect and then not discard items of little obvious value. The term 'syllogomania', used in the way we have suggested above, would be an appropriate descriptor in this case.

Compulsive hoarding has been described as a mental disorder marked by an obsessive need to acquire and keep things, even if the items are worthless, hazardous or unsanitary (A & E Network, 2010). We will discuss definitions of hoarding below, but first we will propose a definition of severe domestic squalor. As we have stated before, the term describes an environment and does not refer to individuals who live in that environment (we will discuss personal (bodily) uncleanliness later). Our working definition of severe domestic squalor is presented in Box 1.2.

Box 1.2 Severe domestic squalor – a definition.

The term 'severe domestic squalor' is applied when a person's home is so unclean, messy and unhygienic that people of similar culture and background would consider extensive clearing and cleaning to be essential. Accumulated dirt, grime and waste material extend throughout living areas of the dwelling, along with possible presence or evidence of insects and other vermin. Rotting food, excrement and certain odours may cause feelings of revulsion among visitors. As well as accumulation of waste, there may have been purposeful collection and/or retention of items to such a degree that it interferes with occupants' ability to adequately clean up the dwelling.

Reviews of series of cases of domestic uncleanliness have shown how domestic squalor varies. These series have included consecutively referred cases seen by (1) a heavy duty cleaning service in London; (2) a Sydney old age psychiatry service; and (3) staff of a 'Squalor Project' developed to coordinate interventions whatever the age of the occupants.

We have used the term 'wet squalor' (as suggested by Graeme Halliday) when describing homes where moist or liquid excrement, decayed material, grease, or water spillage or overflow are prominent features of the uncleanliness; commonly there has been accumulation of rubbish but not much purposeful accumulation of items. We use the term 'dry squalor' in talking about homes where there has been a disorganised accumulation of 'dry goods', often including clothing, papers, material contained in plastic bags, and/or electrical devices, in a way that does not allow adequate cleaning. Such items may have been selected and collected purposefully or not; failure to discard unused or unusable items may have been purposeful or not.

The following list provides a working classification of types of squalor and/or hoarding situation. The range (but not necessarily the pattern) of cases is reportedly similar among those seen by mental health teams, environmental health workers, public housing officers, community services, fire officers and others. Squalor may be 'severe' in the absence of clutter or hoarding, and vice versa. Thus, severity is not the only determinant of how cases should be classified.

1. Dry, neglectful squalor

The home is very dirty. Windows, walls and ceilings are grimy. Surfaces and floors in the kitchen, bathroom, living room and elsewhere have obviously not been cleaned for many months. Dust and carelessly dropped items are seen everywhere. Pots, pans and crockery remain unwashed, piled in the sink or elsewhere, and food may have putrefied. There has been little or no purposeful accumulation of goods or items. Clothes may have been left around in heaps or untidily, covering much of the furniture and floors.

2. Rubbishy, neglectful squalor

The home is very untidy, with an accumulation of garbage, waste or rubbish, especially in the kitchen but often in other rooms too. When brought into the dwelling, items had a purpose: the rubbish includes discarded glass, metal or plastic containers and bottles, packaging, remnants of meals, etc. As in (1) above, the dwelling is usually dusty, with grimy walls and greasy surfaces. Basins, stove and the toilet have not been cleaned for many months.

3. Wet, neglectful squalor

The home may be as filthy as in (1) above, but rather than there being a large quantity of rubbish, there is excrement (animal or human faeces, urine and maybe vomit) throughout the dwelling, especially around the toilet bowl or in other places where animals or humans excrete. Neglected overflow or spillage, and rotting food may accord with the descriptor of 'wet squalor'.

4. Dry clutter

The dwelling is cluttered in a disorganised way. A variety of items and material is spread around the home, including clothes, papers, boxes, videos, DVDs, electrical goods, and various items either purchased, freely distributed or found on streets or elsewhere. The clutter covers most surfaces and floors and consequently cleaning has been difficult or impossible. It is messy but not in a 'wet squalor' way. The mess is disorganisation rather than neglect.

5. Dry extensive clutter or hoarding

Large parts of the dwelling are inaccessible because of items and material collected and brought in for storage. The accumulation of goods is too great to refer to it merely as clutter. At one time the collection may even have been fairly organised, but now the occupant is unable to access most of the items and material because it is in such a disorganised state. The items may be piled as high as the ceiling. It may be impossible to reach basins or the kitchen, and the home has become dirty because of inability to clean it. The main problem is hoarding, not the secondary squalor.

6. Dry, semi-organised hoarding

In some dwellings, accumulated articles and material are kept in a semi-organised way, with 'pathways' through the piled-up items. Parts may be inaccessible, but others are accessible enough to clean them. Although the squalor may be mild,

Box 1.3 Further dimensions of severe domestic squalor.

How severe is the squalor? A way of rating severity would be helpful.

To what extent is the structure of the building in disrepair? Does dilapidation contribute to the uncleanliness? Do the utilities work?

To what extent are the contents of the dwelling disorganised? Is the messiness attributable more to inability to make decisions about what to keep and why, than to disinterest in maintaining cleanliness and hygiene? Or is it attributable to lack of recognition of reasons for getting rid of garbage and rubbish?

Is the uncleanliness clearly related to purposeful and excessive collection of items that have no obvious value to occupants? To what extent do the hoarded items restrict access to facilities within the home – the toilet, basins, stove, bed, etc.?

To what extent is the uncleanliness of the home reflected by occupants' personal uncleanliness? Degree of personal cleanliness does not appear to correlate well with degrees of domestic uncleanliness. Neglect of domestic hygiene is not to be regarded as self-neglect.

risks of fire or accident make a clear-out desirable. When articles or material have been collected in a systematic and organised way, the home can be kept clean even though it is perceived as 'full' of hoarded items. The occupants hoard; they do not live in squalor, not even mild squalor. Whether there is a fire risk depends on what has been hoarded.

This typology is designed to help those wanting to convey information about living conditions in a dwelling. Some dwellings fit two types at once, for example, types 2 and 3 together:

> A woman in Sydney owned at least 50 animals of various species. There was wet squalor, plus a disorganised neglectful mess of animal food and other items scattered over surfaces and floors, which had not been cleaned for many months; cobwebs abounded and all facilities were filthy.

But there are other dimensions of severe domestic squalor and other questions that need to be asked. Observers may benefit from further structure on how best to summarise what they have seen, touched or smelt. The main themes are shown in Box 1.3.

Rating the severity of squalor

The Squalor Survivors website (squalorsurvivors.com/squalor/index.shtml, accessed April 2012) has been developed by people who found that their living conditions were unacceptable to themselves, let alone others. They have provided a rating scale that they have found useful when discussing their self-perceived domestic difficulties, and in helping those seeking ideas on how to change their situations.

They refer to four degrees of squalor:

(1) The first is where little piles are starting to emerge and disorganisation is starting to cause inconvenience. 'You might be embarrassed for other people to see your mess... but you would still let them in the house.'
(2) In second-degree squalor (according to the website), the piles have expanded to cover items up, and restrict use of facilities. Normal movement is impeded by the piles of stuff. People are discouraged from coming inside.
(3) Third-degree squalor is where 'you have all the above, plus you have rotting food and animal faeces and/or urine in the house... Essential household repairs may not be done, because you are too afraid to let a tradesperson see your house.'
(4) Fourth-degree squalor is where 'you have all of the above, plus you have human faeces and/or urine in your house that is not in the toilet'.

The website has been modified over the years, but remains useful and constructive in showing those with messy or disorganised living conditions that they are not alone, and making changes is possible.

A comparable scale has been developed by what is now called the Institute for Challenging Disorganization (www.challengingdisorganization.org). This has been called the ICD Clutter Hoarding Scale (see Chapter 6), and combines ratings of sanitation and cleanliness, pets and rodents, constraints on function within the home and structural issues within the home. Together, its ratings of sanitation, cleanliness and the mess left by pests and animals, could be used as a measure of uncleanliness. Its ratings of clutter and ability to function in a home could be used in rating degrees of clutter. Whether as a whole it measures degrees of disorganisation is debatable, but the concept is certainly relevant when considering how best to record assessments of factors that could contribute to deterioration of living conditions.

We have used rating scales when documenting our observations in dwellings in London and Sydney, and will discuss the relevance of our results (especially regarding how best to intervene) in the next two chapters. However, we draw attention now to the Environmental Cleanliness and Clutter Scale (Halliday and Snowdon, 2009; Appendix A) in order to point out aspects that we believe need to be assessed when rating the severity of domestic squalor. The total score on this scale gives an indication of severity but does not show why a person lives in squalor. The scale allows ratings of the degree to which there is restricted access in a dwelling, and whether such restriction is due to accumulation of garbage (i.e. failure to discard) and/or accumulation of hoarded (purposefully collected and retained) items. It provides ratings of aspects of uncleanliness, including vermin, odour and faeces. It allows ratings of squalor associated with hoarding, but was not developed primarily to assess degrees of hoarding.

We recommend supplementary ratings of the extent to which there is restriction of access to particular facilities (bed, stove, basin, toilet), but this would be more to rate degree of hoarding than degree of squalor. Minor, moderate or severe hoarding was reported in about half the dwellings included in Halliday *et al.*'s (2000) study of cases of domestic squalor, but with hoarding defined as an accumulation of singular items such as newspapers, bottles or plastic bags. In the Sydney study (Snowdon and Halliday, 2011), two thirds of the older people living in moderate or severe squalor accumulated items or waste to a moderate or severe degree. More detail is provided in the next chapter, and we speculate about how mental disorders among the occupants relate to the types of squalor encountered in the homes they live in.

Personal cleanliness

It is true that some people appear not to care about either personal or domestic cleanliness, so that those who have not washed themselves for years commonly have very dirty homes, whereas the homes of those who sometimes wash and use soap tend to be not so filthy. However, degree of personal cleanliness does not appear to correlate well with degrees of domestic uncleanliness. Neglect of domestic hygiene is not to be regarded as self-neglect. It may be that a correlation would be more obvious in cases of dementia or acquired brain injury. Some individuals who need to be acceptably clean in order to go out to work have been observed to live in filthy homes; their workmates would never believe their domestic arrangements. Rating personal uncleanliness may not be easy; the person may not want to expose their finger-nails, hair or body.

2

A hundred years of squalor – what we know

Introduction

Over the last hundred years here has been a growth in the number of articles and narratives published about people living in unclean conditions, often centring on eccentrics and recluses. The Collyer brothers, who died in 1947, were said to have defied orders issued by New York's Health and Fire Department to clear out their rubbish. Data concerning 105 recluses were obtained from New York newspapers in the 1940s and 1950s, and the living quarters of 37% were described as being in 'shambles, unkempt and/or piled with trash' (Granick and Zeman, 1960).

This chapter will focus on factors associated with dwelling in squalor, and try to identify explanations for why some people live in this way. Literature regarding management and interventions in such cases will be flagged up but will be discussed further in subsequent chapters.

Pioneers: Macmillan and Shaw

The first notable mention of research on the topic, published in health-related literature, was by Patricia Shaw (1957), a Senior Medical Officer for Prevention, Care and After Care in Nottingham, England. She studied 987 reports by health visitors concerning people aged 60 years or older, whom they had visited, and found that 139 (62 men, 77 women) showed evidence of what she called 'social breakdown'. She defined this as 'a state resulting from prolonged neglect of the physical and mental health of the individual and of his environment, rendering the sufferer offensive to society'. She pointed out that the material for study was inevitably highly selected, and that 'the standards for making a diagnosis of social breakdown are arbitrary; some borderline cases may indeed be classified one way or the other according to the interpretation of different observers'.

Shaw (1957) provided an illustrative case: John C, a widower aged 76, lived in a terrace house but occupied only a front room, which was 'indescribably filthy'. A year later, in spite of his daughter scrubbing out the house and disinfesting the place of fleas, he had become uncooperative and had thrown newly provided bedding into the cellar. The chief public health inspector visited him with a view to removal to hospital under the National Assistance Acts, 1948 and 1951, then applicable in England. The house was cleaned but 'he relapsed as soon as he returned'. He was described as 'a drunkard'. Two and a half years after that first visit, his habits had become worse. In the words of Shaw:

> . . .and he urinated and defaecated into any receptacle available, such as the kettle, and cups, or on to the floor. The mattress was rotted with urine. One neighbour wrote to the Health Department complaining of the stench from the house. After a domiciliary visit by the psychiatrist and a social worker, when it was decided that no action could be taken by them, several more visits were paid by the health visitor. Mr C finally agreed to go away [and] a few weeks after his admission to residential accommodation, he was a changed man. He was well cared for, clean. . . He was, however, aggressive and difficult and constantly wanting 'a pint'.

In summarising the data about 'social breakdown', Shaw described what was likely to be observed in the subjects' dwellings:

> The room in such cases is the epitome of neglect. Dust lies thick everywhere, and cobwebs abound. The windows are barely translucent and the curtains are in shreds. Rubbish, odds and ends and remains of food are found everywhere. The bed is often broken and the sheets, if there are any, are dark grey. Often the subject lies on a bare mattress, with a pillow without a pillowcase and a pile of old coats for bedding.

Not only did she give an overview of what later came to be called severe domestic squalor, but Shaw also recommended actions to be taken to deal with or prevent 'social breakdown'. She put emphasis on the need for good coordination between agencies to achieve optimum results. Referring to women working in the Home Help Service, she wrote that 'Fortunately, some have so strong a sense of vocation and service that they continue, whatever the state of the house.' She noted the roles played by Home Nursing Services, Health Visitors and Welfare Services, and stated that voluntary agencies 'give the statutory bodies much help in suitable cases'. She mentioned the importance of primary care physicians and of the general public in drawing attention to cases.

In a paper in the same journal, immediately following Shaw's, Macmillan (1957) described psychiatric aspects of social breakdown in the elderly, and referred to the evolution of geriatric psychiatry. Wards in an annexe to the Mental Hospital in Nottingham had been converted into a geriatric unit, and many of the subjects of Shaw's research were admitted there. In a subsequent paper. Macmillan (1969) wrote that observation of the incipient stages of senile breakdown ('a situation in which the resources of the family or community have become inadequate to deal with the needs of the old person concerned') is possible only in a domiciliary service in which the resources of the hospitals and of the community are combined.

Macmillan and Shaw together (1966) elaborated on their original research findings in a paper entitled 'Senile breakdown in standards of personal and environmental cleanliness'. This is the paper commonly cited as being seminal in research on severe domestic squalor. They said 'we have called this condition senile breakdown because, with the exception of one psychiatric patient, we found it only in the senile epoch'. One of their cases was of a woman living in circumstances resembling those applying to Mr C (above). They scored all cases from 1 (clean) to 5 (filthy) on ten environmental features and five personal ones. The former comprised floor, walls, ceiling, windows, bed, table, cooker, coal, dirt and smell, while the latter included skin, hair, hands and clothes, as well as the method of disposal of excreta.

They gave details of 72 cases (12 men, 60 women), the median age of the women being 77 years, and of the men 79 years. Cases were referred to the mental health department through health services, some being in response to a circular sent to Nottingham primary care physicians. The clergy and some 'private individuals' gave information to the researchers about other cases. The incidence (i.e. the number of new cases per year) among people aged 60 years or over was calculated to be 0.5 per 1,000 per year. Fifty of the 72 lived alone; 11 were married, 1 separated, 42 widowed and 18 single.

They identified a particular pattern of personality that emerged again and again, being that of a domineering, quarrelsome and independent individual, with gradually developing rejection of the community, resentment of any outside interference and an abandonment of the accepted standards of behaviour of the neighbourhood. The researchers believed this rejection of usual standards was not simply a passive deterioration, but rather, it was an expression of a hostile attitude to and a rejection of the outside community.

However, they reported that the mental state of 9 men and 25 women among their subjects was *normal,* though 11 of them had a mild degree of reactive depression, usually attributable to bereavement. They labelled 38 (3 men, 35 women) as *psychotic*. Of these 38, 23 were diagnosed as having senile psychosis and 1 presenile psychosis (i.e. 24 had dementia); 3 had chronic alcoholism, but 20 others in the whole group were known to be heavy drinkers. Eight of the psychotic group had schizophrenia, paraphrenia or senile paranoid psychosis, and 3 were manic-depressive. None had learning disability. Eleven had poor mobility and another 5 could not climb stairs.

Initially, subjects in this study were all offered admission to the psychiatric hospital, but because it was found that most 'degenerated rapidly into apathetic beings', the researchers decided instead to offer day care in a hospital ward. Of 30 admitted to the psychiatric hospital, 17 were dead within four years and only 3 were living back in the community. Of 21 admitted to non-psychiatric hospitals,

7 died within a few days. After five years, 36 (50%) of the 72 were dead, but 18 were at home, the latter outcome being largely attributed to day care arrangements.

Macmillan and Shaw (1966) lamented that 'there is usually no organization to which cases can be reported and from which efficient action can be obtained. Our survey has demonstrated the need for such a service to be made available for these cases.'

Diogenes syndrome

Clark *et al.* (1975) described 30 patients (14 men, 16 women) aged 66 to 92 years who had been referred for urgent admission to their *geriatric medicine* unit in Brighton (UK). 'All lived in a desperate state of domestic disorder, squalor and self-neglect.' All were known to the social services departments and a third had persistently refused offers of help. 'Several hoarded useless rubbish (syllogomania).' All were acutely physically ill, most frequently with congestive cardiac failure (8), cerebrovascular disease (7) or bronchopneumonia (4). The authors reported on intelligence and personality assessments in half the cases, and these showed a mean IQ of 115 and no gross deviation of personality, though 'they seemed more aloof, detached, shrewd, suspicious and less well integrated'. Fourteen died, 13 were discharged (5 to their own homes) and 3 went to long-stay wards. Follow-up showed those at home to be 'in a reasonable, yet untidy, state'.

The authors posited that their study had revealed sufficient common features to confirm Macmillan and Shaw's suggestion 'that severe self-neglect in old age is a syndrome'. They titled their paper 'Diogenes syndrome' after the Greek cynic philosopher Diogenes of Sinope who lived in a barrel in Athens and built the cynic philosophy around the need for simplicity and the dangers of property. They referred in a footnote to Diogenes's ideals of 'life according to nature, self-sufficiency, freedom from emotion, lack of shame, outspokenness, and contempt for social organisation', but did not mention Diogenes in the paper itself, nor define the syndrome operationally. Other than the mention of lack of shame and contempt for social organisation, Clark and colleagues provided scant evidence for suggesting that Diogenes's name be used in an eponym. Some of Diogenes's reported behaviours (in which he was said to indulge in order to illustrate the finer points of his philosophy) certainly are not typically observed in cases of severe domestic squalor. Laërtius (1925; trans. Hicks, 1972) noted that he repudiated commonly accepted ideas about human decency, was said to urinate on people who insulted him, spit in the faces of his hosts, defaecate in the theatre, masturbate in public and even point at people with his middle finger.

Clark *et al.* (1975) suggested that the syndrome might be a reaction late in life to stress in a certain type of personality. They proposed that 'Enforced isolation by bereavement, with loss of support, or retirement could result in reactive rejection of contemporary standards and social contacts.'

Among letters in response to the article was one that wondered 'whether self-neglect in such cases is not a manifestation of the death-wish, as in some cases of hypothermia. If so, are we necessarily justified in interference as long as the person's habits and behaviour are not a nuisance to others?' Another (partly answering the question) was from a psychiatrist closely associated with the research: he pointed out that half the 30 patients had psychiatric disorders, including schizophrenia and dementia (Whitehead, 1975). He, like another correspondent, noted that young and relatively young people can live in squalor too, yet may not have a psychiatric illness. He suspected that those in Clark *et al.*'s study who had no recognisable psychiatric disorder had 'probably always lived in some degree of so-called squalor and only came to the attention of the medical profession when, because of age, their home conditions deteriorated'. However, there has been ongoing confusion as to whether the term 'Diogenes syndrome' is inclusive or exclusive of those with underlying mental illness or dementing disorder (Cooney and Hamid, 1995).

Roe (1977) conducted a retrospective survey of 25 patients admitted to a geriatric unit in a five-year period 'because of gross self-neglect'. All (11 men and 14 women) were reported to have been living in squalor. Roe added that the majority 'were admitted for non-specific reasons, namely, unsteadiness and falls (11 patients) or general weakness resulting in a chair- or bed-ridden state (7). Three others were admitted because of pneumonia. At follow-up, 16 had been discharged, with 9 returning home and 7 going to residential homes; 2 were still in hospital after one year, and 7 had died.'

Kafetz and Cox (1982) reported two cases where alcoholism appeared to have caused decline into a 'senile squalor syndrome' and expressed surprise that Clark *et al.* (1975), unlike Macmillan and Shaw (1966), had not noted alcohol as a factor in any of their cases.

A number of authors have argued that the term 'Diogenes syndrome' is a misnomer (Post, 1982; Ungvari and Hantz, 1991; Vostanis and Dean, 1992; Wrigley and Cooney, 1992; Cybulska, 1998; Marcos and Gómez-Pellín, 2008), but it must be acknowledged that this imaginative term had utility in that it led to increased awareness by health professionals that living in squalor is commonly a result of medical or psychiatric problems that warrant attention. Jolley and Read (2009) commented that 'Diogenes' is not a perfect match for the syndrome 'but it is a near miss'.

PubMed is the medical research indexing system of the US National Library of Medicine, part of the National Institutes of Health. In June 2012 we found 59 papers referring to Diogenes syndrome (mostly in English but 9 in French and 9 in other languages), and 59 that used the key-word 'squalor' in reference to filthy living conditions. PubMed identified 21 papers when 'squalor syndrome' was used as a key-term, and 18 with 'domestic squalor'. In spite of all of this, we recommend that the term 'severe domestic squalor' be used (rather than mentioning Diogenes) when referring to cases such as those described by Clark *et al.* (1975). Post (1982) considered the term 'Diogenes syndrome' inappropriate and that, 'in addition, senile seclusion is no syndrome, it marks the end stage of a personality disorder'. Reifler (1996) commented that its aetiology is heterogeneous; it is not just one entity. He preferred the term 'syndrome of extreme self-neglect', but we would argue that self-neglect refers to various ways in which an individual may neglect personal care, while domestic squalor refers to filthy, usually unhygienic, living conditions.

Table 2.1 shows a comparison of findings from five studies of older people who lived in squalor. The third of these was by Wrigley and Cooney (1992), who collected information on all patients referred to an Irish Department of Old Age Psychiatry over a two-year period who fulfilled their criteria for Diogenes syndrome, which were extreme self-neglect, gross domestic squalor and social withdrawal. Of the 29 participants (9 men, 20 women; mean age 78 years), 72% lived alone. Fourteen were single, 5 married, and the other 10 were widowed. Thirteen (45%) had dementia, 3 schizophrenia, 3 were alcohol dependent and 10 had no psychiatric diagnosis. Twenty-four of the 29 were seen first in their own homes. At follow-up (which appears to have been between a few months and two years later), 5 had died, 9 were in nursing homes, one in a psychiatric facility, 2 were living with relatives, and 12 were at home. The incidence rate was calculated to be 0.5 per thousand per year.

German authors (Klosterkötter and Peters, 1985) reviewed the literature regarding Diogenes syndrome and declared that the syndrome has been accepted internationally as comprising 'shameless' neglect of body and personal environment, associated with 'collectionism', social retreat and rejection of any well meant help. The authors concluded from their review, and from two new cases they presented, that the socio-culturally complete rejection associated with the syndrome is the final result of a personality-based abnormal emotional reaction development. They stated that medical treatment can be successful, mainly by means of behaviour therapy. Barocka *et al.* (2004), also from Germany, referred to 'the messy house syndrome (Diogenes syndrome)' when describing people who, owing to a disordering of personality structure, are unable to keep order, for example in the household or in their finances. 'Useless objects are hoarded in such quantities that the apartment can no longer be lived in,' but cognitive behavioural therapy may help. Jurgens (2000) used Dettmering's term 'litter hoarding syndrome' to mean the same thing, and provided a case description.

Chan *et al.* (2007) described the clinical profile of 18 cases of Diogenes syndrome (defined as extreme squalor, neglected physical state, unhygienic condition and social isolation with or without hoarding) presenting to an old age psychiatry team in Hong Kong. Eleven had dementia (eight Alzheimer's, two vascular, one alcohol dependency with co-morbid severe dementia) and two others had mild cognitive impairment. Of the other five, one was alcohol dependent, one had schizophrenia, one had a WAIS-IQ of 63, and the other two had no diagnosable mental or psychological disorders. 'Excessive hoarding of garbage including rotten stuffs and other futile objects' was evident in fifteen (83%) cases. At follow-up, two patients had died within a year and ten had moved to nursing homes within two years; two had moved in with relatives and another

Table 2.1 Data from five series of cases of older people who were living in severe domestic squalor.

	Macmillan & Shaw, 1966, UK	Clark *et al.*, 1975, UK	Wrigley & Cooney, 1992, Ireland	Chan *et al.*, 2007, Hong Kong	Snowdon & Halliday, 2011, Australia
Age range	93% aged 70–97 Four aged 60–69 One aged 48	66–92	66–86	68–91	65–95
Male:female	12:60	14:16	9:20	7:11	79:41
Living alone	50/72	28/30	8/29	7/18	96/120
Referred to	Psychiatric services	Geriatric unit	Old age psychiatry service	Old age psychiatry service	Old age psychiatry service
Where seen	At home	In hospital	24 at home, 5 in hospital	At home	At home
Diagnoses	24 senile or presenile psychosis; 5 senile paranoid psychosis; 3 schizophrenia; 3 manic depressive; 3 chronic alcoholism; 11 mild reactive depression; 23 normal; (23 were heavy drinkers).	Half had psychiatric disorders, including dementia or schizophrenia. All had acute medical illnesses.	13 dementia; 3 schizophrenia; 3 alcohol dependent; 10 no psychiatric diagnosis.	13 dementia or mild cognitive impairment; 1 schizophrenia; 1 alcohol dependent; 1 developmental disorder; 2 normal.	42 dementia; 18 schizophrenia or paranoid state; 29 alcohol brain damage or substance abuse; 11 personality disorder; 4 depression; 10 physical illness. 6 no definite diagnosis.
Outcome	***At 5 years:*** 36 dead; 15 in hospital or nursing home; *18 at home;* 3 lost to follow-up.	***Outcome:*** 14 died; 8 in care homes; 3 in long-stay wards; *5 at home.*	***Outcome:*** 5 died; 9 in nursing homes; 1 in psych hosp.; 2 with relatives; *12 at home*	***In 1–2 years:*** 2 died; 10 in nursing homes; 2 with relatives; *3 at home;* 1 lost to follow-up.	***At 1 year:*** 10 died; 29 in aged care facilities; 16 moved; *45 at home;* (20 no follow-up).

had moved elsewhere; the other three were still at home, with enhanced community services, none having significant cognitive or psychiatric abnormalities.

A recent survey, administering questionnaires to health professionals in Paris (Monfort *et al.*, 2010) found that 26% of 121 subjects reported to have Diogenes syndrome (mean age 77.8 years; range 52 to 95) had dementia, and half of the 121 had a psychiatric disorder. Another French report described a 69-year-old woman with Diogenes syndrome attributable to an eight-year period of mania following a depression (Fond *et al.*, 2011); the mess and disorganisation did not recur after she had been treated with mood stabilisers.

Other series and case-reports

As is clear, all series of cases of severe domestic squalor (or whatever the authors called it) described in health-related or other published material are biased; subjects are selected, for example by being inpatients of a geriatric medical service, or by being referred to psychiatrists. Case-reports in journals, too, are selective in that presented cases are considered to be of particular interest; otherwise they would not have been submitted or accepted for publication. Of the various series we have mentioned, most were reported by psychiatrists or geriatricians and their teams, the main focus being on people aged over 60 years. Although psychologists may have contributed to the research the emphasis in these papers appears to relate to psychiatry and geriatric medicine rather than conditions where psychologists commonly take leading management roles.

A high proportion of individual case-reports in the literature refer to middle-aged or younger persons who were living in domestic squalor. Unlike the series mentioned above, there have been others in the literature that described referrals from across the whole adult age range, a few mentioning children living in the same dwellings as the referred clients. We will summarise these before deriving conclusions from the literature about domestic squalor cases.

Snowdon (1987) presented details about cases referred to *community health* services in one part of Sydney. Staff were asked to rate the degree of cleanliness on ten aspects of their clients' dwellings, and in addition to rate degrees of hoarding, disposal of garbage and odour. Eighty-three clients were identified as living in unclean conditions, with a mean score on the 13 aspects of home cleanliness of 3.2 on the 4-point scale. Of the 83, a maximal rating on the hoarding aspect ('items piled high') was recorded in 36 (43%) cases, and another 24 showed substantial evidence of hoarding. Fifteen (18%) of the 83 were aged less than 60 years. Two thirds were female. About 60% lived alone, but several of the other 33 were living with more than one other (un-referred) person; of 75 where marital status was recorded, 20% were married, 52% were widowed or separated, and 28% were single. Almost two thirds had some degree of memory impairment, and 40% were or had been heavy drinkers. Twenty-four of the sample were believed to have delusions or hallucinations, while 11 had recently been bereaved. One subject had poor mobility for physical reasons. There were no definite clues to the cause of uncleanliness in 12 dwellings; the 12 clients (four aged less than 60 years) had good hearing and vision, were mobile, not deluded, not recently bereaved, never heavy drinkers and had no memory impairments. It was thought that 'eccentric' might be an appropriate way of describing most of these 12 individuals.

A study providing a less biased cross-sectional epidemiological picture of severe domestic squalor in an urban setting was conducted by Halliday *et al.* (2000). Those interviewed were not representative of the total population, however, as almost all their homes (94%) were rented from the local council or housing association. The municipality where the research took place employed a *special duty team* to clean the homes of people living in very unclean conditions. A research worker accompanied the team, and where consent was provided, occupants of these dwellings were interviewed at the time of the cleaning or soon after. Of 91 individuals, ranging in age from 18 to 94 years (mean 63 years), 58 (72%) were male and 68 (84%) lived alone.

The description of living conditions observed in this study may be usefully kept in mind when comparing studies focusing on domestic squalor with those focused on hoarding:

> Houses were often cluttered with bags and boxes of property and possessions so that it was virtually impossible to move around, with rooms inaccessible or impossible to enter safely. We commonly found all floor space thickly covered with newspapers, cardboard, discarded packaging, and other rubbish. Often the occupant had accumulated or hoarded a large number of singular items such as milk bottles (sometimes containing souring milk), newspapers, food containers, carrier bags, or fabric. Several homes were dirty and unhygienic due to incontinence or blocked and overflowing toilets. Less striking but not uncommon were rooms and bedsits that were sparsely furnished except for a foul smelling sofa or mattress, and floors and tables that were thickly covered in dirt, dust, and rotting food.

Halliday *et al.* (2000) used a living conditions rating scale, developed by Samios (1996) and similar to that used by Snowdon (1987), in describing the interiors of the 76 dwellings. On the 13-item scale (maximum score 39), the mean was 17, range 6 to 34. One third of the participants stated a belief that their homes were clean or very clean. Thirty-seven (46%) individuals had moderately or severely disabling chronic illnesses, and 21 participants were rated as having a physical health problem (such as incontinence, immobility or severe visual impairment) that had significantly contributed to the unclean state of their living environment. They found (using a structured diagnostic interview) that 57 (70%) participants fulfilled criteria for an ICD-10 mental disorder. There was high co-morbidity between substance (usually alcohol) abuse and organic and schizophreniform disorders. Thirteen (16%) participants had dementia and another 5 had another organic mental disorder, 17 (21%) had schizophrenia or schizoaffective or delusional disorder, 8 (10%)

had substance abuse with no other psychiatric disorder, 4 (5%) had an affective disorder, 5 (6%) had a phobic or anxiety disorder or an anxiety/depressive reaction, and 9 (11%) were reported to have a learning or developmental disability. They noted that no case fulfilled criteria for obsessive–compulsive disorder (OCD), and that there were few cases where there was potentially explanatory impairment of executive and other frontal lobe function in the context of an organic mental disorder. They found mental disorder to be less common among older than younger people living in squalor. The researchers commented that the personality types predominantly identified in this research (anxious, avoidant or anankastic) could point to a role for obsessional traits in the aetiology of squalor. Finally, they gave reasons for thinking that the term 'Diogenes syndrome' should be regarded as a term of historical interest rather than of clinical utility.

Researchers conducting a two-year study in a German city (Wustmann and Brieger, 2005) found 35 persons (mean age 63 years, 60% male) living in squalor and filth or in a neglected condition, or who were known to hoard. Seventeen (49%) had organic brain disease, while 14 (40%) had psychotic illnesses, mainly schizophrenia. In 9 cases a physical disorder contributed to the observed living conditions. Interventions (such as arranging moves to sheltered accommodation) had positive effects, but after nearly a year there had been no amelioration in 60% of cases; the latter applied particularly to individuals with psychotic illnesses.

When writing a review concerning severe domestic squalor, Snowdon *et al.* (2007) identified 15 reports of series of cases, 12 written in English, with 1 each in German, Spanish and Czech. They also studied 48 publications (43 in English, the others in German, Spanish or French) that, between them, presented details of 74 cases of squalor. Of the total of 1,109 subjects in these reports and series, 652 (59%) were women. Because more of the case series came from researchers working specifically with older people, the number of older people far exceeded the number of younger people among the 1,109. Most subjects lived alone, but details were given of over 70 cases where two or more people were living together in a state of severe domestic squalor. Subjects came from all social classes; some owned property and some had substantial financial reserves, though in some studies the majority received social security and occupied public rental housing. Again, results were affected by bias, depending on the locality sampling strategy.

Among the case-reports mentioned above, mainly describing squalor in one home but sometimes in two, excessive accumulation of rubbish or useless possessions was specifically mentioned in 40 (54%) of the 74, while 12% implied or described a lack of such accumulation. Purposeful accumulation was described in 22 (30%) and was implied in 2 other cases. However, it is possible that authors and editors believe that cases lacking accumulation are less likely to be of interest to journal readers, thus creating a publication bias.

Cases of hoarding with squalor

Although researchers have been investigating issues related to living in unclean conditions for decades, and although they have often referred to hoarding or accumulation of rubbish when describing cases or case series in medical or psychiatric journals, citations by them of articles focusing on people who hoard (as opposed to people who live in squalor) have been relatively uncommon. The leaders in the field of hoarding research have most commonly been psychologists, and their research has largely been published in journals devoted to behavioural psychology.

Most people who hoard do not live in squalor. Those who hoard excessively commonly recognise that they have a problem and may seek treatment – particularly from psychologists. Research on hoarding is usually conducted with subjects who are keen to change, and are willing participants. It may be that hoarders who live in squalor are a sub-population likely to decline participation in studies, and that therefore associated squalor is not viewed as much of a problem by the health professionals who specialise in treating hoarders. Yet we know from reports about people who hoard that some have great difficulty keeping their dwellings clean because of the amount of hoarded material. Ratings of the degree of uncleanliness (comparable to those made by Halliday *et al.*, 2000) have not been recorded in epidemiological studies relating to hoarding. Frost *et al.* (2000) have drawn attention to public health problems, including violation of sanitation and housing laws, but commonly it is not clear from such research whether the studies were only of people who purposefully collect and then have difficulty discarding, or whether some of the accumulations of rubbish resulted from not bothering to discard (rather than being unwilling to discard).

Studies of cases referred or self-referred because of hoarding (defined by Frost and Gross (1993) as 'acquisition of, and failure to discard, possessions which appear to be useless or of limited value'), with or without consequent squalor, have been of samples that are quite different to those studied by researchers examining cases of squalor (whether the subjects purposely collect and retain items or not). The diagnostic pattern and results of psychological and neuroimaging testing in studies focused on hoarding have been seen to be very different to those seen in studies focused on squalor (with or without hoarding). Conclusions to be derived from the present chapter will relate to cases where squalor is a major concern (even if hoarding is also an issue). Chapter 4 focuses on cases of hoarding, where squalor is usually not an issue. But there is good reason to examine the overlap – including the use of newly derived measures of cleanliness in rating the dwellings of people who hoard, and by using ratings of factors related to hoarding when interviewing people who live in squalor. Studies of case series of people who hoard have not been included here, even though a proportion of a truly representative sample of people who hoard would be found to be living in moderate or severe squalor. Hoarding researchers have recently expressed interest in rating squalor in cases referred to them because of accumulating clutter (Rasmussen *et al.*, 2012 submitted). Such ratings will allow comparisons of diagnostic patterns in groups of participants rated by hoarding researchers and by psychiatric services as living in moderate or severe squalor. There is a need to connect the insights of those engaged in hoarding and squalor research.

Self-neglect in cases of squalor

Macmillan and Shaw (1966) referred to a 'rejection of the usual standards of personal and environmental hygiene' together with a hostile attitude towards the outside world, rather than a passive neglect of self-care. Clark *et al.* (1975) believed they had enough evidence to confirm that severe self-neglect in old age is a syndrome, and their name for it was 'Diogenes syndrome'.

This syndrome has been characterised by gross self-neglect, domestic squalor and social withdrawal (Wrigley and Cooney, 1992; Jackson, 1997). All the inpatients comprising Roe's (1977) series of cases of self-neglect had been living in squalor. Cybulska (1986) used the term 'gross self-neglect' in referring to similar cases, and Vostanis and Dean (1992) titled their paper 'Self-neglect in adult life' when describing two people in their thirties who lived in squalor and accumulated rubbish. Reifler (1996) stated a preference for the term 'syndrome of extreme self-neglect' rather than 'Diogenes syndrome', and talked of having been confronted, on home visits, by hoarded possessions and animal excrement. Halliday *et al.* (2000) included self-neglect as one of their operationalising criteria for Diogenes syndrome. Lauder *et al.* (2005) stated that 'Descriptions of the lifestyle of people who self-neglect are often very dramatic and normally portray an individual who lives in unclean, verminous circumstances, often associated with hoarding.'

However, many authors have a broader or different understanding when using the term 'self-neglect'. Abrams *et al.* (2002) described it as a 'behavioral entity involving inability or refusal to attend adequately to one's own health, hygiene, nutrition or social needs'. Pavlou and Lachs (2006) stated that self-neglect in older adults is a 'complex spectrum of behaviours characterized by inattention to health and hygiene, typically stemming from an inability or unwillingness to access potentially remediating services'. Dong *et al.* (2010) commented that there was no national standardised definition of self-neglect, though general concepts are usually similar, referring to an older person's inability to provide for themself the goods or services to meet basic needs. They noted that the National Center on Elder Abuse (2006) defined self-neglect as 'the behavior of an elderly person that threatens his/her own health and safety. Self-neglect generally manifests itself in an elderly person as a refusal or failure to provide himself/herself with adequate food, water, clothing, shelter, personal hygiene, and safety precautions.' Naik *et al.* (2008) stated that self-neglect arises when a person has diminished capacity for self-care and self-protection, and defined it as the 'failure to engage in self-care acts that adequately regulate independent living' or 'failure to take actions to prevent conditions or situations that affect the safety of oneself or others'.

Non-intentional self-neglect is observed when deficits in cognition and those other mental, physical, material or social resources required for self-care result in failure to engage in self-care actions; whereas intentional self-neglect is purposeful failure to engage in self-care actions necessary for health and well being (Gibbons *et al.*, 2006). Examples of neglect of health care include failure to take required medication or seek medical help for persistent medical illnesses, failure to comply with disease-modifying or preventative treatment, ignoring signs and symptoms of disease, and failure to attend to hygiene, or eat, drink and exercise appropriately. A self-neglect severity scale devised by Kelly *et al.* (2008) consists partly of items related to living conditions and personal hygiene, but also of tests of ability to function (for example, regarding time since last visit to a doctor, and untreated conditions).

Thus, epidemiological studies and case-reports that define self-neglect in terms of the domestic environment (with or without consideration of personal hygiene) can usefully be included when researching factors relevant to the development, persistence and management of severe domestic squalor. However, most studies of self-neglect appear to include (sometimes mostly) cases of neglect of self but without neglect of the domestic environment. This applies when a self-neglecting study participant co-habits with someone who attends to all the domestic cleaning and organisation. Thus most self-neglect case-reports and studies could not be included in Snowdon *et al.*'s (2007) review of studies of severe domestic squalor. It would be useful to compare participants who neglect self-care (health, nutrition, etc.) and are rated as living in domestic squalor with self-neglectors whose dwellings are acceptably clean and hygienic. The study by Kelly *et al.* (2008) suggests this should be possible.

Epidemiological findings in the 2011 Sydney study

A study by Snowdon and Halliday (2011) in Australia has allowed estimates of the incidence (number of new cases per unit of time per unit of population) and prevalence (the number of cases at any one time compared with the size of the base population) of severe domestic squalor in a defined area of a large metropolis, comprising suburbs of varied socio-economic and ethnic composition. The population of persons aged 65 years or more is about 20,000, of whom 2,000 are in aged care facilities. Over a ten-year period, the referral rate of cases of moderate or severe squalor to the catchment area old age psychiatry team was 0.66 per 1,000 per year, and (after determining one-year and two-year outcomes in these cases) the minimum prevalence of such cases was calculated as 1 per 1,000 (0.1%) in this age range. A number of cases of squalor in the area may have been referred to other services (including psychologists for intervention in cases of hoarding) but not to old age psychiatry, and others may not have been referred to anyone during the year. Thus the true prevalence and incidence rates may be higher than the rates the authors calculated.

During the ten years, 173 cases of men and women living in squalor (the mean age of both genders being 76 years) were referred to the team, 53 (32 men, 21 women) in mild squalor, 120 (79 men, 41 women) in moderate or severe squalor. In eight dwellings, two persons aged over 64 years were living together and were both included as participants. Thus a total of 165 dwellings were rated. Of these elderly people, 41% had never been married (53% of the men, 19% of the women), 27% were widowed (17% of the men, 44% of the women), 23% of both the men and women were separated or divorced, and 9% were still married (7% of the men, 13% of the women) with 4 married to people aged under 65 years (whose data were not included with those of the 173). About 44% lived in homes that the occupants or their relatives owned, while a similar proportion lived in public housing and 6% (each) lived in privately rented accommodation or in boarding houses. This accommodation profile differs from that reported in Halliday *et al.*'s (2000) study of a cross-age population, but also from the profile for the country as a whole, where only 5% of Australians live in public housing.

The principal clinical diagnoses made in the 120 cases of moderate or severe squalor were dementia (35%), substance abuse and/or alcohol-related brain damage (ARBD) (24%), schizophrenia or paranoid state (15%), personality disorder (9%), physical illness or disability (8%) and depression (3%). In 5% of cases, criteria for a DSM-IV or significant physical illness/disability were not fulfilled. Of the 11 participants with personality disorders, 5 showed marked obsessive–compulsive traits. Ratings of degree of accumulation and/or hoarding were made in 115 of the 120 who lived in moderate or severe squalor. One third (each) were rated as accumulating/hoarding to a major, moderate or minimal/negligible degree. In one third of the cases where there was a major degree of accumulation/hoarding, the diagnosis applied was personality disorder (26%) or no definite DSM-IV diagnosis (8%), in contrast to only 5% of those who accumulated or hoarded to a moderate or negligible degree. Of the others who accumulated or hoarded to a major degree, 26% had dementia, 10% substance abuse or ARBD, 23% schizophrenia or delusional disorder, and 8% had physical illness or disability, while none had depression as the principal diagnosis.

Of 157 participants who were followed up a year after first assessment by the old age psychiatry service, 47% (41% of those living in moderate or severe squalor) were still at home, but mostly without much long-term reduction in the uncleanliness or disorganisation of their dwellings. Some 12% had moved in with friends or relative, 32% were in aged care facilities and 8% had died.

We hope in due course to hear more details about referrals to the Severe Domestic Squalor Project, run by Catholic Healthcare in Sydney: staff assessed and provided support to people living in squalor in 17 local government areas of the city. Referrals were from a variety of community and health services (70%), the Department of Housing (20%) and from family, neighbours, doctors, rental managers and the occupants themselves. An evaluation was conducted in mid-2008 (McDermott and Gleeson, 2009), by which time 218 clients aged between 21 and 94 years (mean 62 years, with 58% aged under 65 years) had been referred; 56% were male. About 54% lived in public housing, 39% lived in properties they owned and 7% rented privately. The Project's figures, if they reflect the true prevalence of severe domestic squalor among people aged under 65 years, suggest that the rate at which older people are referred to helping agencies to consider interventions in cases of severe domestic squalor is about five times higher than the rate applying to younger adults.

Aetiology of squalor

As shown in Table 2.2, people referred because of unclean living conditions have been diagnosed as having a variety of diagnoses. However, living in squalor is not necessarily *attributable* to whatever mental disorder they have.

There must be reasons why some people with schizophrenia (for example) live in squalor while the vast majority does not. Features of the psychiatric problem (apathy, lack of motivation, loss of perceptive skills, lack of energy) may seem to have contributed to an accumulation of dirt or clutter. Pathology or injury to particular areas of the brain have consistently been found to be associated with certain emotional reactions or thoughts, and some of these may account for behaviours that lead to unclean living conditions. An interplay of personality, genes and brain changes may be what determines how people behave.

Table 2.2 The range of diagnostic labels that may be applicable in cases of severe domestic squalor.

Adults aged 18–94 (mean 63) years (Halliday *et al.*, 2000) (n = 81)		Aged over 65 years (Snowdon & Halliday, 2011) (n = 120)	
Organic mental disorder (12% + substance abuse) (dementia 16%)	22%	Dementia	35%
Substance abuse (no mental disorder)	10%	Alcohol related brain damage/ substance abuse	24%
Schizophrenia/delusional disorder	21%	Schizophrenia/paranoid state	15%
Affective disorder (4% depression)	5%	Depression	3%
Anxiety/phobic (obsessive–compulsive nil)	6%	Personality disorder (obsessive–compulsive 4%)	9%
Developmental disorder	11%	Physical illness	8%
No diagnosed mental disorder	25%	No DSM or physical disorder	5%

Organic causes

In cases described in the squalor and/or hoarding literature, there have been reports that point to organic aetiologies. Various features in cases of severe domestic squalor are also those of frontal lobe dysfunction. Reduction in self-care and personal hygiene, lack of empathy and concern for others, disinhibition and impaired social skills, are features of dementia of frontal type (Gregory and Hodges, 1993). Neuroimaging has shown frontal lobe dysfunction in a number of cases of severe domestic squalor. Orrell *et al.* (1989) described the living conditions of a woman shown to have severe frontal dysfunction on neuropsychological testing. Computerised tomography (CT) brain scans showed marked but localised atrophy of the frontal lobes, unchanged over 18 months. The woman's flat was 'squalid, with cigarette ends, rotting, uneaten meals, and excrement from her Pekingese lying around. She seemed largely unaware of her state of self-neglect.'

Lebert (2005) studied the prevalence of features of severe domestic squalor in outpatient cases of fronto-temporal dementia, seen over a two-year period. Both self-neglect and domestic squalor were observed in 28 of the 30 cases, though syllogomania was reported in only 15 (50%). All participants showed lack of concern, but suspicion, hostile attitude and distrust were said to be uncommon.

Others have reported infarcts (Al-Adwani and Nabi, 2001) and small vessel disease (Shah, 1992) in the frontal lobes of people living in squalor. Beauchet *et al.* (2002) described four cases of severe domestic squalor in cases of fronto-temporal dementia, with frontal lobe hypoperfusion shown on positron emission tomography (PET) scans.

Frontal lobe changes have been described in cases of hoarding as well as in squalor. In a case of newly developed hoarding, removal of an olfactory meningioma had led to prefrontal cortical damage (Volle *et al.*, 2002). In other cases, hoarding behaviour developed following rupture of an anterior communicating artery aneurysm (Hahm *et al.*, 2001), and in relation to a depressed skull fracture in the frontal region (Sebit *et al.*, 1996). Anderson *et al.* (2005) identified 9 cases of collectionism/hoarding after brain damage and compared them with 54 cases of brain damage without subsequent hoarding. All the collectors acquired items excessively and indiscriminately, and had acquired deficits in planning, organising and controlling their impulses; 8 of them had diminished discarding behaviour. Neuroimaging showed the maximal region of difference between the two groups was the ventromedial prefrontal cortex, extending posteriorly to the anterior cingulate cortex (Anderson *et al.*, 2005).

Hoarding has been reported in series of cases of dementia. Hwang *et al.* (1998), in a study of inpatients of a geropsychiatric ward of a veterans hospital, found that of 133 patients (a majority men) with dementia, 30 collected objects that appeared useless or unneeded, indiscriminately – including 24 out of 75 with Alzheimer's and 4 out of 40 with multi-infarct dementia. Others had noted that hoarding was found in 5.3% cases of moderate dementia, where subjects tended to save everything, resulting in 'conditions of hoarding and filth' (Homma *et al.*, 1994).

Differences in how and why accumulation happens

Maier (2004) drew together the literature on hoarding and on squalor when describing differences in how and why people may accumulate items and material. He stated that some hoarders clearly have pathological acquisition habits and suggested that in many cases so-called 'compulsive hoarding' is really an impulse-control deficit rather than a compulsion. It appears that acquisition and saving are often associated with pleasure rather than the avoidance of an obsessional fear. He agreed with Frost and Gross (1993) that difficulty in discarding may be related to avoidance of decision making. In a substantial proportion, however, it results from purposeful retention and active resistance to the idea of discarding. Conclusions to be derived from Maier's review (but giving attention also to the concept of hoarding disorder as a diagnostic category distinguishable from OCD), include:

(1) that some people with obsessive–compulsive disorder and others with hoarding disorder collect too much and have difficulty discarding
(2) that a proportion of people with newly acquired brain disorders develop an urge to collect items, and may resist discarding them, and
(3) that some people (exemplified by persons with newly acquired or developing brain changes) have difficulty with impulse control and acquire more than they discard.

These behaviours can be called *hoarding*.

However, Maier (2004) pointed out that in various psychiatric and neuropsychiatric disorders, including dementia, autism and chronic schizophrenia, acquisition of items is neither compulsive nor lacking impulse control, but is 'just motor activity without clear intention or aim, hence stereotypic, ritualistic'. People who acquire objects or material in this way may be indifferent to removal of the items. He recommended using notions such as 'collectionism' (Volle *et al.*, 2002) rather than 'hoarding' to describe their 'grasping' behaviour. The conclusion to be derived is:

(4) that if people are observed to collect ritualistically, this should be called *collectionism* and *not* hoarding.

Maier (2004) commented that clutter and uncleanliness are frequently the result of inability to clean up. This could be because of physical disability, or perceptual problems (inability to see or recognise filth), or due to cognitive difficulties resulting from dementing disorders or brain damage due to alcoholism, injury, infection or other cause. He argued that 'hoarding' is an inappropriate term to use in cases where accumulation is not purposeful and there is no intention or desire to 'store' goods. The conclusion to be derived is:

(5) that some people accumulate rubbish and filth because they are not motivated or able to throw it away, and this should *not* be called hoarding. This could be termed syllogomania (see Chapter 1).

The extent to which, in cases of organic brain disorder, accumulations of waste and dirt can be attributed to lack of motivation to discard (and lack of realisation of the propriety of doing so), as opposed to urges to collect together with resistance to discarding, varies. The former is accumulation; the latter is hoarding. The former sounds like disorganisation and lack of social appropriateness, and an appearance of laziness, attributable to frontal lobe changes or abnormalities, though there could also be diminished ability to discard due to dyspraxia and impaired visuo-spatial skills. Collecting plus resistance to discarding sounds more like response inhibition resulting from brain changes, but in a different area of the brain.

Pathways to squalor: factors and disorders

Maier's ideas are consistent with findings from case series and case reports mentioned earlier in this review. Among older subjects living in squalor, the commonest diagnostic associations have been recorded as dementia, schizophrenia and alcoholism. Frontal lobe changes may be found in all three and so may be the determinant of living in squalor. Decline in executive function among community-dwelling subjects during a 12-year follow-up was found to be associated with a greater risk of 'elder self-neglect' being reported and confirmed during the 12 years (Dong *et al.*, 2010). Younger patients living in squalor were more likely to have schizophrenia or to abuse drugs than have dementia.

Lewandowski *et al.* (2011) have reviewed the evolution of neuropsychological dysfunction during the course of schizophrenia, with impairment noted particularly in executive functioning. Patients with negative symptoms, or the 'disorganized subtype' performed worse on neurocognitive tasks than those with the paranoid subtype (Lewandowski *et al.*, 2011). There has also been evidence of increased impulsivity among persons with schizophrenia, linked to cerebral activation within the right ventrolateral prefrontal cortex during response inhibition (Kaladjian *et al.*, 2011).

Drummond *et al.* (1997) reported that, of 50 patients admitted to hospital for treatment of obsessive–compulsive disorder (OCD), 4 presented with self-neglect, domestic squalor and hoarding. In a subsequent study (Drummond *et al.*, 2011), severe self-neglect and inability to perform basic activities of self-care and hygiene were described in 75 out of 98 patients with severe, chronic disabling OCD; their average age was 39 years (range 19 to 70). Self-neglect was found to be correlated with increasing severity of OCD. Many were severely dehydrated on admission to hospital, and some had evidence of renal failure. Dehydration appeared to be due to difficulty in preparing or imbibing drinks due to compulsive rituals or avoidance. The report did not mention the prevalence of hoarding among this group, or results of neuroimaging or tests of frontal lobe function.

Williams *et al.* (1998) reported two cases of people in their fifties with intellectual disability of unknown aetiology, who manifested 'Diogenes syndrome'. One had a full-scale IQ of 65. She collected rubbish from dustbins and stored it in plastic bin-liners along with rancid milk and rotten food. Any suggestion that she get rid of the rubbish was resisted, though the hoarding ceased when she moved back to live with her mother. The other had an IQ of 67; her language development was delayed until 4.5 years of age and she showed odd, isolative behaviour in childhood. The authors raised the possibility that she had autism, a condition associated with compulsive behaviours. We are aware of other clinicians who have looked after patients with Asperger's syndrome who lived in severe domestic squalor, and there have been anecdotal reports of people living in squalor having had attention-deficit hyperactivity disorder (ADHD) as children. These cases suggest, again, that brain abnormalities may be a major causative factor in cases of severe domestic squalor.

The predominantly inattentive type of ADHD has been characterised by disorganisation and failure to complete work (Solanto, 2000a, b), while patients with so-called deficit schizophrenia showed more severe disorganisation than did those without deficit features (Cohen *et al.*, 2010). Disorganisation can lead to the accumulation of items in a haphazard way, as seen in a majority of cases of severe squalor and in 'organic object accumulation' (see Chapter 4; Table 4.2).

We can also understand how physical disability (motor, coordination, visual – or even lack of energy for medical reasons) could contribute to development of a state of squalor, but this would not be attributable to purposeful retention of items. Similarly, depression could lead to lack of motivation and energy, resulting in accumulation of waste.

In some cases described in the literature there was no clear causative factor to explain why occupants were living in severe domestic squalor. Cleanliness varies between homes and between individuals and can be presumed to be influenced by multiple factors, including upbringing, peer and family expectations, living arrangements, social and financial circumstances, cultural background and surroundings (Snowdon *et al.*, 2007). Some of us are disorganised and/or indecisive; some of us procrastinate, whereas others rush into things without thinking too much about consequences. Is it in the genes, or have these traits developed as a result of childhood experiences or training? Are some people simply very lazy (in relation to cleaning and organising)? Have some people been brought up in cultural situations where cleanliness was not seen as worth bothering about? Descriptions of nomadic peoples have shown how they deal with accumulating filth: they move on to somewhere else. Some people in our own cultures get rid of waste by discarding it in a place where someone else can be expected to clear it up. 'Not in my back yard – chuck it into someone else's!' Clearly, personality issues determine behaviour. Cultural and personality factors affect inclination to care about environmental cleanliness.

There has been little systematic assessment of personality, pre-morbidly or at presentation, among people who live in squalor, so that the influence of personality issues on progress into severe domestic squalor is unclear. Greve *et al.* (2004) described an 80-year-old woman who described herself as perfectionistic and liked to be the centre of attention. She had 'a narcissistic personality style with features of obsessive–compulsive disorder'. Her family said she had become more confused over the years; she never threw anything away and kept broken items found in other people's trash. She hid rotten food in cabinets, and her relatives threw out five bags of rotten food from her refrigerator. Her home was cluttered and insects were a problem. She saw no problem with the condition of her house. Comprehensive neuropsychological evaluation showed no evidence of a dementing illness, though recall was characterised by perseverative and intrusive errors. Complex working memory was within normal limits. Speech was fluent. Higher level problem solving and mental flexibility were intact. She had no history or evidence to suggest an Axis I psychiatric disorder. The assessment team attributed her 'Diogenes syndrome' to a long-standing personality disorder.

To summarise, it is likely that those who live in squalor start doing so because of a complex interplay of triggers and vulnerabilities. Literature on hoarding tends to focus on psychological factors, compulsions and indecisiveness when mentioning the squalor observed in some cases. There is contrasting work that describes accumulation of refuse and useless items as a result of apathy and impaired executive function, resulting from brain disease and mental disorder, though sometimes the accumulation is due to impaired mental or physical capacity to maintain home care. Lack of impulse control (related to brain disorder or personality problems) could also be a factor.

The importance of considering why people live in severe domestic squalor is that the answers will help in planning strategies of management. These will be discussed in subsequent chapters. The outcomes in cases of severe domestic squalor have been described in case reports and in follow-up studies of case series (Table 2.1). Such studies have been selective. There has been too little research to tell us what factors determine success in preventing and dealing with squalor situations. The literature reviewed here is as important in showing what we do not yet know (but need to, so the relevant research needs to be done) as in showing what we do know. Suggestions for further research and evaluation are made in Chapter 10.

3

How best to intervene in cases of severe domestic squalor?

Dealing with squalor

Relatively little has been written concerning how best to intervene in cases of severe domestic squalor. Outcomes of interventions have been presented in case reports, and the difficulties posed to a variety of agencies have been discussed in their journals and newsletters, but few scientific studies of what works best in particular situations have been conducted. Numerous case descriptions have shown that effective management is usually time consuming and complex, commonly requiring liaison and cooperation among several agencies. It can be expensive. Reports suggest that organisations worldwide are generally uncoordinated and consequently inefficient when trying to intervene and help in such cases.

The present chapter collates the ideas and views expressed by service providers in Australia and England, many of whom have had extensive experience in dealing with people whose living conditions were very unclean. We realise that their recommendations regarding interventions will have been shaped and influenced by factors that will differ from those encountered in other countries, and between different areas of the same country. However, we believe that the underlying principles underpinning effective intervention transcend these cultural differences. Cultural and socio-economic factors affect both the way people live and community perceptions of what is acceptable. In preparing this book we have read articles and manuals (in English or translated for us) concerning squalor and hoarding in other countries, and have sought information from service providers in diverse cultural settings; we have discussed with them issues concerning presentation and appropriate interventions.

We know that we know much more about squalor in developed countries than in developing countries. Discussions with aged care teams during visits to a number of developing countries have suggested that comparatively few of their older people live in unclean dwellings (even in places where garbage has accumulated in streets), and this may be attributable to the fact that few elderly people in those countries live alone; they live with relatives or extended families, in contrast to cultures where older individuals tend to live independently, even when their spouses or partners have died or moved to residential care. However, we acknowledge that our views concerning living conditions in developing countries are (because of limited opportunities to visit, and lack of comprehensive relevant information) sketchy and superficial. This is an area where there is a need for more and better research.

Nevertheless, even though we know that the generalisability of our recommendations is limited and will be more applicable in some settings than in others, we believe it is useful here to present observations concerning whether and how to intervene in cases of squalor. In this we aim to inform the public and practitioners and to stimulate discussion of how situational factors affect the way services are provided.

A need for guidelines

Requests and suggestions for something to be done in cases of severe domestic squalor reach a variety of service providers and come most commonly from people who live and/or work in proximity to dwellings that appear uncared for. Neighbours and visitors may have concerns about persons who seem unable to look after themselves and their domestic environments 'adequately'. (We use inverted commas to acknowledge that perceptions of 'adequacy' vary.) Others may be more concerned about how lack of hygiene in an adjacent property might affect their own health and safety and the value of their home. Visiting doctors, health visitors or outreach workers may be keen to involve other agencies. Landlords, meter readers, deliverers of goods, postmen, providers of local services, as well as relatives, friends, acquaintances and others may have had good cause for calling, and then may perceive they have a responsibility to report what they have observed, often by chance.

The people or agencies that have been approached first with expectations that they will take action may view it as appropriate to forward such referrals to services they perceive as better informed, equipped and resourced to respond Among the service providers/agencies expected to take a lead in dealing with squalor situations are:

(1) local councils and their social workers or welfare officers
(2) community health services (aged care, mental health, drug and alcohol)
(3) other government-supported community services
(4) not-for-profit caring organisations
(5) government departments taking responsibility for housing and overseeing home care and disability services

(6) guardianship personnel

(7) others, including housing providers, varying between regions and countries.

Cases of severe domestic squalor are among the most difficult referrals for such agencies to deal with. There is generally no simple answer to the problems posed by the person at the centre of the squalor. Issues are complex and often cannot be dealt with by one agency without the help of another. Coordination is needed.

An example of how to seek improved coordination was set by the Middlesex-London Health Unit, based in Ontario, Canada (Pelletier and Pollett, 2000). A meeting of service providers with an interest in what they called 'senile squalor' was informed that individuals exhibiting 'typical symptoms and behaviours' (social isolation and withdrawal, extreme self-neglect, domestic squalor, a tendency to hoard rubbish, lack of shame, and a stubborn refusal of help) often fall through the cracks. A task force was formed and after eight meetings made recommendations regarding a local action plan. The first was to develop a consortium of service providers and other stakeholders to coordinate services for at-risk individuals. Another was to seek funds to undertake a gatekeeper programme in order to foster the early identification of these at-risk individuals.

Discussions between service providers in Sydney pointed to comparably poor coordination between agencies in relation to helping people living in severe domestic squalor. Furthermore, meetings with colleagues working in various locations in Europe, Asia and North America told us that most jurisdictions and government departments around the world had little in the way of documented policies or plans concerning management of such cases. Consequently, relatives who were often desperate to obtain help (see Appendix B), and others encountering problems in relation to people living in squalor, found no written guidance to suggest: who (which service or person) should take initial steps in making a referral; to whom it was best to refer; or how to ensure that appropriate interventions were initiated. Some agencies had developed policies regarding occupational health and safety precautions to be taken when visiting dilapidated or unhygienic places, but these were not readily available to those working elsewhere. Thus it was often the case that the wheel of intervention had to be re-invented each time there was a referral, with consequent inefficiency, cost and delay in resolution.

In New South Wales (NSW), representatives of several agencies discussed these inefficiencies. With the support of the NSW government department responsible for disability services, funds were allocated and a reference group formed in 2002 (Snowdon and Halliday, 2009) in order to:

(1) better understand why some people live in severe domestic squalor

(2) develop recommendations regarding the organisation and funding of appropriate services

(3) develop and publish guidelines regarding how best to intervene in cases of severe domestic squalor.

As an illustration of what guidelines might look like, we now present the guidelines generated. The exact content of any specific guidance will depend on local service provision and configuration, as well as local and national legal systems.

The New South Wales squalor management guidelines

Referrer

Details given by the referrer may indicate the nature of the problem. Is this a case of squalor, hoarding, self-neglect or what? Is the referral appropriate? Has it been made to the agency or person best qualified to make an assessment and then make recommendations regarding who should intervene?

Assessment

Home visit

Risk assessment

Importantly, those asked to accept a referral need to consider whether it would be safe for the agency or person to visit the premises. They need to be told about any known risks. Many jurisdictions have legislated requirements that employers follow procedures to ensure the health, safety and welfare of their employees. Organisations that provide services to people living in squalor must ensure a safe working environment for their employees. Risk management strategies such as having checklists for identifying hazards, including home safety assessment, help eliminate or control risks to employees engaged in service provision in the community. In some cases of severe domestic squalor, occupational health and safety (OHS) concerns may in the first instance prevent service providers from entering premises and carrying out comprehensive assessments.

The following questions summarise some of the OHS concerns to be considered. When the referrers themselves cannot answer them, they may be able to provide or obtain information relating to people who can, such as neighbours, relatives and renting agencies. Examination of the outside of a building may (but may not) give an indication of what it is like inside.

Occupational health and safety concerns

- Are the structure and fabric of the dwelling safe and secure?
- Are the premises safe to enter (floorboards, ceilings, stairs, sharp objects)?
- Are there uninsulated or damaged electric wires that could cause electric shock? Do they trail across walkways?
- Are there diseased or potentially aggressive animals on the premises?
- Are there fire hazards (e.g. unsafe electrical cords, flammable items next to stoves or other heat sources)?
- Are there weapons, explosive materials or potentially harmful chemicals on the premises?
- Might there be 'booby traps' on the premises?

- Are there falling (slipping) or health hazards because of animal or human faeces, urine or vomit? Has there been spillage or leakage of grease or liquids? Has food rotted into a 'mush'?
- Is there a risk of falling over collected or collapsing heaps of items?
- Is there a health risk (e.g. from pathogens, disease, airborne particulate matter, mould spores, ammonia or other gases)? Have numerous insects or vermin been seen in the dwelling?
- Is personal protective equipment (PPE) (i.e. protective clothing, gloves, safety helmet, mask, safety spectacles or goggles) required?
- Might there be physical assault(s) by the occupant(s)?
- How difficult might it be for emergency personnel to move through the home?
- Are exits from the home blocked?

Organisations involved in making initial assessments of squalor situations need to ensure adequate training of their staff in relation to risk management and hazard identification – just as would be expected of organisations dealing with the aftermaths of earthquakes, floods and landslides. Risk control options need to be considered (NSW Government, Ageing, Disability and Home Care website, 2012). Staff can benefit from education regarding manual handling, infection control, challenging behaviour and first aid, as well as about how best to relate to occupants of dwellings they have been asked to visit.

Engagement

The process of engaging a referred client begins even before the first home visit, by eliciting information from the referrer that increases the likelihood of being able to meet up with the client and gain cooperation. Whenever possible, early access to the dwelling should be sought. The home visit then provides an opportunity for establishing a trusting relationship with the occupant(s), and for seeking other details that will facilitate the assessment, such as contact details for relatives, friends and their local doctor. It allows assessment of the extent of the squalor, and of whether there has been accumulation of items and/or garbage. Meeting the occupant(s) allows an assessment of personal cleanliness – i.e. of whether self-care is also a problem that needs attention. If a home assessment is not possible at first, plans need to be evolved in order to seek to enter the home eventually, preferably with the consent and involvement of the occupant(s).

Different approaches are needed for different individuals. Those living in unclean conditions do so for a variety of reasons reviewed earlier. Some have frontal lobe conditions and may appear very unreasonable; some have dementia or schizophrenia and may have paranoid ideas. Some have always had 'difficult' personalities, and some have been thought reclusive and keen to avoid social contact. Clients referred because of their living conditions vary in personality, attitude, willingness to engage with those keen to help them, recognition that they would benefit from help and in other ways. Flexibility is important when attempting to establish rapport. Some may respond to a series of brief, informal meetings. Others appear more likely to respond to people perceived as authority figures, such as a fire officer or police, whose firm but compassionate instructions regarding the need for a clear-out may motivate change or acceptance of assistance. However, occupants may react to such persons with fear and suspicion, resulting in a refusal to accept services. Cultural sensitivity and appropriateness are important. Those who do not speak the native tongue of the country where they live may only relate to those who can communicate in their own language.

Ideas about engaging clients

- If the client is too fearful to open the door, the staff member may try leaving a note in their post box or under the front door asking them to make contact. Enquiries from neighbours (but keeping privacy issues in mind) may be helpful in getting to understand the client's habits and attitudes.
- Calling after working hours or at varying times of day may eventually result in contact.
- It is important not to overwhelm the person. Take time! An immediate focus on a need for cleaning can lead to distress.

Occupants' wishes and views on what support would be beneficial should be respected, and the agency's values and judgement should not be imposed on them. Where an intervention seems vital, there needs to be opportunity for discussion and time to consider priorities. There may need to be compromise. Problems cannot all be dealt with at once, especially if the person shows reluctance to engage.

When an occupant refuses to open the door or to speak to the person seeking to make an assessment, even after repeated visits, it may be necessary to use legal procedures in order to gain access or arrange assessment of their capacity (see Figure 3.2 later, and our chapter on the law).

The first assessment

The referrer will have been given information about the type of accommodation (house, bedsitting room with shared facilities, owned or rented apartment, etc.), and whether there is more than one person living there. The following aspects should be assessed by staff of the contacted agency when they make their initial home visit:

- Do the occupants (one or more) indeed live in squalor and have they accumulated excessive amounts of items and/or rubbish? Is there reason to intervene urgently? Do any occupants need urgent medical attention?
- Do the living conditions present risks to the occupant(s) or others? Are any animals or children at risk and, if so, is immediate action (e.g. recommendation of removal to a caring environment) needed? Are neighbours at risk in relation to hygiene or safety, e.g. from fire or structural collapse? To what extent do the living conditions affect neighbours (e.g. odours, vermin or unsightliness)?

- Is there reason to have public health concerns (rodents, vermin, infestations, excreta, pathogens, fire risk, sewerage problems, animal hoarding, etc.)?
- Do utilities within the dwelling (water supply, hot water, electricity, gas, phone, sewerage) function effectively?
- On meeting the occupant(s), is there evidence of self-neglect, weight loss, inappropriate clothing, mobility restriction or other disability?
- On meeting the occupant(s) is there evidence of impaired or abnormal cognition or learning disability? Is there evidence to suggest excessive suspiciousness, peculiar beliefs, hallucinations, bizarre behaviour or other signs of possible mental illness?
- Are there potential safety concerns in relation to subsequent visits by service providers (e.g. for health care, cleaning or home maintenance)?
- Is intervention needed? If so, for what?
- Is it appropriate for the contacted agency to take a coordinating role in ensuring appropriate action (if indicated) is taken? If not, who should? Is it appropriate for the contacted agency to take on a case management role?

In all cases it is important to have or put in place a system that ensures coordination between services and makes clear who takes main responsibility for managing each case. If an occupant of a dwelling that is reportedly unacceptably unclean or unsafe declines or is unable to give informed consent to assessment or intervention, yet information available (often from various sources) makes it clear that intervention is required, it may be necessary to use statutory legislative arrangements in order to be able to arrange the necessary changes or interventions. When this is considered, the expediency of legal action needs to be weighed against the individual's rights and the ethics relating to the use of involuntary intervention.

Whether the initial home visit results in fuller assessment (for example, in relation to mental state or medical problems) depends on the skills and training of the person(s) undertaking that first contact. Whatever their background, if agency staff have the opportunity to see and talk with the occupant(s) for an adequate time in adequate conditions, they may then feel able to advise whether assessment by a doctor, psychiatrist, nurse, social worker or other health professional with special training appears appropriate. They may recommend obtaining advice on safety issues, including the risk of fire, but with attention to the rights of occupants.

A primary care physician (if the person has one) may be ideally placed to review their physical and mental health, particularly if they are accepting help. A wide range of medical problems has been reported among cases of people who live in squalid conditions. Special consideration should be given to problems with mobility, continence, sensory (especially visual) impairment and nutritional deficiencies. Similarly, various mental disorders mentioned in Chapter 2 have been recognised as being associated with unclean living conditions, and it is important to identify treatable psychiatric conditions. These include schizophrenia, depression, obsessive–compulsive disorders and substance abuse. Recognition that a person living in squalor has dementia, alcohol-related brain damage or brain changes due to other causes (such as head injury, infection or tumour) allows development of appropriate care and management strategies. Initial assessment should include observation of whether the person living in very unclean conditions is physically, mentally and cognitively able to look after themself safely, and to make rational decisions regarding self-care. If there is doubt, an appropriately trained health professional will need to be called in urgently, to assess capacity and health risks.

Table 3.1 lists issues that need consideration when assessing the impact of a squalor situation on an occupant's family and/or the neighbours and local community.

Table 3.1 Impact of squalor.

Issue	Relevant agency
Health and safety issues due to accumulation	Public housing department; local council
Neighbour complaints re mess, odours, vermin	Public housing, local council
Health and safety of occupants	Medical and psychiatric services
Utilities not functional (water, power, etc.)	Local council; water, gas, public housing
Threatened eviction and homelessness	Public housing, community services
Dependent children or disabled relatives	Medical or community services
Pets poorly cared for	RSPCA

Assessment by health professionals

The following is a list of features pointing to a need for priority assessment by health professionals. Assessment could be by local doctors or community health staff (mental health, aged care) visiting the person, or arranged by referral to a hospital emergency department or clinic.

- Observed self-neglect, with poor nutrition, dehydration, untreated medical problems or inability to use toilet appropriately.
- The person appears confused or muddled, unable to think clearly, especially if they appear to be hallucinating (e.g. due to delirium).
- The person appears vulnerable to exploitation by others (e.g. financial).
- Threatened self-harm, suicidal behaviour or features indicating severe depression.
- Aggressive behaviour or threatened harm to others.
- Acute psychiatric symptoms, such as delusional perceptions or severe anxiety.
- Marked decline in functional status, mobility, ability to prepare meals, or inability to use facilities (kettle, stove, shower, etc.).
- Evidence that an occupant's behaviour has resulted in (or might cause) fire within the dwelling.

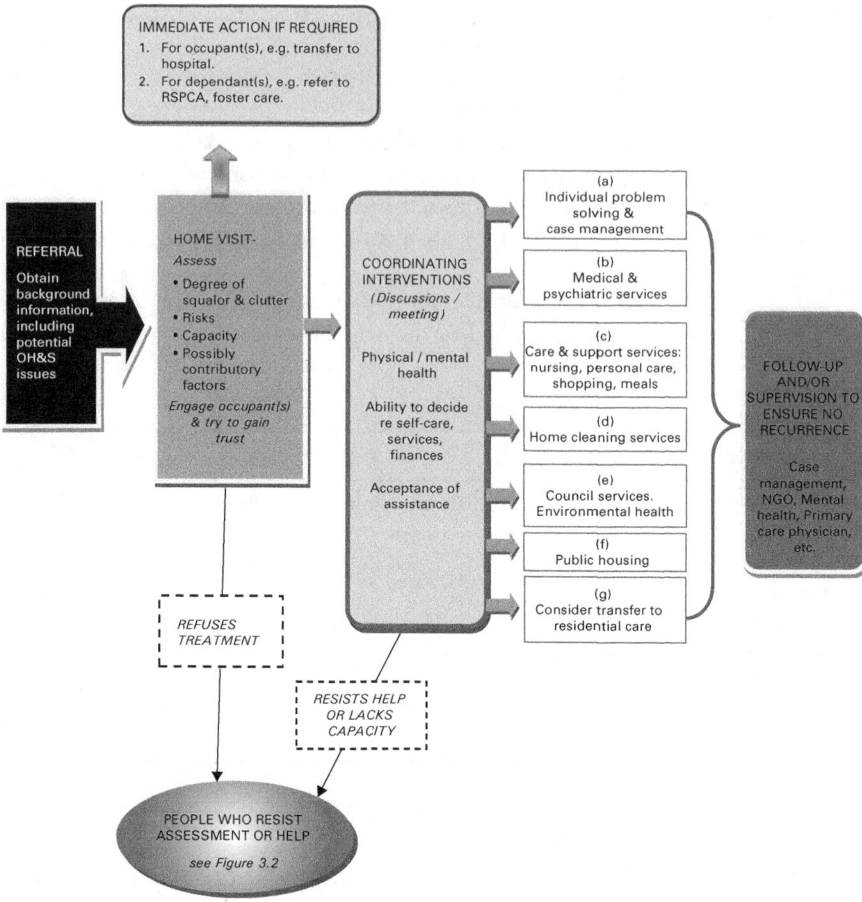

Figure 3.1 Assessment and management of people living in squalor.

A flow chart showing the varied interventions and steps that may be appropriate in cases of severe domestic squalor is presented in Figure 3.1. Case 3.1 (below) raises issues for discussion in relation to assessment. Later in this chapter we will discuss how best to intervene in cases when people living in squalor refuse permission for agencies to enter their dwellings or to assess whether they are able to adequately look after themselves and their homes (Figure 3.2).

(Figures 3.1 and 3.2 have been modified from the algorithms developed by Graeme Halliday for our 2003 report (see Snowdon and Halliday, 2009). Versions of the figures have been published by Gaston *et al.*, 2009.

Case 3.1

An elderly male who has lived in the same private rented flat more than ten years was referred to a local aged care assessment team by his primary care physician. He receives an aged pension and although he reliably pays rent, he spends the rest of his income on cigarettes and alcohol, leaving no money to pay for food or medication. He has chronic smoking-related lung disease, high blood pressure and leg ulcers but even though he uses a stick to walk and is unsteady, he goes out every day. After a recent admission to hospital with a chest infection he was discharged to a nursing home. When his health improved, he insisted on returning to his home.

His flat is very dirty, dark and neglected. It requires painting, has several broken windows and only one working power point. There are no carpets or floor covers. A local charity group removed a large amount of refuse before he returned but quite a bit of rubbish has re-accumulated. He does not want anyone to approach the owner about repairs in case the rent is increased. He has been receiving home delivered meals but refuses to pay the nominal fee and they have threatened to withdraw. Home help refuse to provide cleaning because of the condition of the accommodation.

Community nurses visit every second day to dress a leg ulcer. He denies drinking any alcohol and has been refusing to take prescribed medications even when the purpose for these has been clearly explained. He is dishevelled, irritable and suspicious. On testing of memory and orientation he performs well; however, he has significant impairment on tests of frontal lobe function. During his recent admission to hospital he had abnormal liver function tests consistent with alcohol abuse. He also had a brain scan showing changes due to stroke-related or cerebrovascular disease. His provisional diagnosis is mild frontal dementia due to alcohol and cerebrovascular disease. He is aware his flat is 'untidy' but isn't concerned and doesn't want to consider alternative accommodation.

Discussion

This man's neglected and unclean living conditions are a concern but do not appear to present a high immediate risk, possibly because of the recent cleaning. The fact that his home is becoming dirty again highlights the importance of ongoing supervision and follow up. He shows little awareness of any problems and the potential risks associated with not taking his medication, continuing alcohol abuse, loss of home services and the state of his accommodation.

Coordinating interventions: case conference

Discussions with relevant services

Usually it is appropriate to involve several different agencies when attempting to intervene for the benefit of people living in severe domestic squalor. For example, a public housing authority might become aware that a tenant's dwelling is unacceptably unclean. The housing officer may well seek input from a community health or medical team. A primary care physician may already be treating the tenant for disabling problems or a psychiatric disorder, and specialist help may have already been sought. Drug and alcohol counselling may have been provided. Home Care or a not-for-profit organisation (such as the Brown Sisters in Sydney) may have already been providing help to the occupier in sorting out how to get rid of rubbish or surplus items. The health team may have questioned the capacity of the person to look after themself, and the person may already have a guardian. The local council's environmental health coordinator may have been called in. A clean-up operation may be in the process of being organised. In some situations, it may be useful to seek help from the RSPCA, and there may be reasons for seeking advice from a fire service. Depending on circumstances, relatives, community service personnel and others may be able to contribute to a favourable outcome.

We acknowledge that in some cases of hoarding disorder it may be that effective treatment can be provided by a single therapist, even when the living conditions have become unclean as well as cluttered (see Chapter 4). Much depends on what factors have led to the squalor situation developing. Sometimes squalor develops following grief or depression, and again a single therapist giving effective treatment may be able to effect a lasting cure. However, in most cases where a mental disorder or brain condition is diagnosable, it seems that multiple agencies need to be involved in order to achieve lasting improvements in the quality of life and living conditions of persons identified as living in squalor.

To be effective, if two or more agencies are involved, there needs to be good coordination. They need to work in a collaborative partnership with each other and to value reciprocity and sharing acquired knowledge. Experience will give them understanding of what services other agencies can provide, and what constraints and limitations may apply. They should identify which situations would benefit from input from another agency and why. We believe it important to establish which person or agency is to be regarded as having chief responsibility for case management and ensuring good liaison between partners. Case managers (whether health professionals, local council welfare officers, representatives of community services or whatever) provide a single point of contact for people who require a complex range of services and/or require intensive levels of support. They maximise a person's capacity for independent living in the environment of their choice (Illawarra Good Living Conditions Working Group, 2009).

A potential problem in arranging good coordination lies in non-disclosure of relevant information between agencies because of privacy policies. We respect such policies, but would hope that common sense, trust and understanding will allow agencies to work together for the person's interests. That said, working closely with other agencies has sometimes been reported to us as difficult.

An evaluation of the work of the Severe Domestic Squalor (SDS) project in 18 municipalities in Sydney (McDermott and Gleeson, 2009) reported that staff of the project:

> had difficulty collaborating with other organisations over half of the time. Qualitative data pointed to two reasons for this. First, many services in the community are guided by strict eligibility criteria and boundaries around their particular areas of responsibility. Health and mental health services were reported to have particularly inflexible service boundaries. . . Because of the conflicting views about risk, SDS had difficulties engaging aged care and mental health services to work in partnership in some situations of squalor. . . These organisations often declined to be involved unless the person was legally assessed to lack the capacity to make decisions.

The evaluation report included a second reason for limited service coordination in squalor situations: interventions are costly and often time intensive.

> The cost of cleanups in situations of squalor and hoarding was particularly problematic for Housing NSW and local councils. . . It takes time to build trust with people who are living in squalor and. . . the resource intensive nature of interventions in these situations precludes the ongoing coordination with agencies that do not have the time to sustain such relationships. (McDermott and Gleeson, 2009)

In the guidelines developed in Sydney in 2003, we recommended a joint agency case conference at an early stage, with specific objectives in mind, but particularly to ensure good coordination and understanding between agencies. We suggested that sometimes parts of such meetings might need to be restricted to only those with a recognised right to know certain aspects of the case – for example, in relation to health matters. We recommended that those attending could identify a key worker or case manager for ongoing work with the person(s) living in squalor. We saw the meeting as an opportunity to share OHS information, and to ask some of the questions mentioned above. Does the squalor matter? If so, who is best placed to initiate some action? Does the person have capacity to make informed decisions – for example, about the effect of their living conditions on themselves and others? Who (which agency) will take responsibility for what, and which other agencies should be asked to be involved?

We recognise that a joint agency conference is not always practical and may not be necessary. Agreeing on a time to meet, and the logistics of getting people together, may be difficult, especially if the convenor has been unable to prompt invited participants to recognise good reasons for their attendance. We accept that the necessary discussions can take place in some other way (serial telephone or email communication, for example), but we still hold that the advantages of getting together, face to face, make such conferences desirable in the more difficult or complex cases, especially those where agencies would prefer to opt out, even though others may suggest they could have a major role. Follow-up meetings of involved agency staff to monitor progress, review difficulties in coordination and ensure acceptance of each other's roles may be helpful. Again it is important to note that these are likely to be relatively rare events and so do not consume high levels of resource, but that a coherent plan may well save time and be more clinically and cost effective.

Case 3.2

The Public Guardian's office convened a meeting in Sydney to discuss a re-referral of a 70-year-old man. The Department of Housing had made a decision to evict him from his dwelling because of his failure to comply with requirements. For years his case has been under review because of the state of his single-storey house. Several times it had been cleaned up by a heavy duty cleaning service; the Home Care (domestic work) team had declined further involvement because of his lack of cooperation. As well as having high piles of clothes and other possessions in the bedroom and living room, his kitchen and bathroom/toilet had again become filthy. He had collected large pictures and pieces of furniture he did not need. He had two dogs, which had little opportunity to exercise and one of which was in poor condition; they were usually shut in a cupboard-like room, which was odorous and unclean. He also had in the house and back-yard (with some in a rented garage) about 200 bicycles, which he said he worked on in order to sell.

Those convened by his guardian to discuss the case included representatives of the Department of Housing, the Protective Office (which controlled his access to funds), the non-governmental organisation that provided an aged care package (i.e. funding provided by the government to enable them to visit regularly and case manage him) and his old age psychiatrist. The meeting first considered whether funds could be found to arrange a clean-up, in order to abort the proposed eviction. The Department of Housing stated that he would not be given another place if he were evicted, and the non-governmental agency would not be able to offer alternative accommodation. He would probably be referred to a shelter for homeless men if forced out of the house. The discussion also focused on what should be done about the bicycles – how many should he be allowed to keep? It was agreed that the only hope of sustaining him in his home would be if there were very strict conditions and authority to enforce them. Money should not be available for renting a garage. The sick dog (which had recently been labelled by the local council as dangerous because of its aggression to a neighbour) would have to be sent to an animal shelter.

A clean-up was mandatory (but payment would need to be found), but without the person being present, as it was predicted that he would get violent towards cleaners. His case manager would arrange to look after particular possessions if he would sort them out prior to the clean-up. The psychiatrist agreed to house him in a psychiatric unit for two or three nights

Case 3.2 (*cont.*)

as a voluntary patient while the clean-up was taking place, and this would allow for psychological testing. Obviously, whether any of this could be put into effect would partly depend on the man agreeing to the plan. It was felt that psychiatric medication would not be beneficial, even though at times in the past he had been given antipsychotics because of suspected delusional thinking and possible hallucinations. The guardian was agreeable to the plan, and in due course he was admitted to hospital and the clean-up was effected.

Types of intervention

Individual problem solving and case management

Each person living in a very unclean dwelling has a different story. Initial and ongoing approaches to the problem need to be flexible, and tailored to the needs of the individual – and (in about 20% of cases) co-habitant(s).

The main difficulty encountered when attempting to deal with a squalor situation is the reluctance of a high proportion of occupants to seek or receive help. They deny or do not perceive that domestic uncleanliness and accumulation of waste pose risks to themselves and others, and interfere with the quality of life of their neighbours. If medical or psychiatric assessment and treatment is offered, they may reject it, and pressure to accept it is likely to meet with resistance. Occupants may refuse to allow well intentioned visitors into their dwellings. An authoritarian, demanding, forceful, over-assertive approach by those seeking to improve a person's living conditions and their functional ability is unlikely to be successful in the long term, even if in some cases an urgent clean-up can be arranged. Where possible (i.e. when the risks are not considered so great that immediate action, including removal of occupants, is considered vital), a patient, gentle, unhurried, respectful approach by those taking on a case management role is needed. Such workers, whatever their background and status, need to have skills in building relationships with the occupants of dwellings identified as requiring attention.

Acquisition of trust and cooperation may require several or numerous visits. The agency and workers may well have to cope with criticism from community residents who want immediate results, whereas obtaining an occupant's confidence usually requires patience and time. The worker needs to be creative in developing relationships, especially if the person has for years been reclusive and relatively asocial.

If the worker assigned to a case finds (but not necessarily at an early visit) that the occupant appears to be functioning at an adequate level, is paying their bills, has no clear evidence of health problems that require urgent intervention, and the dwelling appears structurally sound, with contents that appear not to pose a threat to occupants or neighbours, an involuntary intervention does not need to be arranged. In such circumstances, where a person lives in squalor that is deemed not bad enough to insist on an urgent clean-up, it is recommended that contact be maintained but that neighbours be encouraged to call the coordinating agency if the situation deteriorates. Expectations by administrators that such cases should be 'discharged' from an agency's case load need to be resisted; though agency visits to the dwelling could be limited (to between monthly and six monthly, for example, depending on the case).

As discussed in Chapter 1, in a majority of cases of severe domestic squalor, workers will find accumulation of varied items of little monetary value and/or of garbage and waste. The accumulated material may be piled high. The factors affecting why people accumulate refuse are largely different from the complexity of reasons why people gather a multitude of non-garbage items. Those accumulating the latter to a degree considered by most individuals as excessive do not consider this mass of items to be valueless or junk, but nevertheless the amassed material in such cases would usually be regarded as useless, and would not fetch much (if any) money if sold. Garbage, however, is rubbish, and although not motivated to throw it away, accumulators are unlikely to voice a strong need to retain waste material such as residual bones or other parts of animals, fruit or vegetable peelings, emptied containers, wrappers, used tissues and cigarette ends. People who habitually fail to discard such garbage commonly have brain disorders for which medical intervention could be indicated, though sometimes accumulations may be attributable to having grown up in a setting where no one bothered to keep their environment clean or tidy. Laziness and expectations that other persons will do the chores for them may be related to innate personality features or could be learned behaviour.

Those who collect excessive amounts of clothing, non-functional electronic goods, newspapers, magazines, free brochures and other items, that they perceive to be actually or potentially valuable, tend to have diagnosable disorders. These may have developed because of abnormal brain function, but they tend to be different to the brain disorders of those who accumulate only waste material. In some cases, occupants are observed to have collected excessive amounts of these items (clothing, electronic goods, etc.), and perhaps food and drink containers, as well as garbage.

When formulating plans for intervention, workers in these various situations need to note the type of accumulated material, and hypothesise why it is there. Increasing experience of such situations may allow conjecture about an underlying disorder and thus point to a therapeutic intervention that might be effective. In some cases there is 'wet squalor', which may result from deposition of human or animal excrement, rotten and mushy food, or liquids that have overflowed or been dropped and never mopped up. The dwelling in such a case may be uncluttered but filthy. The occupant may be oppositional, hostile and unwilling to have people or service providers in their house, or 'interfering' with what they want to do, but may not be opposed specifically to a clean-up. Getting to know the person (and whether, for example, they are continuing to abuse alcohol) will allow a view on whether they may eventually be more agreeable to a clean-up – or to accepting help for their addiction.

A main need in relevant cases may be to help the person improve organisation of care for their pets. This is discussed in our chapter on animal 'hoarding'. In other cases the occupants may not object to the accumulating mess being cleaned up, but the main need may be to organise ongoing regular services in order to make it possible for the person to remain in their home. Alternatively, in discussion with next of kin and the occupant, it may be thought that a move to supervised care would best improve the occupant's quality of life.

Treatment of hoarding is discussed more fully in Chapter 4. However, it is appropriate to give consideration here to the role of case managers in cases where excessive collecting of items by occupants is a striking feature and the living conditions are sufficiently unclean to warrant use of the term 'severe domestic squalor'. If hoarding (acquisition and failure to discard a large number of possessions) is the reason why a person's dwelling is unacceptably unclean, the worker assigned the role of case manager will want to help the occupant progressively organise and reduce the clutter. Initially, the worker may want to pose non-threatening questions about material in the home, enquiring whether the occupant has plans for storing, displaying, repairing, selling or giving away collected items. A good relationship with the occupant may allow the worker to explore whether any of the items in the home can be seen as valueless, or surplus to requirements. One or more items may be seen as disposable.

Commonly those who hoard acquire feelings of comfort and security from their possessions – which is why attempts to discard them lead to feelings akin to grief. Positive reinforcement is said to be derived from the pleasures of saving and acquiring, while negative reinforcement involves avoidance of negative emotions arising from indecisiveness and anxiety about making mistakes (Gaston *et al.*, 2009).

Frost *et al.* (2000) found that, of people reported to community health departments because of lack of hygiene attributable to hoarding, 32% willingly cooperated in getting rid of possessions, though cooperation was sometimes limited and improvements were not always maintained. Focusing on the aim of minimising the risk of falls and maximising independence may help provide justification for removing excess clutter, and thus result in more chance of cooperation. Negotiation and a problem-solving approach may be useful (see Table 3.2, showing techniques recommended in our NSW guidelines). Tackling problems gradually may help occupants over the initial hurdle of getting started.

Table 3.2 Techniques utilised to promote cleaning and self-care.

1	Encouraging occupants to communicate openly about emotional difficulties experienced while rationalising belongings.
2	Education in relation to safety issues presented by excessive clutter and possible interference with activities of daily living.
3	Breaking larger tasks down into manageable small initiatives.
4	Choosing target areas so that progress is apparent.
5	Provision of emotional support.

Whether case managers and other staff who visit clients to promote cleaning and organising activities are skilled in all these techniques will depend on their training and experience. Some of those who live in very cluttered and/or unclean dwellings seek lengthy opportunities to discuss personal problems with staff, whose orientation is more towards helping and prompting occupants to tidy up and get rid of accumulated material. When this is the case, referral to an appropriate counsellor may be appropriate, so that clean-up organisers can fulfill their main aim while at the same time a counsellor can deal with issues that impact on the person's willingness to engage in the clean-up.

It has been proposed that DSM-5 should make a clear distinction between those who show features of 'hoarding disorder' and those with obsessive–compulsive disorder who hoard. Grisham and Barlow (2005) listed the characteristics of 'compulsively hoarding patients': they have emotional attachment to possessions, concerns about memorising them, a desire for control over them and abnormally high feelings of responsibility for them. They avoid discarding them or making decisions about them, and are generally indecisive. They have impaired organisational and categorisation skills and are over-distractible. They are poorly motivated to change. These characteristics should be borne in mind by case managers in relation to people who live in squalor and hoard, when trying to help them to progressively reduce (or improve organisation of) their piles of possessions.

Passive resistance to therapy makes it difficult, even for experienced psychologists, to design interventions. Case managers may want to refer such occupants to websites designed to help people de-clutter, or even to de-cluttering workshops if such exist in their locality. Therapist guides and workbooks have been developed, but in cases of compulsive hoarding it is recommended that case managers seek to work in cooperation with psychologists skilled in therapy for people who hoard. The latter may conduct cognitive behavioural therapy with the aims of reducing clutter, improving decision making and organisational skills, and strengthening resistance to urges to accumulate items, but will be wise to encourage ongoing involvement of case managers in such cases. Working together to engineer graduated exposure to the anxiety-provoking task of discarding, and aid recognition of the benefits of organisational strategies, has potential for improving outcomes. A multimodal psychological intervention has proved effective when clients have been willing to work with therapists over prolonged periods (meeting 15 to 30 times over 6 to 12 months), every fourth session being based in the person's home (Saxena and Maidment, 2004).

Medical and psychiatric services

A wide range of medical problems has been reported in cases of people living in severe domestic squalor. Consideration needs to be given to mobility, continence, sensory (especially visual) impairment and nutritional deficiencies. People living in severe domestic squalor may have personality disorders or developmental disorder. Among mental disorders, consequences of long-term excessive alcohol use, abuse of other drugs, organic brain disorders (frontal lobe syndromes, Alzheimer's disease and other dementias), schizophrenia, depression and obsessive–compulsive disorder need consideration. Effective treatment and management of any such conditions, if present, may be important in dealing with and preventing recurrence of a squalor situation.

Referral for intervention in cases of squalor may come from staff in hospitals or primary care physicians, specialists or other health professionals, who have had reason to observe or find out what a person's living situation is like. A pre-discharge home assessment by an occupational therapist, or a home visit by a physiotherapist, social worker or primary care physician or as follow-up after discharge from hospital, may have drawn attention to a life situation of which the therapists were previously unaware. This was the case in many of the cases reported by geriatricians working in inpatient settings (e.g. Clark *et al.*, 1975). Clearly it would be important for those asked to advise on management to glean all relevant details from whichever health professionals have already been involved. In particular, they will need to consider whether it is likely that the medical or psychiatric condition for which the referred person has been seeing a health professional could be the major factor that led to the person living in squalor. Have they been known to live in squalor for many years or is this a new development? Is the person meant to be taking antipsychotic medication or an antidepressant? What does the health professional know about the person's family? Has the person been bereaved recently? Has their dog or cat died?

If the referral has come from a person or agency other than via a health professional or service, it will be important to consider whether health issues might at least partly explain why the person now lives in squalor. Case managers and assessors of the situation need to obtain relevant information about the person's health, from relatives, friends, the person's primary care physician (if any), community health staff, or whoever might know what has been happening. Privacy issues may need to be overcome, recognising duty of care to a person who may be at risk.

In many instances it will be appropriate to seek involvement of the primary care physician or local mental health team to assess and then treat mental disorders. Evidence suggests that more than half of those referred to non-health services for intervention because of the unacceptable living conditions in their homes have diagnosable mental disorders (Halliday *et al.*, 2000; McDermott and Gleeson, 2009). People living in squalor commonly are unwilling to visit doctors, clinics or hospitals, but in many areas there are services that are willing to visit people in their own homes – aged care and community mental health specialists and services, primary care physicians and some others. If they visit but the person is not prepared to let them in or see them, decisions have to be made on whether to seek a legal order (e.g. under a Mental Health Act or Guardianship Act) to obtain access or arrange vital investigations. Table 3.3 indicates situations where urgent assessment must be considered a priority.

Table 3.3 Situations requiring urgent home visits and assessment.

1	Considerable self-neglect, poor nutrition, dehydration, untreated and potentially life-threatening medical problems.
2	Delirium or 'confusion'.
3	Suicidal statements or behaviour, or indicators of severe depression.
4	Aggression and threatened harm to others.
5	Acute psychotic symptoms, such as hallucinations, especially if previously unassessed.
6	Marked decline in activities of daily living and functional status, in relation to mobility, personal care, toileting, nutrition, care of pets, etc.
7	Fire setting (accidental or deliberate).
8	Vulnerability to exploitation or abuse by others.

Where feasible it would be hoped that whatever medical or psychiatric care is indicated can be provided in the person's home. At the same time, the living conditions need to be improved enough to make them safe and acceptable. Suppressing psychotic ideas and perceptions (e.g. using antipsychotic medication), controlling or stopping abuse of alcohol or drugs, restoring contentment, providing supervision for those with disabilities, and medication or behaviour therapy for OCD, together with ongoing monitoring by health staff, may be enough to prevent re-emergence of squalor in relevant cases. If home services (such as Home Care) are unavailable to monitor the living conditions of people who were previously living in squalor, it will be important for the primary care physician or community health team to maintain long-term contact – with the person's understanding and consent.

A substantial proportion of older people who are found to be living in severe domestic squalor have progressive brain disorders such as Alzheimer's disease, and some have disabling physical disorders (e.g. after strokes). A clean-up and support at home may enable them to remain in the community for some time, but the evidence base suggests that most of those with moderate or severe cognitive impairment are likely to be admitted to a care home within a few months. Having a cognitively intact co-habitant may delay such a move. The outcome in cases of non-progressive conditions may be better, depending on whether support remains available. Doctors should consider whether admission to a care home is likely to improve a person's quality of life as well as their physical health, and if they resist the idea it is appropriate to obtain an opinion about their capacity to make decisions about self-care. This is discussed in our chapters on the law and ethical aspects of intervention.

There are case-reports in medical and psychiatric journals describing pharmacological, behavioural and psychotherapeutic strategies that have been used by health professionals in treating people who were living in squalor. It is relevant to note what has worked in particular circumstances, and to consider whether there might be justification for using the same approach in other cases of squalor. Treatment with risperidone was reported as beneficial in one case where a 77-year-old woman had taken to collecting rubbish, but was discontinued when it led to impaired cognition (Herran and Vazquez-Barquero, 1999). If an occupant living in squalor is psychotic or highly agitated it might seem appropriate to try treating the person with an antipsychotic such as risperidone, but in most squalor cases there would be little reason for expecting such medication to be beneficial in the absence of demonstrable psychosis. Saxena *et al.* (2007) have reported paroxetine as well as cognitive therapy to be helpful in reducing compulsive hoarding, but did not comment specifically about those living in unclean conditions.

Medical interventions might seem appropriate in some cases of severe domestic squalor, but this should be on the basis of a formulation that the person has a health problem for which a specific treatment might be beneficial (whether or not it also helps them out of their squalor situation).

Home services

Support services aim to help people remain in their own homes. Thus people who are frail or disabled may benefit from community nursing and 'meals on wheels', and from agencies that provide personal care, assistance with medication, showering, cleaning, shopping, meal preparation and dressing.

In Australia, a number of non-governmental organisations (NGOs) are funded by the federal government to provide community aged-care packages that permit individualisation of support services according to need. Help can be offered, too, in association with health care services, to people with physical, psychiatric or developmental disabilities. Such agencies can monitor health, functional status and living conditions, and some may help with the cleaning that others find too difficult to undertake. The Brown Sisters in Sydney is an NGO to be commended for being willing to assist in squalor situations that many would seek to avoid. Some agencies provide transport to get to socialisation opportunities, and run activity centres and living skills programmes. In Australia, Mercy Arms (a component of Catholic Community Services), Uniting Care and the Benevolent Society (among others) have resources to reach out comprehensively and assist in organising alternative permanent accommodation.

Cleaning

Where feasible, cleaners working for a government-subsidised service (whether provided directly by councils or purchased from independent providers such as Home Care, in Australia and the UK) can be contracted to provide a regular service to people who collect clutter and in whose homes garbage tends to accumulate. Thus they can keep mild squalor under control. Their other work is mainly with frail, disabled older people, and in some jurisdictions they carry out personal care tasks such as washing and dressing, and sometimes meeting other needs such as shopping. However, if dwellings are unsafe because of accumulated clutter or hygiene problems (for example, if there is a high level of human or animal excrement around the home), they cannot undertake cleaning services. Case managers or others may need to arrange for specialist cleaning companies with specific protective equipment to take on the work. When dwellings are disgustingly, verminously unclean, forensic or heavy duty cleaners are needed. One of us (GH) worked ethnographically with such a team in London for a year while gathering data regarding 81 cases of severe domestic squalor (Halliday *et al.*, 2000) and can vouch for the difficulties in carrying out such work.

A clean-up cannot be commenced without the consent of the occupant(s) or someone empowered to give substitute consent. When embarking on cleaning up dwellings (as opposed to maintenance cleaning to ensure that squalor is kept at bay), the occupant should be asked to review and record what possessions need to be retained. This applies even when consent has been authorised by someone else (e.g. a legal authority). An inventory of valued possessions should be documented, and decisions need to be made about where they should be stored during the cleaning. Valuable possessions need to be kept in a secure place. An estimate of the cost of the clean-up should be provided before starting it.

By negotiation, the occupant(s) may be able to be on hand during the clean-up, but this needs to be balanced with the potential distress it may cause them and the likelihood of undue interference. In cases where it is expected that the clean-up will take more than a day, it may be appropriate to arrange temporary accommodation elsewhere for the occupant(s). A care home may be able to offer respite care, if relatives or friends are not available to support them. Admission to a psychiatric unit might be considered, either with their consent or (if appropriate) under guardianship or under a section of the Mental Health Act or equivalent. With efficient coordination between services the length of the hospital (or other) stay can be minimised.

Where a large amount of rubbish or accumulated items need to be removed from a property, the cleaning company will need to work with rubbish removers who can convey the material to a garbage tip. Garden clearance and tidying may also be needed.

Because of the likelihood that accumulation of filth and clutter will occur again if there is no one available to monitor and control the situation, we strongly advise that a necessary element of authorising a clean-up should be the specification of ongoing support to the occupants to help them keep their dwelling adequately clean and clutter free.

Council services

Local councils frequently receive requests for action in relation to people living in severe domestic squalor. A well known example in Sydney is that of a woman who lives in a house not far from Bondi Beach, half-way down a desirable street in an affluent area. The house and garden would be worth several million dollars. Repeatedly, over the last 20 years, Waverley Council has needed to take proceedings against the owner because of accumulation of items around the house, leading to unsightliness and lack of hygiene. (Plate 6.1) Each of the several clean-ups over the two decades has cost the equivalent of more than A$50,000 in 2011 costs.

An appeal to the Land and Environment Court delayed action, and eventually this case led to changes in the law in New South Wales regarding such cases. Presumably the council will have sought payment of the expense from the occupant, but we suspect it will have been difficult to recover costs.

Arranging similar clean-ups in cases where occupants have negligible assets has left councils with large bills and the need for considerable financial outlay. For this reason it is not surprising that they are often reluctant and slow to take action in some cases, even if their own environmental health officers consider the living conditions unhygienic and/or unsafe. Fire risk would seem to be an important spur to action, but fire officers have found that they cannot enforce the clearing out of inflammable clutter from a person's home (such as the house in Bondi) until or unless a fire has been reported. Where dwellings are rented, landlords can take action (either a clean-up or eviction); this is discussed below.

Council staff can seek action by referring people reported as living in severe domestic squalor to appropriate health or community services, liaising with drug and alcohol counsellors, mental health, aged care or developmental disability services as appropriate. If the occupant of an unacceptably filthy property does not have a known or identifiable physical, mental or developmental disorder requiring compulsory intervention (e.g. under a Mental Health or Guardianship Act) and does not wish to talk with visiting staff from one of these services, those staff cannot take action unless there has been a breach of the law. Jurisdictions vary in their legislative ability to require that a dwelling conform to certain housing safety standards.

In the UK, the Housing Act 2004 brought in the Housing Health and Safety Rating System, which provides a legal method of inspecting houses. Landlords are responsible for ensuring that their properties are free from hazards.

Bratiotis *et al.* (2011) refer to the Massachusetts State Sanitary Code's 'Minimum standards of fitness for human habitation' and point out (p. 80) that:

> Each geographic area across the United States has public health and fire codes that differ substantially depending on the region of the country. In some states landlords have the primary responsibility for maintaining the property in compliance with the public health code, whereas in other regions (such as Los Angeles County, California) tenants have this responsibility. Cities and towns have the right to write their own codes or to adapt the international code, which is amended annually (International Code Council, 2009). Property owners have an obligation to learn the code for their area and to maintain their property in compliance with the code. . . Properties can be condemned and even demolished if they are deemed hazardous or unfit for human habitation. At the same time, private ownership of property brings with it certain rights not available to renters. In general, private property is protected, limiting the access of certain authorities. . . Someone who has entered the home and can report visual evidence of risk (e.g. family member, friend, repair person, emergency responder, or a home service provider, such as a visiting nurse) must lodge a separate complaint. Because laws vary by state, it is important to verify the legal requirements for obtaining entry before undertaking such proceedings.

It appears to be easier in Sydney than in London or Massachusetts for an owner (who has capacity) to cite legislative regulations when resisting council requests to restore structural and hygienic safety. Council staff may be able to arrange assessment if, for example, there has been a breach of a public health law – and this is discussed in our chapter on the law. Whether anything is done depends on whether the council perceives there is sufficient reason to take action. If the condition of a home or garden is viewed as substantially impacting upon neighbours and the local community, especially if there are public health concerns in relation to vermin, fire risk or sewerage problems, and especially if there is sufficient media outcry (creating a political imperative), something may get done. Observations in Sydney and London show that councils vary in how they respond to such challenges. As civil structures loosen then it will be increasingly difficult to find any statutory (or other) body to take on a role in the planning and execution of activity in this area.

Public housing

Administrators of public housing (e.g. the Department of Housing, in New South Wales) have responsibility for addressing the problem if severe domestic squalor or hoarding in one dwelling impacts on the health, safety and wellbeing of tenants in other such dwellings – or, indeed, on the occupant of the dwelling about which complaints have been made. As landlords, they would want to check that their property is not damaged, and they have a right to inspect the property at intervals, by arrangement.

In London and Sydney (and many other cities) there are large high-rise apartment buildings, the units being rented to public housing tenants at a subsidised rate. Some of the tenants are disabled and have very limited financial reserves. Housing administrators in these situations have a duty of care with respect to the state of the dwelling rented. The duty of care for the welfare of the individuals often lies in a different element of service provision (e.g. local authority social services or local health services). There is a major issue with communication between agencies and the threshold for action in terms of sharing of information and making referrals. We find it remarkable that we see tenants who have clearly been living in a state of neglect for many months or years before any contact is made with health professionals. Clearly we must be sure that occupants' privacy is appropriately protected, but such protection should not be used as an excuse for not looking out for the welfare of our neighbours – and our tenants.

Where appropriate, public housing administrators should be enabled to liaise with health professionals to provide medical and psychiatric assessment and treatment, and seek involvement of support services. Laws relating to tenancy can be used to enable them to put pressure on tenants who do not respond to requests to comply with hygiene and safety requirements. Guardianship arrangements may be helpful in some cases.

Intervening when people resist assessment or help

People have the right to live their lives as they wish, providing they are not putting themselves or others at significant risk, or causing undue harassment to others. This potential for legal constraint varies between countries and will be discussed in later chapters, but the concept of capacity needs to be explored initially here in relation to decisions about whether to intervene when people living in severe domestic squalor resist intervention.

If a person appears to lack capacity to make decisions about self-care and related aspects of life, it is necessary to obtain a formal assessment. Confirmation that a person lacks capacity will allow concerned persons (agencies, relatives, doctors or others with good reason) to seek a legal order to allow compulsory intervention in the person's interests – and to address the problems that the person's living conditions may be causing themself and others.

If a person living in severe domestic squalor retains capacity to make decisions but persistently chooses not to comply with requests or orders made by their local council or landlord or the public housing authority, or by police, fire officers, animal welfare agency staff or other persons with authority to require action, legal proceedings may be needed if compliance with orders is to be enforced (see Figure 3.2). In such cases, where help has been refused initially, it is appropriate to try to persuade the person to agree to accept assistance, since intervention with consent is likely to result in a better outcome as well as maintaining the person's dignity. Sometimes people who were initially opposed to intervention become more accepting when they have had time to consider the potential consequences of their decision.

If a person living in squalor refuses to open their door or speak to persons with expertise to form an opinion about their cognition, capacity cannot be assessed. If then it is still considered essential to view the premises even without the consent of the occupant, application can be made under the relevant Act of Parliament (or equivalent statute) for authority to enter the dwelling (see our chapter on the law). If it is suspected that the occupant or owner does not have capacity to make rational decisions because of mental illness, application can be made for an order under the Mental Health Act (in Australia, UK and where comparable legislation has been enacted) for assessment of the person's capacity and mental state.

Figure 3.2 summarises the ways in which laws can be used to achieve a positive outcome in cases where occupants in cases of severe domestic squalor or hoarding decline or are unable to give consent to measures that agencies argue are necessary. Chapter 7 provides a more detailed discussion of these issues. It should here be emphasised that the law is a blunt instrument and that experts and agencies are fallible. Capacity, consent and confidentiality are sometimes used as an excuse not to act where the processes involved are feared to be complex or costly. What should matter most is the wellbeing of the person

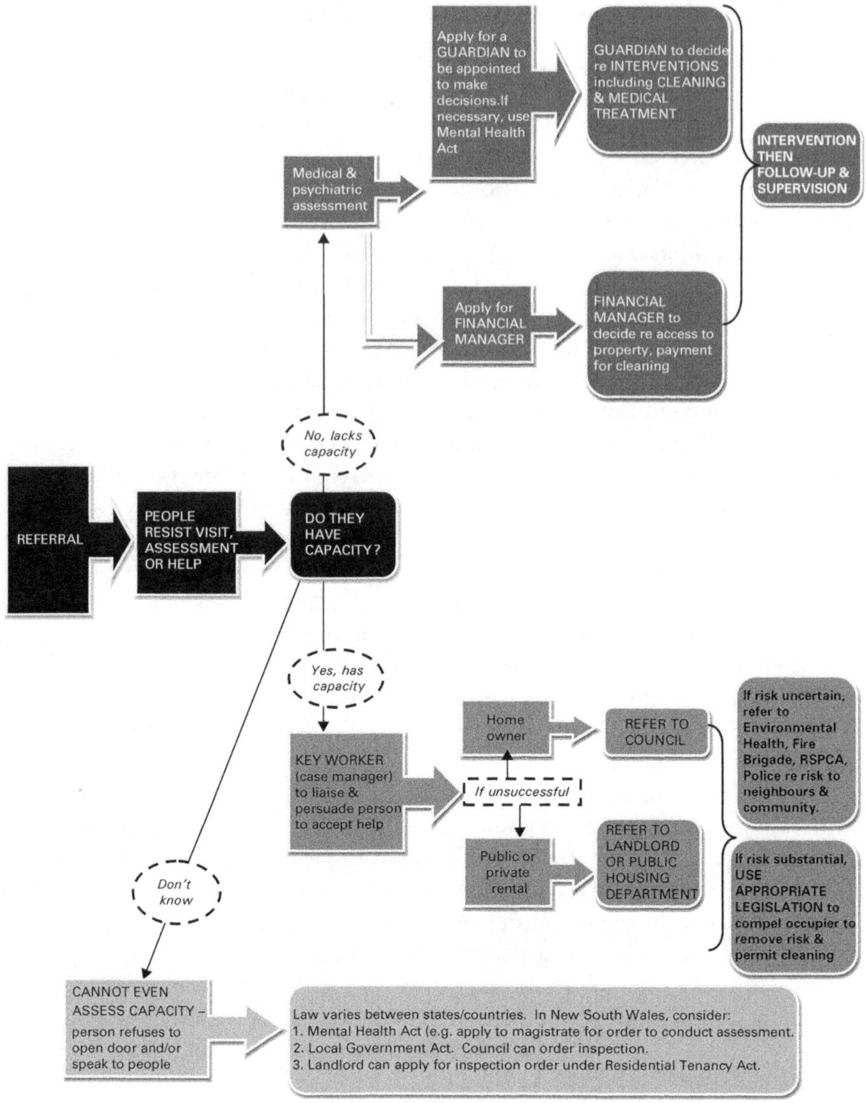

Figure 3.2 People living in squalor who resist assessment or help.

at the centre of the squalor and the wellbeing of those affected by severe domestic squalor in someone else's home. Our job is to seek the best solution for all of them, but it is important that we do so based on a clear, explicit ethical framework that respects human rights. Health and legal systems vary between countries and states, but the principles set out here should be applicable across countries.

Case 3.3

A 62-year-old female lives in her own home unit, which is in a state of squalor. She has a history of head injury and alcohol abuse resulting in moderate to severe frontal lobe damage. She is also noted to be in poor health and her diabetes is poorly controlled. She has a long history of refusing access and has become verbally and physically aggressive to workers when access has been sought previously. Other residents in the block have complained because of the smell. Community Health Services have received calls from the Council and the Body Corporate for the block of units. She has been served a notice from the Council (Environmental Health) requesting her to have her property cleaned or she will be taken to court in accordance with the Local Government Act. The Public Guardian has been appointed to make decisions on her behalf and the Protective Commissioner appointed to manage her finances. Her primary care physician is of the opinion that although she is extremely thin and in poor health she does not need hospitalisation or admission to an aged care facility.

Discussion

In this case the person was recognised to have impaired decision-making capacity and sufficient need (reflecting level of risk) such that the Guardianship Tribunal appointed the Public Guardian to be a substitute decision maker. Guardianship is decision specific and initially only the legal authority to make decisions with relation to consenting to medical treatment and accepting home services (such as Home Help) was granted. A guardianship order is usually limited in time and scope. It is the responsibility of the guardian to review the person's circumstances and act in the best interests of the person. Although the person may not have capacity to make decisions they may still be able to express a view or preference and where possible this should be taken into account. Although the guardian has legal authority for making decisions on the person's behalf, it is the job of others, such as a case manager (if there is one) to implement those decisions.

Sometimes, areas of decision making initially granted by the Guardianship Tribunal may be insufficient. It may become apparent that the substitute decision maker also needs authority to make decisions on behalf of the client in other areas, such as a change of accommodation. Alternatively, it may be impossible to implement an order without the use of force, in which case 'coercive powers' will be required. Authority for decision making in other areas or the use of 'coercion' requires a further application to the Guardianship Tribunal. This case also illustrates occupational health and safety risks. Various workers who are required to enter a dwelling in a state of squalor in the course of their work may be exposed to a wide variety of safety concerns including unstable flooring, exposure to unsafe electrical wiring, violence and

Case 3.3 (*cont.*)

attacks from the individual (or animals) living there. Under NSW law the employer is responsible for ensuring a safe workplace and safety, and risks must be documented and minimised wherever possible. This case also illustrates how level of risk is sometimes uncertain and differences in opinions may arise, even among professionals in the same field.

Case 3.4

Mr A is a 70-year-old male who lives alone in his own home. Mr A was referred to mental health services by his neighbour who was concerned that he was in a severe state of self-neglect and that his mental and physical health had declined. The neighbour had observed that Mr A had been talking to himself, was pale and losing weight. Mental health records confirmed that Mr A was admitted to hospital in 1975 with schizophrenia but has not had any further contact since. Mental health services try to assess Mr A on several occasions without success. His house is extremely neglected and dilapidated. There are several holes in the roof, no glass in the windows, no electricity and no water. The yard and garden are extremely overgrown. Mr A is not known to have any living friends or relatives. The local council knows of Mr A. He comes into the council to pay rates occasionally. His rates are in arrears; he last made a payment several months ago. His yard has had to be cleared by the council on two occasions in the last three years without his permission. He has been charged with the cost of this but the account is outstanding. Otherwise he is not known to have caused any problems and is not known to be a danger to himself or others.

Discussion

In this case there were medical as well as psychiatric problems. Mr A appeared content before the intervention of agencies, and although his psychotic perceptions and experiences were probably interfering with his ability to conduct his affairs and interact with others appropriately, some might think he should have been allowed to go on living in the way he chose, though maybe with compulsion to pay his dues. However, his way of living was certainly affecting his neighbours: his house and yard being unsightly and being a home for vermin. His house was structurally very dangerous for him to live in, and he himself was thought by those who assessed the situation to be potentially at risk because of neglect of his medical condition. On later examination it was shown he was markedly anaemic. A brief stay in hospital was followed by considerable changes in his lifestyle, which appeared to be to his liking as well as that of his neighbours. Using coercive powers proved to be to his benefit.

Case 3.5

Mr B is a 33-year-old male with chronic schizophrenia who lives alone in a Department of Housing (DOH) bedsit. Mr B was last hospitalised over a year ago. He has little insight and has avoided contact with mental health services since his Community Treatment Order expired approximately seven months ago. Mr B is generally suspicious and irritable and DOH has had difficulty organising a routine inspection of his accommodation. When this finally occurs, Mr B is found to be in a severe state of self-neglect. Mr B has minimal furniture but all walls, fixtures and surfaces are severely dirty and damaged by cigarette burns and moisture. The bathroom and kitchen are in a particularly bad state and the floor has been extensively damaged by water. Mr B says he deliberately left the taps dripping to obscure distressing persecutory auditory hallucinations. Mr B agrees to see the local mental health team but refuses to go to hospital.

Discussion

In this case, again, psychotic phenomena were interfering with a man's ability to care for himself and his home. The neglect led to damage to a building that was shared by others. He had no insight. Undoubtedly there were fire risks as a result of his smoking. His untreated mental illness was putting the lives of others as well as his own at risk. Compulsory treatment was necessary. Assertive follow up, to monitor his self-care and to help him to improve his quality of life and wellbeing, would be important to arrange. It would also help identify whether substance abuse exacerbated his psychotic symptoms.

Case 3.6

Ms D, living in public rental accommodation, was hospitalised for an acute episode of a mental illness. In preparation for discharge, the occupational therapist went with Ms D to her home and discovered the severe neglect of property that had resulted from her illness. The property scored 34 on the Living Conditions Rating Scale (LCRS) with a major degree of hoarding, poor disposal of excreta, large amounts of rotten food and a major infestation of vermin. In addition, Ms D's electricity and gas had been disconnected. Application had been made to the Guardianship Tribunal for financial management and this was approved. Ms D expressed considerable dismay at the condition of her flat and agreed to industrial cleaners visiting and addressing the squalor.

Case 3.6 (*cont.*)

Action

As part of the local Transition Pilot Project, 28 hours of cleaning was undertaken and Ms D returned home with follow-up support of workers from Community Mental Health and Assistance with Care and Housing for the Aged Program. Ms D's situation had not come to the attention of neighbours, the community or public housing workers.

Case 3.7

Mr M was referred to the Assistance with Care and Housing for the Aged Care and Assessment Team (ACHA) by the Department of Housing, who had discovered severe domestic squalor while undertaking a regular inspection of his property. Department of Housing staff had also received complaints from neighbours about Mr M's behaviour including his abusive language and threats of violence affected by his considerable use of alcohol. Department of Housing staff attempted to negotiate the organisation and disposal of some of his hundreds of books and other items that he had hoarded over twenty years of residency. They enlisted the aid of the Aged Care Assessment Team's psychogeriatrician and social worker, staff from ACHA and the Fire Department in an effort to provide support.

Mr M vacillated between being cooperative and agreeing to the idea of getting rid of some of his things, to outright refusal and hostility towards those attempting to make him do things he didn't want to do. As he saw it, there had been twenty people tramping all through his place 'like an ant's nest' and then leaving after a brief visit. They had no idea of the value of the things he collected and he thought they were likely to discard prized possessions including war medals, photos and memorabilia. In addition, he thought his place was no more of a fire risk than the bookshop down the road. There were one or two bags that he said he would take to the rubbish, but that would be the extent of it.

Strategies to address his situation included building rapport over a long period of time with the recognition that any change in his home was likely to take upwards of two years. It seemed there would be considerable problems if an eviction notice were granted, since he said he would fight anyone who ordered him to do anything.

4

Hoarding and severe domestic squalor

David Mataix-Cols

Introduction

Collecting and saving are widespread and normal human activities. At age six, for example, approximately 70% of normal children possess a collection (Evans *et al.*, 1997), while by the second decade of life this percentage has decreased to 23%. This figure appears to be largely maintained through the 30s and mid-40s and is followed by a second decline to 13% between the mid-40s and 50s and 15% in the mid-50s to 60s (Pearce, 1998). The ubiquity of this behaviour is reflected in large quantities of collector-based media in the form of magazines, Internet fora, radio shows and television programmes, including the BBC's *Antiques Roadshow*, which is currently in its 33rd season, and regularly attracting an average audience of 6 million people (BBC Press Office, 2007). This form of selective object accumulation is largely viewed as a pleasurable leisure activity that provides psychological benefit to the person engaged in it (Nordsletten and Mataix-Cols, 2012).

Within the clinical psychology and psychiatry communities, however, investigations into object accumulation have increasingly focused on its ability, in some cases, to cause distress and impair normal function. This excessive form of object amassment, widely referred to as 'hoarding', has resulted in a body of research elucidating its core features and highlighting its potential to impair individual, interpersonal and occupational functioning (Frost and Hartl, 1996; Thomas, 1997; Damecour and Charron, 1998; Frost *et al.*, 2000; Steketee and Frost, 2003; Tolin *et al.*, 2008). At its most severe, hoarding can pose serious risks to health and safety, such as falling, fire and sanitation problems, which are especially common among the elderly (Frost *et al.*, 2000; Kim *et al.*, 2001).

As noted in earlier chapters, hoarding behaviour has been described in multiple organic and mental disorders, such as dementia, schizophrenia or autism (Pertusa *et al.*, 2010a; Steketee and Frost, 2003). Although hoarding is frequently linked with obsessive–compulsive disorder (OCD), it is not directly mentioned in DSM IV-TR or the World Health Organization's International Classification of Diseases (ICD-10) as a symptom of OCD. In DSM IV-TR, hoarding is listed as one of the eight diagnostic criteria for obsessive–compulsive personality disorder (OCPD). In the description of the differential diagnosis between OCPD and OCD, DSM IV-TR states that a diagnosis of OCD should be considered especially when hoarding is extreme (e.g. accumulated stacks of worthless objects present a fire hazard and make it difficult for others to walk through the house) (p. 728). Thus DSM IV-TR assumes that in severe cases hoarding can be a symptom of OCD. Of note, this was not the case in any of the previous editions of the DSM (Mataix-Cols *et al.*, 2010).

While there is little doubt that hoarding can be a symptom of OCD or secondary to typical obsessive fears, such as difficulties discarding items for fear of contaminating or harming others (Pertusa *et al.*, 2010a), there is an increasing body of evidence supporting the view that, in most cases, hoarding symptoms are not OCD related. For example, although approximately 5 to 10% of patients with OCD display hoarding symptoms, the majority of individuals (>80%) with hoarding problems do not display other OCD symptoms (Pertusa *et al.*, 2008; Samuels *et al.*, 2008; Frost *et al.*, 2011b). In fact, the most common co-morbidities among hoarding cases are depression and anxiety disorders other than OCD (Frost *et al.*, 2011b). Furthermore, severe hoarding symptoms may be equally prevalent in individuals with anxiety disorders other than OCD, although these symptoms often go unnoticed as clinicians do not ask about them (Tolin *et al.*, 2011).

Research reviewed elsewhere has also revealed important differences between hoarding and OCD, including symptom phenomenology, degree of insight, clinical course, cognitive–behavioural–emotional processes, neurocognitive correlates, genetics and treatment response (Saxena, 2008; Rachman *et al.*, 2009; Mataix-Cols *et al.*, 2010; Pertusa *et al.*, 2010b). In light of this accumulating evidence, the DSM-5 Obsessive Compulsive Spectrum Sub-Work Group of the Anxiety, Obsessive–Compulsive Spectrum, Posttraumatic, and Dissociative Disorders Work Group is currently recommending the creation of a new diagnostic category in the nomenclature named hoarding disorder (HD; Mataix-Cols *et al.*, 2010; www.dsm5.org). The provisional diagnostic criteria for HD are listed in Table 4.1. It is proposed that HD will be placed under a broader umbrella of Obsessive–Compulsive Spectrum Disorders (Phillips *et al.*, 2010). The Sub-Work Group is also proposing the removal of the hoarding criterion of OCPD, a recommendation that is also endorsed by the DSM-5 Personality Disorders Workgroup (Mataix-Cols *et al.*, 2010).

The prevalence of clinically significant hoarding is estimated to be in the region of 2 to 5% of the general population (Samuels *et al.*, 2008; Iervolino *et al.*, 2009; Mueller *et al.*, 2009; Fullana *et al.*, 2010) and 10 to 20% in anxiety

Table 4.1 Provisional diagnostic criteria for hoarding disorder in DSM-5.

A. Persistent difficulty discarding or parting with possessions, regardless of their actual value.

B. This difficulty is due to a perceived need to save the items and distress associated with discarding them.

C. The symptoms result in the accumulation of possessions that congest and clutter active living areas and substantially compromise their intended use. If living areas are uncluttered, it is only because of the interventions of third parties (e.g., family members, cleaners, authorities).

D. The hoarding causes clinically significant distress or impairment in social, occupational, or other important areas of functioning (including maintaining a safe environment for self and others).

E. The hoarding is not attributable to another medical condition (e.g., brain injury, cerebrovascular disease, Prader-Willi Syndrome).

F. The hoarding is not better accounted for by the symptoms of another DSM-5 disorder (e.g., hoarding due to obsessions in Obsessive–Compulsive Disorder, decreased energy in Major Depressive Disorder, delusions in Schizophrenia or another Psychotic Disorder, cognitive deficits in Dementia, restricted interests in Autism Spectrum Disorder).

Specify if:

With Excessive Acquisition: If symptoms are accompanied by excessive collecting or buying or stealing of items that are not needed or for which there is no available space.

Indicate whether hoarding beliefs and behaviors are currently characterized by:

Good or fair insight: The individual recognises that hoarding-related beliefs and behaviours (pertaining to difficulty discarding items, clutter, or excessive acquisition) are problematic.

Poor insight: The individual is mostly convinced that hoarding-related beliefs and behaviours (pertaining to difficulty discarding items, clutter, or excessive acquisition) are not problematic despite evidence to the contrary.

Absent insight (i.e. delusional beliefs about hoarding): The individual is completely convinced that hoarding-related beliefs and behaviours (pertaining to difficulty discarding items, clutter or excessive acquisition) are not problematic despite evidence to the contrary.

disorder or OCD clinics (Tolin *et al.*, 2011; Chakraborty *et al.*, 2012). Thus hoarding difficulties appear to be frequent. However, most of these epidemiological studies could not reliably exclude other causes of hoarding, such as other organic or mental disorders (Criteria E and F). Therefore, the true prevalence of HD in the community remains to be elucidated. It is essential that the proposed criteria are able to discriminate HD from other 'organic' and mental disorders that are known to result in hoarding or in the passive accumulation of possessions. Criteria E and F (Table 4.1) are clear in that general medical conditions (e.g. brain injury) and DSM-5 disorders must be ruled out as potential causes of the hoarding before a diagnosis of HD can be made. However, note that HD can be co-morbid with any medical condition or DSM-5 disorder, as long as the hoarding is deemed independent (i.e. not secondary or caused by) these conditions.

The provisional DSM-5 criteria for HD include two specifiers, excessive acquisition and degree of insight, which aim to increase the clinical utility of the diagnosis (Table 4.1). Although the presence of excessive acquisition is not required for diagnosis, a significant majority of HD patients suffer from it, and ignoring it in treatment is likely to result in treatment failure (Frost *et al.*, 2009). On the other hand, including an insight specifier is relevant to hoarding given that many sufferers underestimate the extent of their difficulties (Tolin *et al.*, 2010a). It is worth noting that the concept of insight in HD is somewhat broader than the concept of insight in OCD or body dysmorphic disorder (BDD) in that it primarily refers to awareness that hoarding-related beliefs and behaviours are problematic. In other words, this definition focuses on the individual's degree of awareness of the consequences of the symptoms (e.g. in terms of safety for self and others, impairment, consequences for family members, neighbours, etc.), in addition to hoarding-related beliefs (e.g. beliefs about the importance of possessions for future use). This is because one of the most striking features of some patients with HD is their failure to recognise that they have a problem and seem 'blind' to the consequences of their behaviour despite clear evidence of the contrary. These individuals also resist intervention. Therefore the types of therapeutic approaches required for patients with absent (delusional) insight may well differ from those required for individuals with good insight (for example the use of motivational interviewing techniques is recommended for patients with poor/absent insight; Steketee *et al.*, 2010).

It is clear that a proportion of people who hoard, or have accumulated lots of possessions, also live in various degrees of domestic squalor, as defined in this book. But it is useful to note that hoarding appears to be more common than living in severe domestic squalor and that those living in squalor may exhibit little in the way of hoarding. This poses a number of intriguing questions that remain largely unresolved. From the DSM-5 point of view, an important question is whether squalor should be included as a potential third specifier to indicate that some individuals with this diagnosis live in squalid conditions (Snowdon *et al.*, 2012). Because the threshold for including a specifier in DSM-5 is very high, one would need to demonstrate that a significant proportion of individuals with HD do indeed live in severe domestic squalor and that there is some clear clinical benefit from including such a specifier.

This chapter begins by defining some key concepts and outlining the differences between 'organic' forms of object accumulation and HD. It then reviews the available literature on the relation between hoarding and squalor and discusses whether it is appropriate to include squalor as a specifier in a classificatory system such as DSM-5. Finally, it identifies some of the gaps in the knowledge base and suggests potential avenues for further research.

Terminology

In this chapter, the term 'collecting' will be exclusively used in the context of the widespread and benign activity of accumulating objects for their symbolic value, commonly with the intention of forming a complete set or creating a legacy (Nordsletten and Mataix-Cols, 2012).

The term 'pathological (or abnormal) object accumulation' can be used to refer to any form of excessive acquisition or object amassment and accumulation that results from brain pathology (e.g. brain damage or dementia). In these cases, the aetiology of the problematic behaviour is largely known and often documented using brain scans.

We prefer to avoid using terms such as Diogenes syndrome or syllogomania (Clark *et al.* 1975) because, as we have seen in the preceding chapters, there is a great deal of confusion regarding their exact meaning and they have poor heuristic value. For example, it is likely that many people said to have Diogenes syndrome have serious mental disorders that can explain the symptom presentation (Cooney and Hamid, 1995). It is also possible that some (a minority) of these patients would meet criteria for HD. Similarly, the pseudoscientific term syllogomania is vaguely defined as the hoarding of 'useless rubbish' but appears to have little construct or predictive validity (Snowdon *et al.*, 2012).

The term 'object accumulation' will also be used in the context of several mental disorders that can result in the excessive acquisition and/or amassment of large numbers of items, including schizophrenia, autism, severe depression, etc. Despite the widespread use of the term 'compulsive hoarding', this chapter will only use it in the context of OCD, i.e. when the accumulation of objects is clearly secondary to OCD symptoms (e.g. difficulties discarding due to fears of harming others) or the avoidance of onerous rituals (Pertusa *et al.*, 2010a).

Finally, when the behaviour is pathological but independent from (even if co-morbid with) any other medical and psychiatric conditions, it will be referred to simply as hoarding or HD, as these are the suggested terms in DSM-5.

'Object accumulation' in general medical conditions and neurodegenerative processes

As mentioned earlier, people with some general medical conditions (e.g. brain lesions) and neurodegenerative processes (e.g. dementia) sometimes excessively acquire and/or accumulate large numbers of objects.

Case studies and case series of patients who started acquiring or accumulating after suffering brain damage suggest that the anterior ventromedial prefrontal and cingulate cortices are implicated in this behaviour (e.g. Cohen *et al.*, 1999; Hahm *et al.*, 2001; Volle *et al.*, 2002; Anderson *et al.*, 2005). In a comprehensive case series (Anderson *et al.*, 2005), nine cases of pathological 'collectionism' (their term) following brain damage were identified and their neuropsychological profiles were compared with those of 54 brain-damaged patients who did not display this symptom. All displayed excessive and persistent acquisition or accumulation behaviour that was not present prior to the onset of the brain damage and led to obvious negative consequences for the patients and their families. All nine patients acquired items excessively and indiscriminately, and eight of them also had diminished discarding behaviour. Abnormal food collection was evident in five of the cases. The relatives described the patients as having acquired deficits in planning, organising and controlling their impulses, but not having significant 'obsessive tendencies'.

In terms of neurocognitive performance, there were no obvious differences between the accumulating and non-accumulating cases with regard to verbal and non-verbal intelligence, memory or executive functions (including the Wisconsin Card Sorting Test). Although the differences were not significant at the group level, perhaps due to limited statistical power, four 'accumulators' had significant memory impairments and six had impairments on the Tower of Hanoi, a planning task. Analysis of the magnetic resonance imaging (MRI) scans indicated that the maximal region of difference between the two groups was the ventromedial prefrontal cortex, extending posteriorly to the anterior cingulate cortex. Linking the existing animal and lesion literature, Anderson *et al.* (2005, p. 201) concluded that 'the evidence suggests that damage to the mesial frontal region disrupts a mechanism which normally modulates sub-cortically driven predispositions to acquire and collect, and adjusts these predispositions to environmental context'.

Additional evidence for the involvement of ventromedial prefrontal regions in pathological accumulators comes from a handful of published cases of patients with the frontal variant of fronto-temporal dementia that included neuroimaging evidence (Nakaaki *et al.*, 2007; Mendez and Shapira, 2008). The features of the accumulating behaviour appear to be similar to those described in brain lesion studies. It is often accompanied by other neuropsychiatric symptoms such as disinhibition, gambling, disorganisation, rituals/stereotypies, tics and self-injurious behaviours (Mendez and Shapira, 2008). Neuropsychologically, these patients often show preserved abilities on traditional frontal lobe tasks because these tasks tend to be more sensitive to dorsolateral rather than ventromedial frontal lobe dysfunction (Nakaaki *et al.*, 2007).

Pathological accumulation of objects has also been described in Alzheimer's dementia. For example, Hwang *et al.* (1998) reported that 30 out of 133 (23%) people with dementia admitted to a geropsychiatric ward in Taiwan displayed hoarding (their term) behaviours. Of these, 24 had Alzheimer's dementia, 4 multi-infarct dementia, and 2 dementia not otherwise specified. Patients displaying this behaviour also had a higher prevalence of repetitive behaviours, hyperphagia and pilfering. These findings could indicate that medial temporal brain regions may also be implicated in this form of object accumulation, which would also be consistent with the animal literature.

To summarise, studies of animal and human brain damage and dementia appear to provide useful clues as to which brain regions may be important in mediating or regulating abnormal object accumulation and the typical neuropsychological profile associated with these patients. The evidence so far suggests that ventromedial prefrontal and medial temporal brain regions are implicated in these 'organic' forms of accumulation. However, much caution is needed before extrapolating these findings to 'non-organic' hoarding cases, as there appear to be some clear phenomenological differences.

Differences between 'object accumulation' and hoarding disorder

Although direct comparisons between the type of excessive accumulation described in the previous section and those with HD have not been conducted, examination of the published cases suggests clear phenomenological differences between these two states (Mataix-Cols *et al.*, 2011).

In 'organic' cases, the onset of the problematic behaviour appears shortly after the brain damage occurs or the onset of the dementing process. In a way, its causes are known and a clear time-line can be established in most cases. By contrast, the onset of hoarding disorder is insidious, has its origins in childhood/adolescence and usually has a long natural history before it becomes problematic (see Mataix-Cols *et al.*, 2010; Pertusa *et al.*, 2010b for reviews). Some of the 'organic' patients seem to be able to discard their possessions easily or do not seem to care if others discard them, whereas others appear to be very reluctant to discard any of their accumulated items (Anderson *et al.*, 2005). By definition, all people with HD have difficulties and experience great distress when discarding their possessions (Frost and Hartl, 1996; Mataix-Cols *et al.* 2010).

The nature of the acquisition may differ, in that in some (but not all) organic cases it may be more indiscriminate; these patients appear to have little interest in the accumulated items and never use them (Anderson *et al.*, 2005). In other brain-damaged cases, however, the collecting behaviour can be truly goal-directed rather than indiscriminate (Volle *et al.*, 2002; Anderson *et al.*, 2005). In HD, the majority of patients who acquire do so purposefully and have a strong interest in the collected items, driven by the emotional or intrinsic value they attribute to these items, although they may not use them either.

While the items being accumulated/hoarded appear to be similar, the accumulation of food, often decaying, is more commonly described in 'organic' cases (Hwang *et al.*, 1998; Anderson *et al.*, 2005). Interestingly, some of the people with OCD-related hoarding (that is, hoarding as a compulsion in an individual with OCD) have also been found to accumulate rotten food and body products (e.g. nails, faeces) but this appears to be much rarer (or non-existent) in cases of HD (Pertusa *et al.*, 2008). Related to the previous point, a large number of individuals who have accumulated large numbers of objects due to a general medical condition or severe psychiatric disorder may live in various degrees of domestic squalor (Snowdon *et al.*, 2012), whereas the number of individuals with HD who live in such conditions appears to be substantially smaller. We shall return to this point later.

In individuals with brain damage or dementia, the collecting behaviour may be accompanied by severe personality changes as well as behaviours commonly attributable to brain dysfunction, such as gambling, inappropriate sexual behaviour, excessive shopping leading to financial difficulties, theft, stereotypies, tics and self-injurious behaviours (Anderson *et al.*, 2005; Nakaaki *et al.*, 2007; Mendez and Shapira, 2008). Although excessive buying is very common in HD (hence the acquisition specifier), and stealing has been anecdotally been reported (Steketee and Frost, 2003; Mataix-Cols *et al.*, 2010), severe personality changes or behaviours clearly attributable to brain dysfunction appear to be far less prevalent.

Whereas HD is characterised by a set of erroneous beliefs about the importance of possessions, strong emotional attachment to possessions as well as information processing deficits (Steketee and Frost, 2003), there has been little research to show whether or not object accumulation in organic syndromes is usually devoid of identifiable cognitive and motivational processes.

Help-seeking behaviour may also differ between these patient groups; many patients who accumulate objects in the context of an organic brain disorder or severe mental disorder (e.g. schizophrenia) may never seek help for their problem (Snowdon *et al.*, 2012). Presumably this is due to a severely compromised level of insight or apathy, which may in turn be caused by the associated neuropsychogical dysfunction that is characteristic of these cases. By contrast, in HD, insight ranges widely along a continuum from good/fair to absent or delusional (Mataix-Cols *et al.*, 2010; Tolin *et al.*, 2010a). Patients with good/fair insight are far more likely to come forward for research and treatment studies, whereas those with absent/delusional insight may never seek help until family members, local authorities or psychiatric teams insist they seek help. In this regard, they resemble 'organic' accumulators. These and other differences between the two phenomena are summarised in Table 4.2.

Excessive object accumulation in cases of severe domestic squalor

The majority of studies on squalor have focused on elderly populations recruited from specialist mental health or geriatric medical services (Snowdon *et al.*, 2007). These studies initially suggested that those living in squalor were likely to be over the age of 60, primarily female, living alone and unmarried (Shah, 1990). The prevalence of squalor among middle-aged and younger people may be one fifth of the rate in old age, judging by referrals to a squalor intervention service in Sydney (McDermott and Gleeson, 2009).

Hypotheses on the aetiology of squalor have moved from the phenomenon possibly being unidimensional to having heterogeneous causes such as physical

Table 4.2 Phenomenological differences between excessive acquisition/accumulating behaviour due to macroscopic brain damage and hoarding disorder.

	'Organic' object acquisition/accumulation	Hoarding disorder
Onset	Generally sudden in cases of brain damage. Can be more insidious if secondary to a dementing process.	Insidious. Usually starts in childhood/adolescence and has a long natural history.
Ability to discard hoarded items	Variable (some are able to discard their possessions easily or do not care if others discard them, whereas others are very reluctant).	Inability to discard hoarded items is a core feature of hoarding disorder.
Nature of acquiring behaviour	Generally indiscriminate but can be more selective (acquisition of specific items – e.g. umbrellas – or according to their shape/colour) in some cases.	Items are always acquired/ hoarded according to their perceived intrinsic, practical or emotional value, but can be more indiscriminate in some cases.
Utility of hoarding behaviour	Often purposeless (individuals display little or no interest in the accumulated items) and items seldom used.	More purposeful (items are hoarded for specific emotional or practical reasons), although items often not used.
Hoarded items	Any item, including rotten food.	Any item, though hoarding of rotten food is rare.
Squalid living conditions and/ or self-neglect	Frequent (especially in cases with dementia).	Thought to be relatively uncommon although more research is needed.
Associated features	Severe personality changes as well as behaviours commonly attributable to brain dysfunction such as gambling, inappropriate sexual behaviour, excessive shopping leading to financial difficulties, theft, stereotypies, tics and self-injurious behaviours.	No severe personality changes or other behaviours clearly attributable to brain dysfunction. Excessive acquisition very common; stealing occasionally reported.
Cognitive processes and motivations for hoarding	Hoarding apparently devoid of identifiable cognitive and emotional processes, although more research is needed.	(a) information-processing deficits: decision-making, categorisation, organisation, memory difficulties (b) emotional attachment to possessions (c) behavioural avoidance (d) erroneous beliefs about possessions.

Table 4.2 (*cont.*)

	'Organic' object acquisition/accumulation	Hoarding disorder
Insight and help-seeking behaviour	Poor or absent insight.Patients seldom seek help.	Insight ranges from good to poor or absent. Initially, hoarding behaviour can be ego-syntonic; it becomes increasingly distressing as clutter increases. Help-seeking probably related to degree of insight.
Prevalence	Unknown (<1%).	Approximately 2 to 5%.
Familial	No? Some cases have been reported of relatives living independently in squalor.	Yes. Hoarding tends to run in families and appears to be moderately heritable.

Adapted from Mataix-Cols *et al.*, 2011.

disabilities, brain damage, psychiatric conditions and personality disorders (Snowdon *et al.*, 2007). Studies on squalor have often noted the presence of 'hoarding' or accumulating behaviours. Macmillan and Shaw (1966) reported squalor patients' reluctance to throw things away. Clark *et al.* (1975) observed the accumulation of useless items and severely diminished living space for several of their squalor cases. Snowdon (1987) provided data indicating that 72% of squalor cases were rated as 'hoarding a lot' or 'possessions piled high'. However, none of these studies have the data necessary to establish whether any of these participants would meet the criteria for HD.

Data regarding successive referrals of older people living in squalor (Snowdon and Halliday, 2011) showed that in a majority of cases the uncleanliness was attributable to a diagnosable DSM-IV psychiatric disorder (see Chapter 2). Of 39 cases where a major degree of hoarding or clutter was observed, ten had dementia, four substance abuse or alcohol-related brain damage and nine schizophrenia or delusional disorder. Because the accumulation of items was attributed to mental disorder in these cases, they would not have fulfilled criteria for HD. In three other cases it was considered that physical disability was the cause of the accumulation of material. Ten had personality disorders and three were given no psychiatric diagnosis; it was thought that in some, at least, of these cases, criteria for HD may have been fulfilled. Whether a diagnosis of OCD rather than HD was justifiable was not examined, since full assessment regarding compulsive features (other than hoarding) was usually not possible. Thus using unstructured interviews and all available evidence, the authors concluded that two thirds of referred older people living in severe squalor, and displaying a major degree of accumulation of material or possessions, had mental disorders. The other one third might well have fulfilled criteria for HD (Snowdon *et al.*, 2012). Of those showing only moderate or minor degrees of accumulation but severe uncleanliness, almost all had a mental disorder that would preclude the diagnosis of HD.

Chiu *et al.* (2003) described 30 patients who 'faced complaints or hygiene problems as a result of hoarding behaviour' and were referred to a psychiatric outreach service in Hong Kong. All had acquired and failed to discard possessions of little or no use or value, and the consequent restriction in living space precluded activities for which such space had been designed. However, the authors did not state that the difficulty discarding was due to a perceived need to save the items and distress associated with discarding them (HD, Criterion B). Items and material were accumulated, but was this purposeful acquisition and/or passive retention? Sixteen of their sample had schizophrenia or delusional disorder. Other patients had dementia (three), mental retardation (two), depression (two), or personality disorder (one), while six had no diagnosed mental illness. Thus, the majority of these patients may have not met DSM-5 criteria for HD.

The dementia literature may also offer some clues. The excessive accumulation of objects, often associated with hiding and rummage, is a relatively common symptom in patients with moderate to severe dementia. In a study comprising 133 patients with dementia admitted to a geropsychiatric ward, 30 (22.6%) exhibited hoarding (their term) behaviour (Hwang *et al.*, 1998), which was associated with a higher prevalence of repetitive behaviours, hyperphagia and pilfering. In some patients, the behaviour preceded the disease onset, initially in an organised fashion, which eventually became disorganised as their dementia progressed (Homma *et al.*, 1994). However, other researchers have not found a link between the degree of cognitive decline and hoarding. For instance, Hwang and colleagues (1997, 1998) found no correlation between hoarding behaviour and Mini-Mental State Examination (MMSE) score in nursing home residents. In another study that included nursing home residents (n = 408) and community-dwelling senior day-care participants (n = 177), 15% of the nursing home residents and 25% of the community-dwelling senior day-care participants manifested 'hoarding' behaviour several times a week or higher (Marx and Cohen-Mansfield, 2003). The behaviour described in these patients, which consisted mainly in collecting many or inappropriate objects such as food in one's purse, pockets or drawers, and/or hiding the collected items, is certainly different from the typical behaviour of patients with HD. Interestingly, elderly persons who manifested 'hoarding' behaviour were those with relatively fewer health and functional disabilities, and also manifested agitated behaviours as well as a larger appetite.

To summarise, it seems clear that approximately two thirds of individuals who live in severe domestic squalor also have at least moderate levels of accumulation of possessions and one third may have a 'major degree' of object accumulation, which precludes the normal use of space. The majority of those who live in squalor and have accumulated large numbers of items have a major mental disorder or physical disability that can entirely account for the accumulation and/or difficulty discarding the objects and would, by definition, not meet criteria for HD. However, there is a possibility that a minority of individuals who live in severe domestic squalor would indeed satisfy diagnostic criteria for HD, once other general medical and psychiatric conditions are ruled out. Finally, it is also conceivable that some of these elderly persons had pre-existing hoarding tendencies and that the onset of general medical conditions or mental disorders aggravated rather than initiated the hoarding behaviour. Longitudinal studies are needed to clarify this.

Squalid living conditions in cases of hoarding disorder

Research on hoarding (or hoarding disorder) has rarely included systematic assessments of severe domestic squalor but the issue is sometimes mentioned in the literature. Winsberg *et al.* (1999) noted that clutter inhibited normal activities of daily living, including personal hygiene. Frost *et al.* (2000) surveyed health department officers in Massachusetts who reported 38% of their hoarding cases to be 'heavily cluttered with filthy environment, overwhelming', although it is unclear how many of these 'hoarding' cases would meet diagnostic criteria for HD rather than for another mental disorder.

Grisham *et al.* (2006) recruited subjects from self-help groups for people with clutter problems, and among people seeking help in dealing with a hoarding problem. Participants had mild to moderate hoarding problems as determined by scores on the Saving Inventory-Revised (Frost *et al.*, 2004). Other mental disorders were not recorded. Participants were asked whether the general condition of their home was good, fair or poor, and whether parts of their dwelling were unsanitary. Findings regarding living conditions were not published in their report, but have now been provided (Jessica Grisham, personal communication, September 2011): valid data were available regarding 82 dwellings out of 125 in the sample. Parts of the houses were reported as very unsanitary in 11 (13.4%) and somewhat unsanitary in 30 (36.6%) cases. In 5% there was evidence of severe insect infestations.

Steketee *et al.* (2001) focused on cleanliness ratings of the personal appearance and the homes of 62 elderly hoarding individuals. In their sample, 17% of individuals were described as 'extremely filthy' and 33% of residences were rated as 'extremely filthy and dirty'. For 32% of the residences, there was an overpowering odour from rotten food or animal or human faeces. Many subjects could not use their refrigerator (45%), kitchen sink (42%), bathtub (42%) or toilet (10%).

Rasmussen *et al.* (2012, submitted) have developed an instrument for measurement of squalor in cases of hoarding. They found that scores on their measure of squalor correlated quite well with degree of hoarding. By contrast, squalor correlated less well with measures of OCD symptoms and depression.

In a large self-referred sample, 16% of patients fulfilling criteria for HD reported moderate or greater levels of unsanitary conditions in the home; 5% reported substantial or severe levels. Observers in the home rated 20% of these patients as having moderate or greater levels of unsanitary conditions, while 7% were rated as substantial or severe (Randy O. Frost, personal communication, August 2011).

Thus it appears that approximately 10 to 20% of patients who participate in hoarding research studies may live in various degrees of domestic squalor. However, according to Frost and Steketee (2010, p. 172) 'in the social service and public health sector, such cases are the norm'. Arguably, in some of these cases squalor could have been attributable to other mental disorders, thus precluding a diagnosis of HD.

The overlap between hoarding and squalor may be most obvious in cases of animal hoarding. This has been defined as the accumulation of a large number of animals and:

(1) failure to provide minimal standards of nutrition, sanitation and veterinary care
(2) failure to act on the deteriorating condition of the animals (including disease, starvation or death) and the environment (severe overcrowding, extremely unsanitary conditions), and often
(3) lack of awareness of the negative effects of the collection on their own health and wellbeing and on that of other family members (Patronek and Nathanson, 2009).

Some authors have proposed that animal hoarding be considered a special manifestation of HD (e.g. Kuehn, 2002; Patronek and Nathanson, 2009; Frost *et al.*, 2011a), given that most individuals with animal hoarding also hoard inanimate objects (Patronek and Nathanson, 2009) and animals are defined as 'possessions' in the US (Frost *et al.*, 2011a).

On the other hand, some of the key phenomenological features of animal hoarding, such as neglect and lack of awareness of the negative effects of the collection on their own health and wellbeing and on that of other family members are similar to those described in 'organic' patients. Probably, the most prominent difference is that many animal hoarders live in extremely squalid conditions, whereas most of those with HD do not. Patronek and Nathanson (2009) reported on the living conditions in the houses of 49 animal hoarders; 78% were 'heavily littered with trash and garbage', and in 45% there was 'profuse urine or faeces in the living spaces'. Frost *et al.* (2000) found animal hoarding cases to involve significantly less sanitary conditions than hoarding that does not involve animals. It may be that many of these animal hoarders would meet criteria for mental disorders other than HD. Interestingly, only 2.9% of older people identified as living in severe domestic squalor in metropolitan Sydney (Snowdon and Halliday, 2011) had more than three animals in their dwellings. The subject of animal hoarding and squalor is discussed in detail in the next chapter.

To summarise, a significant minority of individuals with HD appear to live in various degrees of squalor. Assuming that these preliminary observations are confirmed, at least two major questions remain. First, what are the reasons why some patients with hoarding disorder live in such conditions? Second, is there any evidence in the literature that specifying whether a person lives in domestic squalor is useful and relevant to the proposed DSM-5 category of HD? These points will be discussed in turn.

Why do some people with hoarding disorder live in squalor?

There is very little research on this topic. Several reasons may be possible, with combinations and interplay likely as in many complex situations. Probably the simplest explanation is a practical one. Patients with severe degrees of hoarding, who have hoarded for many decades, may simply be unable to reach and clean all areas of their homes, where dust, grime, dirt, vermin, etc. may accumulate over time. Indeed, the most severe hoarders we have seen often report being unable to enter entire rooms in their houses, or even open the doors, for several years. In these cases, unsanitary living conditions may be seen as a logical consequence of their condition.

Another possibility is that individuals with HD may experience strong attachment to any sort of object, regardless of its value, whether it is considered clean or unsanitary, whether it is animate (i.e. an animal) or inanimate, etc. In this regard, rotten food or a dirty nappy may be seen as too valuable to throw away. Again, in this case, the unsanitary conditions would be an integral part of the syndrome.

A third possibility relates to impaired neuropsychological function in HD. The cognitive–behavioural model of hoarding postulates that difficulties in decision making, categorisation, organisation and memory difficulties contribute to the causation of the disorder (Frost and Hartl, 1996). A small but growing neuropsychological and neuroimaging literature broadly supports this view, although the results to date have been relatively inconsistent (see Mataix-Cols *et al.*, 2011 for a review). Recent reports of high rates of attention deficit symptoms in HD (Tolin and Villavicencio, 2011; Frost *et al.*, 2011b) are also consistent with the view that at least some cases may be characterised by cognitive deficits that may possibly contribute to the inability to organise and keep a clean home environment. The hypothesis that individuals with HD who live in unsanitary conditions have more marked neuropsychological deficits, compared to patients who are able to keep their homes clean, deserves empirical attention. Whether neuropsychological dysfunction is an integral part of HD (as postulated by Frost and Hartl, 1996) or rather a separate dimension that can overlap with HD and modulate its symptom presentation is another important question for the future.

Finally, it may be worth exploring the link between hoarding, squalor and insight. As discussed previously, many individuals with HD have poor insight into the consequences of their behaviour and refuse help (hence the insight specifier). In these individuals, the degree of insight is inversely correlated with their self-perceived distress (Tolin *et al.* 2011). Could it be that those individuals with poor insight are more likely to display 'blindness' to clutter and filth, than individuals with good insight? Of course, insight may also relate to neuropsychological dysfunction. Research is needed to address this question.

Is there evidence that specifying the state of a person's living conditions is relevant or useful in relation to the proposed DSM-5 category of hoarding disorder?

The question is whether having a squalor specifier would improve the clinical utility of current diagnostic criteria for HD. For example, would the treatment for those patients who live in squalor be any different? If we assume, as we have seen in the previous section, that squalor may be a resultant condition or associated state of HD, then the answer may be no. In theory, treating the main condition should result in improvement of the unsanitary living conditions too. However, if the hypothesis that patients who meet criteria for HD and also live in squalor constitute a specific subgroup of individuals with marked neuropsychological function, then conceivably, different diagnostic procedures may be required (e.g. neuropsychological assessment) and perhaps even different therapeutic approaches (e.g. cognitive rehabilitation). However, at present, there are insufficient data to support either view and, because the threshold for including a specifier in DSM-5 is high, it would not be justified to do so now. Instead, there is a recommendation that the text accompanying the HD criteria in DSM-5 should discuss the fact that some people with HD live in various degrees of domestic squalor (Snowdon *et al.*, 2012). A similar conclusion was reached regarding animal hoarding (Frost *et al.*, 2011a).

Conclusions and future directions

The literature reviewed here indicates that the vast majority of people who live in severe domestic squalor fulfil criteria for mental disorders (e.g. dementia, psychosis, obsessive–compulsive disorder); if the squalor is attributable to another mental disorder, they would not qualify for a diagnosis of HD. Longitudinal studies are needed to examine the possibility that some of these individuals may have had pre-existing hoarding tendencies that were aggravated by the onset of these mental disorders. Conversely, perhaps as many as a quarter of people fulfilling HD criteria live in moderate or severe domestic squalor. The convergence between hoarding and squalor is particularly obvious in cases of animal hoarding, although conclusive research indicating what percentage of animal hoarders suffer from severe mental disorders has not been conducted.

At present, there is insufficient evidence to propose that squalor per se should be an exclusion criterion when considering a diagnosis of HD (Snowdon *et al.*, 2012). Although the inclusion of a squalor specifier is not recommended at this point due to insufficient data, there is good reason for clinicians to record the presence and degree of squalor when observed in cases of HD, particularly because it may be relevant when planning treatment and in considering prognosis. Perhaps domestic uncleanliness might indicate greater severity of the HD or could point to a greater likelihood of executive impairment being a factor in development of HD than in non-squalid cases. These are possibilities worth researching (Snowdon *et al.*, 2012).

Research is needed regarding domestic cleanliness (or lack of it) in cases of HD and in other cases where hoarding is reported. Ratings of the degree of uncleanliness should be made, preferably following direct observation. The Environmental Cleanliness and Clutter Scale (Halliday and Snowdon, 2009) has proved useful in monitoring changes following interventions in cases of severe domestic squalor (McDermott and Gleeson, 2009).

As mentioned earlier, future research should examine to what extent squalor in cases of HD is just a logical consequence of severely cluttered spaces in such cases, and the practical inability to clean properly. In this case, the severity of the hoarding and resulting clutter should correlate highly and positively with the severity of squalor. Further investigation is needed regarding the extent to which patients with HD attribute practical or emotional value to unsanitary things, e.g. rotten food, body products and animal carcasses, in the same way that they attribute value to other classes of objects. Furthermore, research is needed regarding the possibility that impairment in executive functions is responsible for the squalid conditions in some cases of HD. Studies employing appropriate neurocognitive batteries would be useful to test this hypothesis. Long-term follow up would allow consideration of whether the case should be re-diagnosed as 'organic hoarding' (see Table 4.2).

Other avenues for future research include the systematic assessment of hoarding symptoms in cases of domestic squalor referred to old age psychiatry services and other intervention agencies. Given the likely ascertainment biases we described earlier, it will also be important to study the link between hoarding and domestic squalor in non-selected epidemiological samples. This would allow estimations of the prevalence, co-occurrence and inter-relationships between these two phenomena. Of course, it is still possible that identified 'hoarding plus squalor' individuals will prove more reluctant than others to be interviewed as part of an epidemiological survey, particularly if this involves home visits. Finally, it will be important to determine whether specific therapeutic strategies will be required for those patients who meet criteria for HD and also live in squalid conditions. If the hypothesis that these patients have increased levels of executive dysfunction is confirmed, different approaches may be required.

5

Animal hoarding

Charles Chan and John Snowdon

Most readers of this book will have visited facilities where large numbers of animals are looked after in defined areas – zoos, farms, aquaria, aviaries and the like. Some animals roam freely in protected territories such as game reserves and bird sanctuaries. Custodians of animals, however many there may be, have a duty of care towards them. They are responsible for ensuring that animals have adequate and appropriate food, drink, space and living conditions; they are their protectors and carers. They have regard for the animals' physical state, health and psychological condition.

Accounts of large numbers of animals being housed in confined spaces that allow for little movement are of concern. Battery hens provide an example. They are caged with a space allowance per bird of less than an A4 sheet of paper. The cages are stacked in several tiers, each unit holding thousands of hens. Such conditions have been banned in several European countries but not in others. Intensive farming of various types of animal in order to make as large a profit as possible clearly requires effective regulation to ensure that duty of care is respected. Codes of practice are in place in many countries.

Some animals are kept for breeding purposes – in puppy farms and on stud farms, for example. Most such animals are provided with adequate space, shelter and care. Temporary housing in cages is seen in animal hospitals, kennels, catteries and even in rescue shelters. The vast majority are cared for well and with kindness. The same might be said of humans confined in hospitals, nursing homes, boarding schools and (varyingly) in prisons.

However, some owners of animal 'collections' appear not to care too much about how the animals 'feel'. Living conditions for these creatures are sometimes appalling.

A commonly observed problem is that animals removed from such places are poorly socialised and commonly cannot be satisfactorily 're-homed'.

The term 'animal hoarder' has been used to describe people who collect, accumulate or keep together an excessive number of animals. The meaning of 'excessive' in this context is discussed below, and we refer to a suggested definition of 'animal hoarding'. Of those identified as animal hoarders by animal welfare organisations, a majority have been reported either as people whose motivation is to rescue animals from an unacceptable fate such as euthanasia, or as people overwhelmed by animal accumulation that they seem unable to control. Some, however, have been considered as exploiters – individuals who aim to profit financially or emotionally (through personal gratification) from their animals, having acquired or bred them for that purpose.

A chapter of this book is devoted to animal hoarding because a high proportion of those who accommodate excessive numbers of animals live in severe domestic squalor. Although research indicates that only a minority of persons living in very unclean dwellings in cities are pet owners (Snowdon and Halliday, 2011), the mess in the homes of this minority is commonly caused by the animals, and by failure of the owners to clean it up. Those accommodating large numbers of uncaged animals within their homes will have even more difficulty than do those with few or no pets in controlling wet squalor (described in Chapter 1), even if they have the inclination. Mess accumulates – and this includes animal excreta, empty pet-food containers and other garbage. The material is not purposefully retained, though disorganisation is commonly a feature of such living situations and contributes to the accumulation. Some occupants have been reported as purposively acquiring and then failing to discard large quantities of possessions, irrespective of their ownership of animals. The retention tends to be disorganised. Visitors to such establishments would observe a mixture of wet and dry squalor – and a mixture of animal and object hoarding.

Definition and description

Little can be found in the medical, psychiatric or psychology literature prior to 1999 concerning excessive animal collection. There had been news reports and discussion in humane society newsletters and the like, over previous years, and there had been papers in legal and veterinary journals focused on how to deal with animal neglect and abuse. For example, Handy (1994) wrote about interventions that can be effective when handling 'animal collectors'. However, there was scant evidence of research concerning the epidemiology of, and human characteristics associated with, what has been called animal hoarding.

Reference to animal collecting was made by Granick and Zeman (1960) in their analysis of newspaper articles concerning aged recluses, which was published in a chronic diseases journal. Decades later, Arluke (1993) commented on social science's general disinterest in studying human–animal relationships, in spite of 5,000 complaints per year in Massachusetts alone of animal abuse and neglect (Arluke and Luke, 1997). Media portrayals of people who own large numbers of animals but without providing appropriate care for them are discussed in Chapter 9. Many have included sensational content and should have raised questions about why people behave in such a way. A Milwaukee newspaper reported in mid-1997 that police had recommended prosecution of a mother whose 6-year-old son lived in their filthy home with 26 cats. *The Arizona Republic* reported in 1998 the 'worst case of animal cruelty' when 201 cats were pulled from a home. A headline in *The Washington Post* in 1999 read: '68 live and dead cats seized from family home'. *The Age* in Melbourne recently reported that, despite dead animals being found in her bath, a woman who owned 270 cats believed she was doing the right thing. The paper noted that the RSPCA believed that 20,000 animals are kept in hoarding conditions in New South Wales (population 6 million), and that 200 hoarding cases had been uncovered in the last year. Reference is made to other cases in Chapter 7 (p. 134). Searching the web provides access to numerous stories and photos describing cases of individuals with hordes of dogs, cats and/or other animals that appear to have been in poor condition.

Searching for research reports prior to embarking on his seminal work in this field, Patronek (1999) found only one paper describing a scientific study of 'pathological collecting of animals'. This was by Worth and Beck (1981), who interviewed 36 owners of large numbers of pets (mainly dogs and cats), most participants being identified from the New York City Department of Health and Animal Control Agency complaint files, while others were owners who became known to them. About two thirds of their sample were women and 70% were unmarried. Most reported their collecting had started in childhood. Social isolation was common, many having no telephone or plumbing. Many accumulated inanimate objects as well. The researchers speculated that the owners adopted a parental role with respect to their animals. This resulted in reluctance to relinquish any pets, even when adequate homes were available. Many of the collectors emphasised that their animals gave them 'unquestioning and uncritical love'. They tended to personalise their pets and viewed themselves as rescuers of suffering or unloved animals.

The Hoarding of Animals Research Consortium (HARC) was established in Massachusetts in 1997 'to better characterise the psychological and sociological underpinnings of animal hoarding; quantify the frequency and outcomes for animals, people and communities; increase awareness; and develop improved strategies for intervention' (HARC, 2004). It consisted of a group of researchers and professionals (including mental health, sociology, veterinary science and animal control specialists), but since 2006 its mission has been continued through the work of Gary Patronek (a veterinary epidemiologist) and Jane Nathanson (a social worker and rehabilitation counsellor) (HARC website, 2011).

In 1997, Gary Patronek was the director of the Center for Animals and Public Policy at Tufts University School of Veterinary Medicine, and a member of the Consortium. His stated aim, when studying a convenience sample of 54 case reports, was 'to better characterise the problem of hoarding, or pathological collecting, of animals'. He questioned animal shelter operators about their experiences with people who hoard animals. In the survey, an animal hoarder was defined as someone who:

(1) accumulates a large number of animals
(2) fails to provide minimal standards of nutrition, sanitation and veterinary care, and
(3) fails to act on the deteriorating condition of the animals (including disease, starvation and even death) or the environment (severely overcrowded and unsanitary conditions), or the negative impact of the collection on their own health and wellbeing.

Patronek (1999) reported that about 46% of the sample were aged 60 years or more, and 41 (76%) of the 54 were women. Thirty-nine (72%) were single, divorced or widowed, and 30 (56%) lived in single-person households. Three households included children. Most of the dwellings were houses, though 7 were 'house-trailers' and 5 were apartments; 52% were in urban areas, 20% suburban and 28% rural. The median number of animals per case was 39, but in 4 cases there were over 100 animals per household. Cats were reported in 65% of the cases, dogs in 60%, farm animals in 11% and birds in 11%. In 35% of households all the animals were the same species, but there were 2 species in 31.5%, 3 in 22% and 4 or more in 11%. Animals had been acquired primarily through unplanned breeding, or by intentionally seeking or acquiring animals from outside the household (for example, by advertising or by picking up strays). Twenty-three participants reportedly knew all their animals by name. Participants' stated justifications for having the animals revolved around their love for animals, treating the animals as surrogate children, feeling that no one else would care for the animals and fear of the animals being euthanased if taken to an animal shelter. Yet in 32 (59%) of the households at least one dead animal was found, and in 43 (80%) there were malnourished, injured and/or obviously diseased animals.

Case-reports concerning the 54 dwellings showed that of the 49 where living areas could be inspected, 38 (78%) were 'heavily cluttered and unsanitary'. Clutter inhibited movement around the home in 84% of cases, prevented access to the kitchen in 74% and to the bathroom in 63%, yet the lack of sanitation was acknowledged by only 26% of the owners. Extensive accumulation of newspapers was noted in 26%, of 'trash' in 39% and of pet food in 17%. In 34 (69%) there was accumulation of animal faeces and urine in human living areas. The owner's bed was reported as having been soiled with human or animal urine or faeces, or both, in 26.5% of the premises that were inspected. Only three (6%) of the residences were rated as reasonably clean and tidy, while 15% were considered moderately cluttered, with some trash or garbage, and 70% were heavily cluttered, with unsanitary living and food preparation areas and (in 63%) fresh faeces or urine in living areas. Owners did not permit inspection in 9%.

A later study by members of the Consortium (HARC, 2002) provided broad support for Patronek's conclusions. Seventy-one case-report forms, mainly from animal control departments and humane societies, were submitted. The number of animals involved per case ranged from 10 to 918. The median age of the subjects was about 55 years, with 83% female. In 66 cases (93%) the residence was rated as very unsanitary. Danger from falling as a result of clutter was reported in 80% of cases, and in all of the households, objects, in addition to animals, were said to have been hoarded. In one case, debris was piled so high in the dwelling that the occupant could move around only by crawling. Activities of daily living (for example, bathing/showering, preparing food, sleeping in a bed) were rated as very much restricted in half to three quarters of the cases.

Referring to outcomes, Patronek (1999) reported that even after removal of animals 'resumption of hoarding was common'. In a quarter of the cases, the owner was ultimately placed under guardianship or in institutional or supervised care. In 23 of the 54 cases, action or intervention was initiated by government agencies such as public health, mental health, child welfare, the department of ageing or the fire service.

Based on these data, Patronek (1999) estimated that there were 700 to 2,000 new cases of animal hoarding in the USA every year. He said

> [the] public health authorities should recognize that animal hoarding may be a sentinel for mental health problems or dementia, which merit serious assessment and prompt intervention. Improved cooperation between humane societies and public health authorities could facilitate the resolution of animal hoarding cases.

He declared that

> common sense suggests that the accumulation of large numbers of animals in human living spaces can have important public health implications, including placing neighborhoods at risk due to unsanitary living conditions, facilitating the spread of zoonotic diseases, and endangering the health of vulnerable household members. The potential for these consequences is not widely appreciated by government agencies. As a result, systematic procedures for resolving these cases are lacking.

Pathogens may be transmitted to humans through droplet inhalation, by ingestion or via the skin, mucous membranes or inoculation (for example, after insect or other animal bites). Dangers also arise through the accumulation of ammonia from waste products. A concentration of 50 parts per million (ppm) or higher is likely to be an extreme irritant, and more than 300 ppm is an immediate threat to life and health (Berry *et al.*, 2005, citing US guidelines). Other gases (methane, hydrogen sulphide, etc.) and airborne particulate matter can cause adverse respiratory effects (Castrodale *et al.*, 2010). Injuries may result from physical hazards and obstructions to ambulation, and also from animal attack. Recommendations for personal protective equipment for those entering the animals' environment will depend on the circumstances of the visit, health vulnerabilities of those visiting and the state of the animals.

Patronek's (1999) report, together with the activities of other members of HARC (Patronek *et al.*, 2006), has led to increased awareness of problems resulting from animal accumulation, and to discussion of how best to intervene to assist affected animals and to prevent harm to individuals living or working in close proximity to them, and how best to assist individuals with personality or mental health problems that could have led to the abnormal animal collection behaviour. HARC's latest definition of animal hoarding, published on its website (HARC, 2011) includes criteria that differ somewhat from those used in Patronek's original study:

(1) having more than the typical number of companion animals
(2) failing to provide even minimal standards of nutrition, sanitation, shelter and veterinary care, with this neglect often resulting in illness and death from starvation, spread of infectious disease and untreated injury or medical condition
(3) denial of the inability to provide this minimum care and the impact of that failure on the animals, the household and human occupants of the dwelling
(4) persistence, despite the failure, in accumulating and controlling animals.

It is important to note that the definition is not limited to any particular number of animals on a property. Farmers, breeders and trainers may be responsible for large numbers of animals. Clearly, this type of owner is not being envisaged when the definition refers to 'more than the typical number of companion animals'. We assume that what is meant is *'a number of animals that exceeds that which the owner is capable of looking after adequately'*. Owners (plus those delegated responsibility for looking after their animals for them) have a *duty of care*. The number of animals for which a person can provide adequate care will depend on the needs, size and types of the various animals, on the person's capabilities and on the resources available to them (including money, shelter, space and whether they have people to help them).

Most published reports of studies concerning animal hoarding since 1999 have been conducted in North America and have used the above or similar criteria to define what was to be researched. The definition has proved useful and acceptable, and has facilitated consistency and a shared understanding of what the results have meant. We therefore support its continued use, though with hesitation about using the label given to the condition. A more appropriate term might have been 'pathological animal accumulation'. In common parlance and in dictionaries, hoarding means storing, which may be for future use (a squirrel's nuts) or for the satisfaction of possessing items (like those gathered by bower birds). Hoarding is a purposeful behaviour.

We agree with Patronek's (1999) view that accumulation of large numbers of animals becomes a concern when the number becomes too great for the owner to be able to provide acceptable care. The actual number is (rightly) not a measure of whether and to what degree there is a problem. People with space, facilities, resources and help may be capable of caring appropriately for hundreds of animals. Others, for various reasons, may not be able to look after even four or five animals adequately. Or even one or two!

The HARC report (Patronek *et al.*, 2006) identified a variety of factors that appeared to distinguish a number of types of animal hoarding. It offered what it called a very preliminary classification system that could be useful when considering different approaches to intervention. Overlap exists among the types and, at different times, an animal accumulator may exhibit characteristics of all three types. The suggested classification was said to support a view that animal hoarding results from a variety of causes, manifests itself in a variety of ways and responds to a variety of solutions.

Exploiters (mentioned above) are usually not hoarders. They breed and/or actively acquire animals for their own gratification (financial or emotional) and fail to look after them properly. Sometimes the driving force leading to acquisition of animals is a 'psychologically rooted need to control other living things' (Frost and Steketee, 2010, p. 131). They are not overwhelmed. They are not 'storing' them. They are keeping them in poor conditions because they have no empathy regarding their suffering, and they do not care about them. They fail to look after them adequately (criterion 2 above), they deny their failure to provide proper care (criterion 3) and ignore (rather than failing to recognise) the effects of this failure on the welfare of the animals. Commonly they do not care for themselves or their dwellings well either. They may persist in accumulating animals in spite of deteriorating conditions. They act cruelly. They collect or retain animals in a 'pathological', sociopathic manner, but they do not display hoarding behaviour as defined by Frost and colleagues (see Chapter 4). They can bear to part with their possessions. Offered enough incentive they would dispose of their animals.

People who are *overwhelmed* as a result of excessive breeding (as opposed to purposeful acquisition) of animals, or by some change in their lives that makes them less capable of caring for their animals, may not resist the idea of getting rid of some of the collection. Their problem commonly is that they cannot work out how to deal with the overwhelming situation. Again, they are not purposely 'storing'. In contrast to overwhelmed 'rescuers' (see below), they accumulate passively rather than actively. They do not purposely persist in accumulating animals and they may recognise their inability to cope, so criteria 3 and 4 above may not be fulfilled. Nevertheless, descriptions of series of cases include them among the group they label as animal hoarders.

Rescuers may fulfil the criteria better. They resist requests to surrender any of their animals because they fear what would happen to them. They believe it is their mission to 'save' them. They may go to extraordinary lengths to retain them under their care, and they avoid and resist intervention by authorities. They do this in spite of obvious (to others) failure to provide adequate and appropriate care (criterion 2). They fail to recognise, and they deny or minimise, the effects of this failure on the welfare of the animals (criterion 3), and they stubbornly persist in trying to keep the animals and even increase their number by further acquisition (criterion 4). Some have extensive networks of animal missionaries who enable their collecting. Ironically, when animal numbers overwhelm their ability to provide proper care, they end up causing the very kind of harm they set out to prevent.

Frost and Steketee (2010) have a chapter on animal hoarding in their book, *Stuff*. They describe Pamela, a woman under the influence of a doctor who collected cats, but was more an exploiter than a rescuer. Pamela's cat accumulation began when she learned that a neighbour was going to castrate several kittens. They grew, and Pamela 'thought it would be nice for them to have kittens, because, you know, for nature' (p. 124). When the collection grew to 35 cats she moved to a sixteen-room house. 'The parties and the men no longer interested her.' By this time people had learned that Pamela rescued cats and began leaving them on her doorstep. She seemed to attract pregnant cats. 'Pamela and others in the Doctor's cult shared the belief that they had the ability to understand and communicate with cats in ways that other people could not, and that cats understood them and their mission.' Eventually the number of cats grew to 200 and costs began to overwhelm her. Looking back on it later, Pamela realised that many of her cats were suffering. 'I was careless with them.'

Frost and Steketee (2010) observed (p. 129) that:

> the hoarders became more animal-like in their daily habits over time. Their homes were turned over to the animals, which seemed to have greater access and privileges than the people living there. Many said that they wanted their animals to be free and 'natural', and so they had no rules for the animals' behavior. They were allowed to eat, sleep, and even relieve themselves wherever they wanted. Most animal hoarders experienced neglectful, abusive, and/or chaotic childhoods in which rules were absent or hopelessly inconsistent...

Case 5.1

A 49-year-old man was referred to the RSPCA by neighbours because of the smell coming from his property. An inspector found that his dwelling was filthy and his many cats were poorly cared for. However, he agreed to the instructions she gave him regarding treatments the cats needed for ear, eye and respiratory infections, and to provide appropriate care and conditions for the animals. He was seen by a psychiatrist, who found that he had personality issues but did not have an Axis I DSM-IV psychiatric diagnosis. He had accumulated an excessive number of cats, partly as a 'rescuer' of abandoned kittens, partly because he welcomed their child-like dependence on him, and partly because he did not want to de-sex the females. He had a source of income, but nevertheless, a few months later, found that he was becoming overwhelmed by the number of cats (over 200) and the expense and emotional impact of trying to look after them. He remained unwilling to part with any. The inspector called every month, and at the most recent visit found his dwelling and the surrounding fenced-off grassy area relatively clean. Of considerable concern, given his feeling of being overwhelmed, were the facts that several cats needed urgent veterinary attention and that ten or more of the females were pregnant following the incursion (he said) of a 'wild cat'.

Case 5.2

An 80-year-old widow (Mrs M) was re-referred to a Sydney Aged Care team. Her MMSE score was 17/30. She was known to have nine dogs and two cats and the house was reported as posing a health hazard due to animal waste products. Formerly she and her husband were breeders of dogs and used to proudly show some at dog shows. However, their dwelling was very unclean, and their children were teased at school because of this. Although apparently successful (their dogs won for them a lot of money), it is known that they kept the animals confined, one to a cage. Mr M was the 'carer' for the dogs, and after he died, when Mrs M was 76 years old, she was left with 174 dogs. The family found that she was erratic and disorganised in trying to care for them. Her daughter stated that the dogs could not be given away because they were too behaviourally disturbed, so a number were, in batches, (and with Mrs M's agreement) sent to be euthanased. It was apparent even then, that Mrs M's cognitive functions were impaired. She was referred to an aged care service, and accepted as a patient at the day hospital for ongoing care and monitoring. Services were provided to her at home as well. A guardianship order was sought. At age 79 her MMSE was 24/30, she showed poor abstract verbal reasoning, and an MRI showed extensive cerebral atrophy with diffuse periventricular white matter disease. At that time she gave away one of her puppies to a passer-by whom she had never met before. That left 40 dogs. Her daughter said that she had taken over her mother's responsibilities in feeding the dogs and cleaning out the cages, a job that Mrs M had long since neglected. At the time of re-referral at age 80 Mrs M was still living at home alone (with support from her family), the dogs being locked in cages, with minimal bedding. There was water, but some of the dishes were contaminated with dog faeces.

It can be formulated that Mr and Mrs M were exploiters, that Mrs M had never been a well organised or caring individual, and that when she developed dementia she was 'overwhelmed' but relatively insightless. She became even less able to fulfil her duty of care. It could be suggested that most of the animals (if not all) should have been taken away from her much earlier than was the case.

The criteria included in the above definition are essentially features of lack of insight by owners into their incapability of looking after so many animals adequately. In our view, the emphasis in the definition and in the applied label, should be on *accumulation of too many animals by a person who does not have the capacity or will to look after them appropriately.* The person cannot and does not try to fulfil a duty of care. In some instances, the stubborn determination to retain the animals ('possessions') can be seen as hoarding. In other instances, the accumulation is more passive than purposeful – just as can be said about accumulation of rubbish and filth in many cases of severe domestic squalor. Indeed, there is considerable overlap between so-called animal hoarding and severe squalor, and there is reason to postulate that mental disturbance (most often attributable to frontal lobe changes, dementia, schizophrenia or severe personality disorder) helps explain both the pathological accumulation of animals and the associated squalor, just as it could explain accumulation of garbage in many cases of severe domestic squalor that are unrelated to the presence of animals.

Other examples of animal hoarding were provided by Reinisch (2009). One woman, following admission to a psychiatric facility, had admitted that she was financially and physically incapable of caring for her 96 cats and four dogs; she was 'overwhelmed'. Another 'overwhelmed' older woman did not feel comfortable allowing others to adopt her cats, but agreed that her feline population had exceeded her ability to provide care. A third was a 'rescuer' who was not cooperative with a proposed attempt to remove her 48 cats and 8 dogs. She took 18 of the animals to be euthanased, stating that no one could care for them as well as she could and that they would be better off dead. Two cases of owners who were 'exploiters' were described, one with numerous rabbits, the other with 41 horses in poor condition.

A comparable horse story (which we can formulate as 'overwhelmed plus exploitative') emerged from Australia. *The Age* newspaper reported (June 12, 2007) that the RSPCA had examined 40 emaciated horses on a property in Victoria. 'Despite a lack of natural feed due to the drought and the owner's inability to provide supplementary food, the owner said she was too personally attached to reduce the number of horses.' *The Age* also referred to a cat shelter reported by the RSPCA to be housing over 50 animals in putrid conditions, the owner having advertised for unwanted cats. And the RSPCA had been called to see a filthy, junk-cluttered one-bedroom flat with 50 cockatiels and budgerigars flying around the room, the floor being unsurprisingly filthy with feathers and bird-droppings.

Whether exploiters, rescuers or overwhelmed, it appears that there are three common characteristic benefits that the animal hoarder derives from the pathological collecting behaviour: identity, self-esteem and control, all being continuously reinforced by the exclusive dependence of the animals on the hoarder (Nathanson, 2009).

Although critical of the wording, we accept that 'animal hoarder' is widely used as a catch-all term applicable not just to 'rescuers' but to 'overwhelmed accumulators' and 'exploiters' as well. It is indicative of abnormality, just as 'pathological animal accumulator' would be, whereas 'animal collector' would not. We, too, will use the term 'animal hoarder'.

Why do they do it?

In a recent study, Steketee *et al.* (2011) investigated the characteristics and antecedents that might explain animal hoarding behaviour. They questioned 16 people who fulfilled criteria for animal hoarding and 11 non-hoarding controls who owned large numbers of animals. Hoarders were more likely to have treated their animals as if they were full family members. They did not impose restrictions, and (as described by Frost and Steketee in *Stuff*, 2010; see above) permitted them to roam the house, even allowing them to urinate inside the home.

More than one third of the animal hoarders, but none of the controls, admitted to having had chaotic home lives in childhood. This disorganised, hectic lifestyle early in development might have contributed to inappropriate caring for animals. Consistent with the difficult home life were the higher number of mentions of negative family relationships by hoarders (88%) than by controls (27%).

No studies to date have examined the frequency of mental disorder in animal hoarding cases. This lack of information is at least partly attributable to lack of involvement of mental health professionals when attending to cases of animal accumulation. Several agency reports obtained by Patronek (1999) in his study 'expressed frustration at the perceived inability or unwillingness of mental health, social service, and public health authorities, including departments of ageing, to intervene. The rationale frequently offered by these agencies was that hoarding is a lifestyle choice and not a public health or mental health issue.' Until recently in the USA the approach to such cases has seemed to assume that 'animal hoarding is strictly a matter for animal welfare and humane law enforcement to resolve' (Nathanson, 2009, citing Berry *et al.*, 2005 and Patronek *et al.*, 2006). Now that it has been better recognised that effective intervention is dependent on interdisciplinary action to resolve the multiplicity of problems that become evident in such cases, including hoarders' unmet physical and mental health care needs, it is desirable that appropriate research initiatives be set up. In Sydney, a joint venture between the RSPCA and a psychiatric service is planned, but a stumbling block has been the need to avoid impeding or prejudicing criminal proceedings. Those aware of the risks of prosecution might not want research data to be subject to subpoena. Those most likely to have mental health problems may be more likely to decline assessment by mental health professionals, thus creating selection bias. The study will be worth attempting, but with care to avoid detriment to the person whose case is being investigated.

Results of prosecution of cases from the US sample reported by Patronek (1999) included court-ordered psychiatric evaluation of 13 (24%). In a study of media reports of animal hoarding cases, Berry *et al.* (2005) were able to acquire further details concerning about one quarter (56 cases), and in 41 a charge of animal cruelty was brought against one or more defendants. In 26% of the latter, the court ordered a pre-trial psychological assessment or mental health evaluation. These findings suggest the possibility that a minority of animal hoarding cases may indeed be due to mental disorders (Frost *et al.*, 2011a). Some have speculated that animal hoarding may, to a varying extent, be associated with or attributable to personality, dissociative or attachment disorders, and perhaps delusional disorder (Patronek and Nathanson, 2009; HARC, 2000).

Lack of insight seems to characterise most if not all people who hoard animals. Most live in unsanitary conditions but claim that their animals are well cared for and are healthy, despite clear evidence to the contrary. They do not admit to the existence of a problem. They may describe a special bond with animals that allows them to communicate at a higher level. Many cases have been reported in which animal corpses were permanently stored in a dwelling where there was also an excessive number of live animals; Nathanson (2009) speculated that this could have been reflective of denial, delusion or dissociation associated with complicated grief. These various observations have led to the suggestion that animal hoarding may be a form of delusional disorder (Frost *et al.*, 2011a), though most cases would not fulfill DSM-IV criteria for Delusional Disorder (American Psychiatric Association, 2000) since functioning is impaired and behaviour could be described as odd (criterion C).

Nathanson (2009) discussed evidence in favour of *impaired cognitive function* in cases of people accumulating animals. Although well orientated, a majority of such clients seen by her conveyed negligible awareness or erroneous information related to animal safety and health, and most demonstrated poor information processing and impaired executive functioning skills (planning, organising and implementing tasks). However, comprehensive neuropsychological evaluation had not been conducted. The isolation factor might contribute to their diminished 'reality testing'. It was unclear from the study what were the underlying causes of these cognitive limitations.

An *addiction model* was also proposed as an explanation for animal hoarding. Hoarders can be said to have poor impulse control and can only focus on the object of their desire (Nathanson, 2009). Based on this model, it has been suggested that motivational interviewing be used in treating animal hoarders (Patronek *et al.*, 2006). This technique has proved effective when working with people displaying compulsive or addictive behaviours, and has been recommended for treatment of compulsive hoarding.

Excessive acquisition, difficulty discarding, and cluttered and disorganised living spaces are features of *hoarding disorder* (Mataix-Cols *et al.*, 2011), but also of most cases of animal hoarding (Frost *et al.*, 2011a). People who hoard possessions often exhibit significant compulsive buying and acquiring of free items, and struggle to resist these urges. Similar acquisition behaviours and struggles can be found in animal hoarders when buying or adopting animals. Animal hoarders exhibit significant difficulty keeping their homes organised and their animals well cared for, similar to the difficulties with item organisation and maintenance experienced by people who hoard possessions (Worth and Beck, 1981; Patronek, 1999;. HARC, 2002).

However, there are limitations in applying the proposed definition of hoarding disorder to cases involving animals. The definition, as Patronek and Nathanson (2009) pointed out, does not take into account the capacity of the hoarded animals to suffer, nor the fact that the animals may have considerable monetary or sentimental value. Concepts such as 'useless' and 'of limited value' are not particularly relevant in defining animal hoarding cases.

Further, squalor is infrequent in cases of object hoarding, in contrast to its high prevalence in cases of animal hoarding (Frost *et al.*, 2011a). In the latter, the relationship between clutter and function can be somewhat indirect, since it may be the filth rather than the animals that render the living spaces unusable. Clutter can be a consequence of accumulation of trash and items used in care of the animals (such as food containers and newspapers). Patronek and Nathanson (2009) suggested that animal hoarding overlaps more with squalor than with compulsive hoarding of inanimate objects.

Brown and Katcher (2001) in a replication study showed that 43% of participants with high levels of attachment to pets presented with clinical levels of dissociation, compared to zero per cent of those with levels of pet attachment well below the mean. Dissociation (rather than delusion) could explain lack of insight in relation to animal hoarding. Nathanson's (2009) conclusion was that 'animal hoarding is likely related to a complex, multifaceted spectrum of underlying psychological disorders, the most relevant taking into account the interactive relationship between the human and the animals, along with the driving force of excessive caregiving, which has been associated with attachment disorder'. Patronek and Nathanson (2009) suggested that dysfunctional attachment early in life may lead to a compensatory over-attachment to animals. Before considering how such thinking might help provide guidelines on how best to intervene in cases of animal hoarding, we should try to understand why bonds between humans and animals can become so strong.

The human–animal bond

The deep affiliation humans have with nature is said to be rooted in our genes (Wilson, 1984). Animals have been part of human communities for thousands of years. Keeping animals as companions is recorded in history dating back to the ancient Egyptians, the Chinese Emperors and the Greek and Roman nobility. Pet keeping was seen in the past as a status symbol as only the wealthy could afford to keep non-working animals (Department of Primary Industries, 2011).

Humans view companion animals as a source of social support. Collis and McNicholas (1998) divided this into various components, including 'emotional support', 'esteem support' and 'opportunities for nurturance and protection'. Most pet owners truly believe that their companion animals feel the same emotions that they do (Serpell, 2002). They believe their animals 'love' them, 'admire' them, 'miss' them while away, are 'joyful' when they return and are 'jealous' when their attention is given to others. This trait is called anthropomorphism – the attribution of human mental states (thoughts, feelings, motivations and beliefs) to non-human animals. This anthropomorphism allows people to derive social, physical and psychological benefits from animals. They relate to companion animals as though they are equal to people in some ways. A survey by the American Animal Hospital Association in 1996 showed that 75%

of pet owners considered their animals akin to children. Nearly half the women in another survey even said they relied more on their dogs and cats than on their husbands or children (Serpell, 2002).

Views towards animals are affected by cultural preferences, personal values and moral sentiments (Jasper and Nelkin, 1992). Recent research revealed that different ethnic groups have varying levels of pet attachment (Brown and Katcher, 2001).

Brown (2004) used the theory of self psychology (derived from the seminal writings of Heinz Kohut, 1971) to define the depth and meaning of human–animal bonds. A person ('self') is viewed as needing certain responses from others ('self-objects') to maintain a sense of wellbeing. Psychopathology is explained as being the result of unmet needs. The dependency on a self-object can be intense and crucial to a person's sense of wellbeing.

A companion animal may serve as a crucial self-object to a person so that when separated from the animal, the person feels a sense of emptiness, depression or disintegration until reunited with the animal. To many animal hoarders who are socially isolated, their animals may be the only self-objects in their world that can bring out an internal experience of meaning and love. This experience can be more real to the person than other experiences of love they have known.

A mature self-object relationship is shown by an ability to empathise with self-objects, seeing them as independent others with needs and lives separate and different from their own. In contrast are those individuals who relate to their companion animals as, more or less, extensions of themselves, and consequently ignore the true species needs of the animal – for example, giving a dog more rights than humans in the household and overlooking a dog's need for a hierarchy in the pack (Brown, 2004).

Attachment theory, originating in the work of John Bowlby, is also of relevance. This asserts that an infant needs to develop a relationship with at least one primary caregiver for social and emotional development to occur normally (Simpson, 1999). When a parent cannot adapt to the changing needs of a child, the more flexible child will adapt to what is available. Although sometimes this may be the extended family members, neighbours or teachers, often the child turns to a companion animal, if there is one (Patronek and Nathanson, 2009), to explore their emotions without being criticised, rejected or feeling overwhelmed (Alper, 1993).

People with histories of abuse often have issues with self-esteem. This may make them more prone to seeking out reliable, trustworthy and safe self-objects such as companion animals. Compulsive care giving has been described as selecting a vulnerable individual with a (perceived) sad or difficult life and giving care obsessively, whether wanted or not, and whether the cared-for has actually suffered a real loss, or is just believed to have done so (Flores, 2004).

Animals might appear to be the perfect focus for these attempts at self-reparative relationships. There is clearly an ample supply of animals perceived to be disadvantaged (e.g. unwanted, sick, stray, feral) and that cannot refuse 'care', being easily held captive or controlled (Patronek and Nathanson, 2009). Thus animals may be the solution for the person wanting to satisfy their longing for intimacy in the face of a paralysing fear of rejection and abandonment by humans. Indeed, by positioning themself as a rescuer, an animal hoarder may believe they have acquired a socially acceptable persona and use this later to deflect external criticism of their failed efforts to properly care for animals (Patronek and Nathanson, 2009).

Patronek and Nathanson (2009) proposed a model of animal hoarding, starting with failure to develop attachments early in life. A chaotic childhood environment may contribute to a lack of adequate coping strategies necessary to effectively interact with people and recover from adverse situations. Subsequently, poor adult functioning leads to impairment in work, daily activities, and social life, along with reliance on animals for emotional comfort. According to the model, the emotional pain accompanying early ambivalent attachments and poor coping set the stage for some people to turn to animals for unconditional love and support, and progressively develop animal hoarding behaviour.

Intervention

The enforcement of the societal values described in animal welfare legislation is a veterinary regulatory function in most European countries (Reinisch, 2008). In the USA, animal hoarding has been regarded largely as an 'animal problem', not a 'human health problem', and it was thought that removal of the animals would solve the problem. The reality, however, is that in spite of prosecution and removal of all the animals, without other and effective interventions the recidivism rate is close to 100%.

Patronek and his colleagues at HARC developed guidelines for intervention in animal hoarding cases (Patronek *et al.*, 2006). They suggested that, in most communities in the USA, the then-current approach to addressing such cases was fragmented, resulting in high community costs, ineffective responses and high rates of recidivism. If, however, agencies can coordinate their approaches, the authors declared that comprehensive and lasting solutions can be achieved. Such an approach requires education, communication and infrastructure. Cooperative agency responses necessitate good communication, allowing them to discuss and sort out concerns over confidentiality, roles, responsibilities and who should report what to whom. Strategies will be dependent on local laws and systems. Those developed in any of the states of the USA may need adaptation if used in other countries and jurisdictions – just as can be said in relation to guidelines regarding interventions in cases of severe domestic squalor.

Some strategies are more likely to be effective with one type of hoarder than with another. The first step to be taken is assessment. The responsible agency needs to evaluate the animals' physical and psychological condition and any immediate health-related needs. Along with this will be an assessment of the

Table 5.1 Matching strategy to type of hoarder.

Type of hoarder	Strategy		
	Persuasion with verbal agreement	*Threat of legal action*	*Prosecution*
Exploiter	Unlikely	Unlikely to be intimidated	Probably essential
Rescuer	Unlikely, at least in the initial stages	Driving motivation is to continue with rescue efforts, so threat must offer potential for a scaled-down operation	May be required when threats fail
Overwhelmed care giver	Most likely to be receptive to help and downsizing	May be sufficient to reduce the likelihood of recidivism	Often unnecessary and may be counterproductive

Reprinted from *Animal Hoarding: Structuring Interdisciplinary Responses to Help People, Animals and Communities at Risk* (Patronek *et al.*, 2006)

custodian's reasons for not fulfilling their duty of care towards the animals. Does the custodian need medical or psychiatric help, or financial or psychosocial support? Who is available to provide support? Table 5.1 provides an overview of how well a specific approach may work in different situations. For instance, relationship building and persuasion to achieve a mutually satisfactory resolution might be adequate in some cases of overwhelmed caregiver; executing a search warrant and removing the animals, followed by aggressive prosecution for cruelty to animals, might be necessary to deal with some exploiter hoarders.

These strategies can be categorised into criminal, civil/regulatory and mental health interventions (Patronek *et al.*, 2006). The three approaches are not mutually exclusive. A combined approach, based on the condition of the animals and the characteristics of the individuals involved, works best.

Criminal proceedings

Criminal prosecution may be the only effective intervention in the worst cases, especially those involving the exploiter hoarder. However, successful criminal prosecution has proved challenging. There are two features that distinguish animal hoarding from other types of animal cruelty. First, most of the suffering arises from chronic neglect; and, second, the perpetrator generally does not intend to harm the animals.

In general, US animal cruelty laws were designed to deal with deliberate abuse against a small number of animals within a short span of time. But most animal hoarding cases are not characterised by deliberate intent to harm or by direct abuse. Criminal proceedings may therefore be less easy to carry through in animal hoarding cases than in other cases of animal cruelty. Although the collective degree of suffering in animal hoarding cases can be enormous, laws in many states do not adequately address this type of animal suffering.

Furthermore, as shown by Berry *et al.* (2005), there has been a disparity between the ways different jurisdictions have handled hoarding cases.

Cases involving large numbers of animals are often prosecuted as a single case of animal cruelty. For purposes of expediency, or because judges discourage multiple counts for the same case, prosecutors frequently have no choice but to charge only a single count of neglect even when dozens of animals are involved. The court then hears a case involving one charge of neglect that happens to involve many animals. A single count rarely allows penalties to match the severity of the crime. Furthermore, it may be under-appreciated that despite the lack of intent to harm, animal hoarders often deliberately acquire and maintain control of animals even though they are unable to provide proper care. Also, prosecution can take years, during which time animals may have to be held as evidence.

Humane agencies often found themselves in a position of making 'bargains with the devil'. For example, in order to prevent animals from being re-victimised by the system through extended institutionalisation while a case was being prosecuted, the humane agents would negotiate dropping charges and prohibitions on future animal ownership in return for immediate custody.

The only effective approach in dealing with some hoarders may be aggressive prosecution, rigorous monitoring and strict sanctions at the slightest indication of recidivism. It was suggested that attending to the small crimes can change community culture and limit the likelihood of progression to major offences.

Reviewing results in 56 cases traced through reports in the media, Berry *et al.* (2005) reported that 48% of defendants were found guilty and another 27% entered a plea agreement. Dead animals had been found on the properties of three quarters of those found guilty. Of the 75% found guilty or entering a plea bargain, 40.5% were sentenced to jail (half receiving sentences of less than 6 months) and 38% were placed under probation. In three cases the defendants were prohibited from ever owning or possessing animals, and another 11 were forbidden from owning or possessing animals just during their probation period. In several cases there seemed to have been little communication between code enforcement agents, health department staff and animal shelter personnel. Judges in several cases were said to be openly hesitant to recognise a mental health component in animal hoarding behaviour. Berry *et al.* (2005) noted that there was little follow up of cases once the investigation and trial were over. They state that 'If we hope to increase the number of hoarders who are ordered to undergo psychological assessments and counseling, more research on the mental components of animal hoarding is needed to produce hard data for the courts.'

Civil and regulatory interventions

Whether criminal prosecution is necessary in an animal hoarding case depends on the individual and the situation. An animal control officer will attempt to establish a relationship with the hoarder in order to monitor the situation. During this process, assistance can be offered to re-locate some of the animals, provide neutering services and arrange support services as appropriate. If such offers are refused, a plan of action is needed (Snyder, 2009).

Civil laws and regulations have proved a useful intervention strategy in US animal hoarding cases. Three common tools have been suggested to be particularly helpful. These include the civil forfeiture laws, bonding laws and municipal regulations.

Civil forfeiture laws can assist in streamlining the rescue of animals, achieving custody and re-homing the animals. These civil procedures can be more rapid than the criminal justice approach. This is partly because of their lower standard of proof; they require only a preponderance of evidence rather than guilt beyond a reasonable doubt. Also, while criminal cases generally take into account the intent (mens rea) of the wrongdoer, civil cases focus more on the end result of the bad act with less emphasis on the wrongdoer's intent to cause harm. This can be very advantageous in animal hoarding cases in which neglect, rather than intent to harm, is more often the prominent feature.

Bonding laws are civil forfeiture laws that have been developed for animal cruelty cases. Bonding laws require a hearing to determine the need to seize and retain the animals; then a bond is set in monetary terms to provide for the animals' care pending outcome of the case. If the bond cannot be met, the animals are forfeited, allowing their quick resettling and precluding months of boarding expenses by the local humane authority. Bonding laws can also be applied in conjunction with animal abandonment laws to hoarders who have been taken into custody for physical or mental health evaluation.

The regulatory approach, particularly the municipal regulations, also can provide fairly rapid responses. Municipal officers have broad powers to regulate animal handling in their local communities and these local laws can be used to intervene quickly and effectively.

Mental health interventions

Given the high prevalence of mental health issues among animal hoarders, mental health professionals have a clear reason for involvement in many of these cases. Because severe domestic squalor has been observed in most of the dwellings of recognised animal hoarders, it is likely that guidelines for use of laws and regulations in dealing with squalor (Snowdon and Halliday, 2009) will be applicable also in cases of animal hoarding. Variations between jurisdictions in their laws and administration (e.g. health) mean that guidelines need adaptation to fit with local systems.

Psychiatrists can assist in the diagnosis and treatment of co-morbid psychiatric illness and carrying out a cognitive assessment. These assessments can be conducted via court-ordered competency evaluations, short-term involuntary admission and in-home assessment. It is important to explore the relationships between hoarders and their animals. Psychological treatment and counselling can target obsessive acquisition of animals, denials of failure to provide adequate care and the resulting consequences. As mentioned previously, motivational interviewing has been suggested to be a useful model in working with animal hoarders.

There are some practical obstacles to linkage of hoarders with mental health professionals. Most animal hoarding cases are referred to animal welfare agencies rather than to health professionals. Animal welfare workers' priority is the safety of the animals. While it is obvious that the welfare of the owners is intertwined with that of the animals, animal welfare workers are not trained to perform mental health assessments. In Australia, a community crisis mental health team can be contacted if there is any concern about acute risk towards the individuals. However, in other cases there is no clear protocol on how to deal with and make appropriate referrals of those individuals who may have mental health problems (personal communication, NSW Branch of RSPCA staff). In some countries, such as the USA, lack of health insurance may limit the coverage of the court-ordered counselling.

Allen (2004) emphasised the importance of patience, gentleness, listening and empathy in approaching the hoarder, in order to secure their cooperation and resolve the situation satisfactorily, preferably without an extended legal battle. Understanding the human–animal relationship (both functional and dysfunctional) will facilitate rapport and communication with animal hoarders. Multidisciplinary assessment supported by inter-agency cooperation is recommended when intervening in animal hoarding cases. Agencies need to have guidelines available regarding potential preventive and intervention strategies. With recidivism rates of close to 100%, it is also important to focus on decreasing the likelihood of recidivism in an integrated targeted approach.

Different jurisdictions will have differing systems, so each will need its own protocols on how best to deal with animal hoarding cases. We recommend that agencies with potential involvement in such cases meet to develop local guidelines and increase awareness of who can do what. Guidelines will be largely similar to those dealing with severe domestic squalor (see Chapter 3), but with a need for extra expertise and a somewhat different emphasis. Among those to be convened might be representatives of:

- public and private animal welfare agencies
- veterinarians
- adult/elderly protective services (guardians, finance oversight)
- mental health professionals, including psychologists, social workers and psychiatrists

- community health and welfare services, and non-governmental outreach services
- environmental health officers and local municipal councils
- code enforcement officials
- public housing departments
- lawyers with special expertise in laws relating to animal cruelty
- the media.

Conclusion

Animal hoarding is a poorly understood and destructive community problem. It causes extreme suffering of, at the least, hundreds of thousands of animals each year, as well as jeopardising the health of the hoarders and their families. Further studies are needed to elucidate the developmental aspects and triggers of animal hoarding behaviours. Current policies and interventions need to be updated to improve human and animal health, and limit the potential for recidivism. Most of the published material relating to animal hoarding has come from North America, but discussion in other areas of the world makes it clear that the problem exists worldwide. There is good reason to raise questions concerning care of animals in developed and developing countries, and guidelines for intervention in cases of excessive animal accumulation by individuals. We hope that this chapter will raise awareness of the complexity of the problem of animal hoarding, particularly to the relevant stakeholders. Engagement and cooperation of these stakeholders would be a key element in the solution of the problem.

6

The use of rating scales and instruments in assessing and managing severe domestic squalor and hoarding

Introduction

When discussing rating scales, 'rating' can be taken as meaning measurement, grading, ranking or appraisal. Such scales can be used to compare degrees of excellence (in various fields) or of ill health, feelings, appearance, behaviour and other aspects and qualities. Guidebooks may award 'stars' to indicate what to expect from a restaurant or hotel. The Hamilton Depression Rating Scale (Hamilton, 1967) measures depression levels, and allows comparison of degrees of severity between individuals, but does not provide a diagnosis. There are different types of depression, and people with similar depression ratings on a scale are not necessarily at equal risk or requiring similar treatment. Nevertheless, a score above a certain 'threshold' is likely to indicate that clinical attention is warranted.

Why rate squalor? Why rate hoarding? Who should be doing it? Who benefits? Why do quantitative ratings enhance assessment? Are they useful in describing cases? Are they useful in judging outcome? Are they primarily research tools? Are there tools available to rate degrees of squalor and/or hoarding? Are we able to rate the factors that are thought to contribute to development of squalor and/or hoarding? Does one need expertise to do the ratings? And surely we should not be spending all our time doing ratings!

In this chapter we will present rating scales that have proved useful in relation to cases of hoarding and/or squalor. Some are readily usable by staff working in various agencies involved in assessing and then trying to intervene for the benefit of people who hoard and/or live in squalor. Service providers include clinicians, mental health workers, psychologists, social workers, public housing officers, community service staff and fire officers, all of whom may have cause to visit the homes of people living in very unclean homes. Some scales could be appropriate for use by people who are not service providers but are concerned about the living conditions of individuals they care about. Some can be used by people concerned about their own ways of living. Others have been designed for administration only by health professionals trained in their use, and able to interpret meaning from the answers obtained from identified patients or clients.

The major utility of most of the scales used to rate living conditions is to obtain and then convey information to others about those conditions. They can be used in relation to an individual or when more than one person shares the same dwelling. The scales allow comparisons between cases, and across time – in other words, repeat administration can show whether there has been a change in the living conditions or (with some scales) in a person's capacity to look after their domestic environment. The particular aspects to be appraised relate to cleanliness, degree of disorganisation, accumulation and hoarding.

Some of the published scales discussed below measure more than just uncleanliness, hoarding or neglect of self-care. We believe it important to stress that squalor may be rated as severe in the absence of hoarding, and that substantial degrees of hoarding are usually *not* accompanied by noteworthy uncleanliness. Self-neglect is commonly observed in the absence of neglect of the individual's domestic environment. But there can be overlap. Unacceptable squalor may co-exist with substantial degrees of hoarding, but commonly used hoarding scales provide an overall rating that does not distinguish the degree of squalor. We recommend that squalor/uncleanliness be rated, but separately from ratings of hoarding.

However, concerned observers, whether service providers or not, will also want to know why the person of interest resides in what they (the observers) regard as an unacceptable domestic environment. Why do they accumulate? Why do they hoard? Why is their dwelling so disorganised? Why is it so unclean? To answer these questions, other assessment tools may be useful, mainly used by health professionals. For example, such tools may help determine if the occupant of the dwelling lacks capacity to clean, organise or discard, due to (for example) a mental illness or disability.

There is undoubtedly a need for more research into the nature and interplay of factors leading to, and affecting the outcome of, squalor and/or hoarding, and such studies need to use standardised instruments to measure living conditions. It will be important, also, to measure or note other features and attributes of importance, such as personality, obsessive–compulsive manifestations, cognitive function, psychiatric and physical problems, sensory impairments and perceptions of disgust. The use of standardised instruments allows us to compare and combine data from separate studies, confident that we are measuring what we wish to (i.e. that the measurement is valid), and that the data generated are accurate over time and between sites (i.e. that measurement is reliable). In practice such measurements can be used to communicate the attributes of a case and to monitor progress over time.

The rating scales used in the assessment and management of severe domestic squalor and hoarding have been grouped according to the principal purpose of each measure:

(1) Environmental cleanliness
(2) Hoarding and clutter
(3) Self-neglect
(4) Obsessive–compulsive symptoms
(5) Other psychiatric ratings (depression, anxiety, etc.)
(6) Cognition and capacity
(7) Activities of daily living (ADL)
(8) Insight and informant measures

Environmental uncleanliness

Environmental Cleanliness and Clutter Scale

(ECCS; Halliday and Snowdon, 2009)

There are few available published measures whose principal focus is environmental cleanliness. Those that are available have not been tested in a way that allows confidence in their validity and reliability. No published validated scale can be described as the 'gold standard', but the *Environmental Cleanliness and Clutter Scale (ECCS)* has been used in a range of settings and is emerging as a useful instrument. Appendix A presents the scale, along with prompts regarding related details worth noting during home assessments regarding squalor, clutter and disorganisation.

The ECCS was designed as a brief, user-friendly way of quantifying severe domestic squalor and, perhaps, differentiating those that were related to hoarding from those mainly attributable to failure to dispose of filth. The scale has been developed for use by workers from a variety of services, including those working in health, housing and community agencies. Items were sourced from relevant publications in the medical and psychiatric literature (Macmillan and Shaw, 1966; Snowdon, 1987; Samios, 1996; Steketee *et al.*, 2001; Chiu *et al.*, 2003).

The scale was developed at the same time as a task force had been convened to develop guidelines on intervention in cases of squalor in New South Wales. The opportunity was taken to test content validity and utility iteratively by consulting with experienced representatives from a broad range of relevant services, including community services, housing, environmental health, the Guardianship Tribunal and the RSPCA. Opinions were also sought from health care professionals with experience in dealing with subjects living in squalor, including old age psychiatrists, geriatricians, clinical nurses and allied health staff. Piloting and initial field trials generated a scale with ten items that were comprehensive, unambiguous and focused on the interior domestic environment. The instrument recognises that for the majority of dwellings where it is likely to be used, occupants are not likely to be responsible for the maintenance of the garden and exterior of their accommodation. The final items were:

(1) accessibility (clutter)
(2) accumulation of refuse or garbage
(3) accumulation of items lacking obvious value
(4) cleanliness of the floors/carpets
(5) cleanliness of walls and furniture
(6) bathroom and toilet
(7) kitchen and food
(8) odour
(9) vermin
(10) sleeping area.

Each item is scored from zero to 3 according to operationally defined criteria, where zero indicates that there is no problem or conditions are acceptable, and where a score of 3 indicates a severe abnormality. The ten ratings add to an ECCS score that indicates the degree of uncleanliness or disorganisation within a dwelling. Considerable work went into developing sufficiently explicit but brief anchor descriptions for every rating of every item. It was recognised that inter-rater reliability would be improved by minimising overlap in the wording of the anchor points and by differentiating between item scores as much as possible. It is impossible to spell out all combinations of degrees of uncleanliness and disorderliness that might merit a particular rating. Raters who observe a sparklingly clean toilet bowl but a basin with blocked outlet and a filthy mirror (for example) will evolve strategies for 'averaging out' aspects they would rate low and those they would rate high. Decisions concerning the cleanliness of furniture and surfaces may be difficult if they are completely covered by clutter, and in such cases, observers tend to assume or estimate a certain degree of uncleanliness. Cleanliness (or not) of the piled-up clutter provides an indication of what score to record. We welcome suggestions for improvement to the scale.

The ECCS is designed to be part of a broad clinical, research or agency assessment of a dwelling and its occupant. Separate from the ten items rating the cleanliness and clutter in the environment, the ECCS provides *supplementary questions* concerning functionality of household utilities, demographic and housing information, pets, personal cleanliness and a rating of how unsafe the dwelling may be to the occupant or any visitors. Answers to these additional questions do not add to a 'score', but allow systematic documentation of the observed living conditions. A final question on the scale is 'Do you think this person is living in squalor?' and if so, is it, mild, moderate or severe. Where applicable, the assessor is also asked to indicate if there was 'lots of clutter', or not.

The field test of this new instrument involved independent ratings on the ECCS and the Living Conditions Rating Scale (LCRS) in 55 dwellings occupied by people consecutively referred to an urban Sydney old age psychiatry service, whose living conditions were identified by the referrers as being unclean or disorganised (Halliday and Snowdon, 2009).

Reliability

The average inter-rater reliability for the finalised scale of ten items was recorded as 0.48 (κ coefficient), varying from 0.31 (vermin) to 0.58 (kitchen and food), all being significant ($p<0.001$). The correlation coefficient between two experienced raters' total ECCS scores was 0.93 and was better than the correlation for the total score on 13 interior items of the LCRS (0.89). The Cronbach's α for the ECCS was 0.87 indicating a high level of internal consistency.

Validity

In the field trial there was complete agreement between raters as to whether there was no, mild, moderate or severe squalor present in 80% of cases ($\kappa = 0.73$). When each rater's total ECCS scores were compared with the others' categorisation of the homes as showing no, mild, moderate or severe squalor an ECCS score of >12 would usually correspond with an independent rating that the degree of squalor was moderate or severe, while an ECCS rating or ≤12 usually corresponded to a rating of mild or no squalor. Further comparisons of the ECCS with the LCRS (Snowdon and Halliday, 2011) determined that the 12/13 cut point on the ECCS indicating the threshold between mild and moderate squalor was equivalent to an LCRS score of 15/16. Content validity was assessed as positive by the task force.

Squalor type

The first sample of cases in which the ECCS was applied was not large enough for formal principal component analysis, but exploratory analyses suggested a pattern, with two clusters of squalor type. High scores on the impaired access item appeared to be associated with high scores on excessive accumulation of items of little value. All of the other eight items seemed to load together as a second component. These data suggested that there may be value in considering different types of squalor. One of these may be related to purposeful accumulation of items (active acquisition, whether on impulse or not) and another may be where the uncleanliness is largely a consequence of failure to clean and remove refuse (passive accumulation, ignoring filth). A factor analysis of over 200 ECCS ratings of dwellings visited by a non-governmental agency in Sydney confirmed the existence of these two types of squalor (Snowdon and Halliday, unpublished findings).

Limitations

The ECCS was developed principally as an instrument to rate the degree of uncleanliness in a dwelling where living conditions have been reported as unsatisfactory. However, we have come to realise the importance of disorganisation and clutter in determining how occupants are affected by their domestic environment. Assessment of functionality within the home is vital in determining what actions need to be taken by concerned agencies. To help with this, raters can record observations of functionality within dwellings (including access to kitchen appliances) by noting degrees of impairment of access on the eight items added to the supplementary questions section following the ECCS (see Appendix A, p. 200).

Living Conditions Rating Scale

(LCRS; Samios, 1996)
The LCRS is based on scales used by Macmillan and Shaw (1966) and Snowdon (1987). It consists of 20 items. One rates utilities, four rate personal hygiene and grooming, and two rate external aspects of the dwelling. The other 13 rate interior features (bathroom, disposal of excreta, floors, walls, furniture, kitchen, lighting, odour, vermin, clutter, accessibility and hoarding/accumulation of similar things). Each is rated from 0 (clean) to 4 (very dirty). It was first tested for validity in a small urban Australian sample whose case managers stated they were living in squalor (n = 7, Samios 1996).

Halliday *et al.* (2000) used the scale in a study of 76 households, which included people across the adult age range who had been referred to social services in the inner city London Borough of Lewisham. The LCRS exterior scale items were disregarded as household occupants were generally not responsible for the maintenance of these. The mean LCRS interior scale score was 17 (from a maximum interior scale total of 39, SD 6, range 6–34). The LCRS mean personal hygiene score in this group was 5 (SD 2, range 0–11). The LCRS was further validated by Snowdon and Halliday (2011) who used the LCRS interior scale to rate uncleanliness in 173 cases of people who were referred to an old age psychiatry service in Central Sydney over a ten-year period. Raters also gave opinions on whether the person was living in nil/mild, moderate or severe squalor. Two old age psychiatrists independently co-rated 55 of these homes and determined that their mean LCRS interior item total score for 'moderate squalor' was 16.3 (range 12–22) whereas for 'mild' it was 11 (range 7–15). They found that almost all 'mild squalor' dwellings were rated <14 on the LCRS, while 'moderate squalor' dwellings were rated between 14 and 20. Most 'severe squalor' dwellings were rated >21. Ratings of total LCRS scores showed a high correlation (0.89), though the reliability and internal consistency of the ECCS were found to be superior.

Activities of Daily Living for Hoarding

(ADL-H; Tolin *et al.*, 2007)
The ADL-H is a 29-item self-report questionnaire, the three subscales rating ADLs (clutter-related inability to do specific household tasks), safety issues (household safety concerns), and living conditions (impact of hoarding upon habitability and living conditions). The *Living Conditions subscale* consists of seven items that, according to the authors, indicate substandard living conditions: structural damage (floors, walls, roof), rotting food, insect infestation, water unavailable, heating unavailable, human faeces (not in toilet bowl), and animal urine/faeces. A high score on the ADLs subscale (16 items such as preparing food, moving inside the house, sitting on the sofa, using the toilet and finding things) indicates clutter is resulting in substantially impaired

functioning in the home. Each item is rated according to a five-point scale ranging from 1 (none) to 5 (severe). The authors suggest that a mean score above 2.5 per item on any of the scales warrants particular attention.

The problem with this instrument as a measure of environmental cleanliness is that two of the items included in the Living Conditions subscale do not rate cleanliness or clutter, while some items in the ADL subscale (ease at moving around the house, being able to find important things such as bills) and the safety subscale (unsanitary areas of the house, offensive smell, obstruction of the main entry/exit, walkways and stairs, and accumulation of paper or flammable objects near appliances thereby causing a fire risk) are closely related. The mean scores, even for the living conditions, may not be sufficiently discriminatory, if a measure of domestic squalor or accumulation of possessions is the main objective. This questionnaire is also affected by the inherent limitations of self-reporting. In addition to the categorical overlap and lack of specificity, there are no publications as yet validating the scale in rating uncleanliness.

The Home Environment Index

(HEI; Rasmussen *et al.*, 2012 submitted)
The HEI is similar to the ADL-H, and was developed to measure squalor or uncleanliness associated with hoarding. The 26 item HEI is a self-report instrument, which includes some questions from the ADL-H and additional questions based upon published literature and on clinical cases. It includes questions about personal hygiene (body odour, changing clothing, showering) and daily activities (cleaning, laundry, changing sheets). However, the majority of items concern cleanliness in the home (rotten food, dirty linen, insects, human/animal waste, dead animals, mould and household odour). Items are rated according to a four-point scale ranging from 0 (clean) to 3 (severely abnormal). While this instrument may reflect environmental cleanliness, the inclusion of questions about functional impairment and personal hygiene are likely to limit its application as a measure of environmental uncleanliness. Whether it is a valid measure of squalor among people who do not hoard has yet to be demonstrated. It is also limited by being a self-report instrument and vulnerable to under- and over-reporting. The HEI has only been validated by comparing it with another self-report measure for compulsive hoarding, the Hoarding Rating Scale-Self Report (HRS-SR), among volunteers recruited after advertising in the media and from data collected online.

Institute for Challenging Disorganization – Clutter Hoarding Scale

(ICD-CHS; Valente, 2009; Paxton, 2011)
The Clutter Hoarding Scale is an assessment tool developed by the Institute for Challenging Disorganization (ICD), a non-profit educational organisation, referred to in several self-help books for compulsive hoarding (Tolin *et al.*, 2007;

Paxton, 2011) and online (challengingdisorganization.org, accessed April 2012). It is also referred to in a nursing review of hoarding (Valente, 2009) and although it has some face validity and might be used to rate environmental cleanliness, we have been unable to find any published empirical evaluation of the instrument. Instructions for use of the ICD-CHS are limited but it appears that an observer may rate a dwelling as being at one of five levels, ranging from 1 (accessible, uncluttered, clean) to 5 (structural damage, backed up sewage, no running water, leaking roof or walls, dangerous pet and vermin infestations, rotting food, unusable rooms due to clutter, accumulated combustible materials and visible faeces). Descriptions of possible signs of the uncleanliness or clutter one might expect to observe at each level are provided in four categories: (1) structure and zoning (including accessibility); (2) household functions; (3) pets and rodents; and (4) sanitation and cleanliness. Descriptions of the scale do not reveal a consistent relationship between the different parameters (for example, between accessibility and lack of sanitation).

Clutter Cleaner Scale

(Paxton, 2011)
In *The Secret Lives of Hoarders* (2011), Paxton published a modified version of the ICD-CHS called the Clutter Cleaner Scale. Although relevant to cleaning up, this scale does not (except through the subscales mentioned above) provide a measure of uncleanliness. The Clutter Cleaner Scale can be used by those trying to help occupants to clean and organise their dwellings. It attempts to take into account the physical health and mental state of the person living in the dwelling under consideration. Five stages are described, being modifications of those defined in relation to the IGD-CHS. At stage 1, 'the problem isn't about volume; it's more about the habits that the hoarder is developing as he or she tries to handle the clutter' (p. 9). In stage 3, 'finances are probably becoming an issue. At this stage the hoarder is often depressed.' At stage 5, 'the hoarder spends the entire day struggling to complete simple tasks like eating, sleeping and going to the bathroom... Depression is often so severe for a stage 5 hoarder that he or she struggles to get up each day' (p. 15).

Paxton (2011) pointed out that none of the stages is clear cut. However, he noted that use of the scale gives a clean-up agency a sense of the severity of the problem. He says that 'the key to a successful clean-up is to understand what makes hoarders do what they do' (p. 15). The validity and reliability of the scale have not been published and it is not designed for use in research studies. However, it has proved useful in stimulating appropriate questions before embarking on cleaning/clearing, and in describing changes resulting from interventions. Because the Clutter Cleaner Scale combines ratings of distress, physical impairment, cleanliness, disorganisation and clutter in one scale, it will not be useful to those wanting to rate different aspects of cases of severe domestic squalor prior to intervention, with a view to repeat ratings later on.

Hoarding and clutter

Most of the instruments in this section were designed with the concept of 'compulsive hoarding' in mind. Compulsive hoarding (Frost and Hartl, 1996) has been defined as

(a) the acquisition of a large number of possessions and failure to discard these
(b) household clutter preventing the use of rooms for the purpose that they were built, and
(c) significant distress or impairment in functioning secondary to hoarding.

Recently, criteria for a DSM-5 'hoarding disorder' have been proposed (see p. 67; Mataix-Cols *et al.*, 2010). The instruments developed specifically for rating hoarding do not allow adequate assessment of uncleanliness and should not be used alone if there is associated domestic squalor. Equally, in cases of squalor, there may be good reason to examine an occupant's tendency to purposely accumulate and fail to discard possessions. There is good reason to make separate quantitative ratings of degrees of squalor and of hoarding – partly to be able to examine changes in the two, over time.

Almost all scales developed to rate hoarding depend on self-report. These have the advantage of being quick and of capturing the viewpoint of the subject. Self-report measures may be more acceptable to some because they can be completed alone and in private. A major disadvantage of self-report instruments is the under-reporting that may occur when insight is impaired. There are likely to be particular problems with using this approach for the assessment of unclean conditions or compulsive hoarding, which may be perceived negatively and as stigmatising. Sometimes self-reporting may result in over-reporting. Language and individual variation in understanding of the words 'often' and 'sometimes', for example, will result in a different result for what in essence may be the same or a very similar problem.

Self-reports may, however, be useful as screening instruments to identify people with serious hoarding problems. Those who suspect or recognise that they have a problem may be glad to access an appropriate scale and use it to rate its severity. Such instruments may be useful in identifying potential research subjects (for example, after advertising in the media or online) and in monitoring changes over time or following interventions. Their utility in most cases of severe domestic squalor is likely to be limited, since many clients will be found unwilling or unable to self-report regarding hoarding inclinations or activities. A majority of those who live in squalor in the community accumulate valueless material, but not purposefully, and their accumulation can be described as syllogomania rather than hoarding. A high proportion have mental disorders. Nevertheless, using a hoarding instrument, if feasible, could be helpful in confirming that strategies reported to be effective in treating tendencies to hoard are unlikely to work well in cases where accumulations are not purposeful.

Clutter Image Rating

(CIR; Frost *et al.*, 2008)

The CIR was developed to overcome problems with subjectivity in estimating degrees of hoarding or, more specifically, clutter. The CIR consists of photographs of three main rooms found in most dwellings – a kitchen, living room and bedroom. There are nine images of each room that illustrate an increasing degree of clutter ranging from 1 (no clutter) to 9 (severe clutter). The stimulus pictures were created by filling a small furnished apartment with piles of the objects thought to be accumulated by people who hoard, such as newspapers, boxes, clothes, dishes, chairs, bottles, cans, books, pillows, appliances, cereal boxes, food containers and junk mail. Items were piled up as high as 60 cm from the ceilings so as to resemble 'the most severe hoarding cases'. Up to 35 photographs were taken of each room as the objects were removed. The least and most cluttered photographs were retained as the extreme anchor points for each room and seven from the remaining 'in between' photographs were then selected to serve as possible indices of clutter ranging from none to severe. (Plate 1.3)

Both mean scores and room-by-room scores can be recorded and have been studied. A room rating of 4 or more has been determined by the authors of this instrument to represent a 'clinically significant' level of clutter (secondary to hoarding). When used as a self-report instrument or as a tool in manual based treatments of compulsive hoarding (Steketee and Frost, 2007a, b, c) the person is asked to select a picture that most closely matches their own room/home to provide a rating of the amount of clutter in the room at that time. A major strength therefore of this instrument is that the visual comparison may reduce error introduced by language and different perceptions of words such as 'clutter', 'hoarding' or even 'accumulation'. It is very easy to use and quick. It has been used to monitor progress as a result of treatment or intervention. The authors suggest that the CIR works best using the full colour photographs. The main limitation for professionals dealing with people living in severe domestic squalor is that it is only a measure of clutter or hoarding, that is, one aspect or type of domestic squalor.

Psychometric properties

The CIR was rated concurrently but independently by an observer and the occupant during 58 home visits. Occupant ratings were also compared with ratings they had made in a clinic one week to three months beforehand. The occupants who participated in the reliability and validity testing of the CIR had responded to an advertisement and were included if they rated 4 or more ('definitely disturbing/disabling') on items of the Hoarding Rating Scale (HRS) (see below) that measured clutter or difficulty discarding – but were excluded if they were known to have dementia, brain damage or mental retardation. Some were paid. Subject test–retest correlations ranged from 0.62 to 0.81 for the three rooms, and the composite score (clinic/home) correlation was very high ($r = 0.82$). Inter-observer correlations (agreement between the observer and occupant) were also high ranging from 0.69 to 0.81. The correlation coefficient was $r = 0.78$. The CIR was validated by demonstrating a good correlation with the Clutter subscale of the Savings Inventory-Revised (SI-R, $r = 0.57–0.63$).

The Savings Inventory-Revised

(SI-R; Frost *et al.*, 2004)
The SI-R was developed in 2004. It has superseded previous hoarding questionnaires from this group of authors, such as the Hoarding Scale (Frost and Gross, 1993), having addressed perceived limitations of the previous scales. For example, questions about lack of resistance to acquiring possessions, central to current definitions of 'compulsive hoarding' are included in the SI-R. Reference to the specific types of possessions commonly hoarded (e.g. papers, containers) are omitted in recognition of their limited relevance in most cases. The SI-R is a 23-item self-report scale with three subscales: clutter (9 items), difficulty discarding (7) and excessive acquisition (7). The questions relate to the previous week, and ask, for example, how much of their home is unusable or whether clutter is an obstacle to having people to visit. They require answers using a five-point scale ranging from 0 (none) to 4 (very severe/complete). Good test–retest reliability and a high internal consistency have been consistently demonstrated in research on subjects recruited from people seeking help for hoarding or OCD.

The SI-R has been validated in comparisons with other indices of compulsive hoarding and can discriminate hoarding cases from non-hoarding controls and non-hoarding OCD cases. The SI-R scores, particularly the Clutter subscale, have also been shown to correlate well with self-rated and observer-rated clutter in the home (Frost *et al.*, 2004; Frost *et al.*, 2008). The main limitation of this instrument is that it relies upon self-report and because of individual failure to recognise the problem or negative perceptions associated with hoarding, under-estimation may limit utility of the questionnaire in a clinical sample. The SI-R includes many similar items and may be unnecessarily long. A 15-item version of the SI-R, the Hoarding Severity Scale (each subscale includes five items), has been published (Tolin *et al.*, 2007). A score of 13 or more on any subscale is severe or very severe.

Hoarding Rating Scale-Interview and Hoarding Rating Scale-Self-report

(HRS-I, HRS-SR; Tolin *et al.*, 2010a, b)
Two scales address five core tenets of 'compulsive hoarding' as defined by Frost and Hartl (1996), these being acquisition, difficulty discarding, clutter, distress and impairment. Because it is not a self-report, the HRS-I may have more application to the assessment of someone who is found be living in a state of domestic uncleanliness and where 'compulsive hoarding' also needs to be quantified. Results of the HRI-SR and HRS-I are reported to correlate strongly (r = 0.74–0.92), with 73% agreement between interviewers and subjects about the presence or not of compulsive hoarding (Tolin *et al.*, 2008). The HRS-I is estimated to take five to ten minutes to complete and consists of only five questions, including, for example, 'because of clutter or number of possessions, how difficult is it for you to use rooms in your home?' The interviewer may ask follow-up questions if required to clarify before making an independent rating on a nine-point Likert scale ranging from 0 (none) to 8 (extreme). Scores from all five questions are added to calculate a total HRS-I score. High internal consistency and inter-rater reliability have been demonstrated, and discriminated compulsive hoarders from both clinical and non-clinical controls. HRS-I scores, particularly the clutter question, correlated well with CIR ratings of the home by both the subject and the interviewer, made at the same time. The sum of all five items generates a total HRS-I score.

Savings Cognitions Inventory

(SCI, Steketee, Frost and Kyrios, 2003)
The SCI is a 24-item self-report questionnaire focusing on the beliefs people have about hoarded items and potential barriers for disposing of these. It includes the following four subscales: (1) a need to keep things to trigger memory, (2) avoiding waste, (3) strong attachment to possessions and (4) beliefs about control. Subjects rate whether and how much they experience a thought in relation to disposing of things in the previous week on a seven-point scale ranging from 1 (not at all) to 7 (very much). The total mean SCI score for hoarding clients was 104.0 (SD = 26.6) compared with 50.6 (SD = 25.7) among non-hoarding controls. This tool may be useful in assessing cases where the accumulation of refuse and items of little value is a problem, particularly in the application of cognitive behavioural therapy (Gaston *et al.*, 2009) to help occupants organise their belongings. A 21-item version divided into seven subscales (three items each) has been published (Tolin *et al.*, 2007) with a view that a score of 16 or more for any subscale is 'high'.

Self-neglect

In the USA, the term 'self-neglect' is generally used in a broad and all-inclusive manner that describes a person's failure to perform essential self-care tasks, such as obtaining sufficient food, medical care and personal care, and maintaining an adequate place in which to live (Rathbone-McCuan and Bricker-Jenkins, 1992). In Australia and in the UK, professionals writing in the fields of medicine, psychology, social sciences and law, tend to delineate between behaviours involving neglect of self-care (self-neglect), extreme neglect of the environment (squalor) and excessive acquisition and inability to dispose of things (hoarding). In an Australian survey of the use of the term 'self-neglect', 'squalor' emerged as the word that was most often used to distinguish dwellings characterised by extreme environmental neglect. Further, 'squalor' was also used to differentiate environments that were profoundly or markedly unclean from those that were described as untidy or messy (McDermott, 2008).

While 'self-neglect' is a term that is sometimes used in the lexicon of American Adult Protection Services together with 'elder abuse' to identify vulnerable older people still living in the community, some of whom may be living in squalor, it is not exclusively used in this context. The term may also be used to refer to vulnerable individuals living in clean environments but exposed to a broad range of risk factors that may jeopardise their wellbeing. There are tools designed to measure neglect of a person by another, but few address 'neglect' by an individual of themself. Few measures have been designed for the specific purpose of detecting self-neglect, and their applicability varies depending on understanding of the term 'self-neglect'.

Self-neglect Severity Scale

(SSS; Kelly *et al.*, 2008)

This is one of the few tools developed to assist in identifying people living in the community who are at risk of self-neglect. It was developed with awareness of the problems associated with self-report instruments and tools standardised for use in emergency or other medical settings. One particular strength of the SSS is recognition of the need to obtain comprehensive objective data about the many ways in which a person may neglect themself, when the evidence is not discernible from behaviour or appearance in a setting outside of their home. The scale was designed to be used when assessing an individual in their home. As for most people living in squalor, the absence of caregivers and sources of collateral history poses a problem. Because of the all-inclusive nature in which self-neglect is understood in the USA, while it very probably includes some cases of people who live in severe domestic squalor, a composite measure of self-neglect includes measures and observations of environmental cleanliness, neglect of personal hygiene, ill-health, mental state and cognitive function. The SSS 'environmental status' subscale is based upon visual evidence of the subject's inability to make necessary household repairs, or to clean the house and yard, and the extent of disorganisation and accumulation of possessions and other material in their dwelling. The subscale includes ten items, all of which are rated according to a five-point scale, ranging from 0 (intact, clean, neat) to 4 (dilapidated, malodorous, very cluttered, severe structural damage). Four of the environment status items are exterior ones: yard and footpath, roof, windows, walls; while four relate to the interior of the dwelling: odour, cleanliness, clutter and structure. There are two other items: number of neglected pets and number of utilities that do not work. Psychometrically the SSS has been shown to have adequate scale reliability (Cronbach's α), inter-rater reliability and capacity to distinguish those living in the community who self-neglect from those who do not self-neglect. Sensitivity and specificity were low, however, and this instrument needs further research and development for use when assessing people reported to be living in squalor.

Personal and Environmental Assessments

(Dong *et al.*, 2011)
As part of a population-based study of self-neglect in Chicago, Dong *et al.* (2011) rated participants' personal and home environments, with assessments of hoarding (four items), personal hygiene (four items), whether their dwellings were in need of repair (five items), unsanitary conditions (five items) and whether their utilities were adequate (three items: heating and/or air conditioning, water supply, electrical services). Overall self-neglect was defined as 'the presence of any of the five domains' and was reportedly present in about 9%, with a significant difference between racial groups. The following were the unsanitary conditions that were rated: 'being extremely dirty or cluttered, spoiled or rotten food, many dirty dishes, insect or rodent infestation, and foul odor'. Definitions of the various items ('extremely dirty or cluttered', for example) were not provided and rating instructions were not given. Reliability was found to be good. However, the main limitation of the schedule of questions was that various aspects of self-neglect, such as personal health care and adequate food intake, were not assessed. In fact, the schedule is more like an assessment of cleanliness, clutter and disrepair than of self-neglect. The researchers did not examine degrees of association between scores on hoarding and insanitary conditions.

Obsessive–compulsive symptoms

As discussed before, hoarding, like squalor, has been found to be associated with a diverse range and large number of psychiatric disorders, but is common in populations not identified as having clinical problems. The relationship between hoarding and OCD has also been discussed. Apart from hoarding, the majority of individuals who hoard do not display symptoms commonly described as being manifestations of OCD, and hoarding occurs in only a minority of patients with OCD. However, in some cases, hoarding appears to be attributable to the compulsions and rituals seen in the disorder. Studies suggest that only a minority of people found living in the community in squalor have OCD, so routine use of scales used to document obsessional symptoms when assessing cases of severe domestic squalor might be questioned. Such scales could, however, be useful in research on the prevalence of OCD among those living in squalor, and in monitoring change or response to intervention among people who hoard and are being treated for OCD.

Yale–Brown Obsessive Compulsive Scale

(YBOCS; Goodman *et al.*, 1989)
The YBOCS is a tool widely used in OCD research. It is a clinician rated, ten-item scale, each item being rated from 0 (no symptoms) to 4 (extreme symptoms). Separate subtotals for severity of obsessions and compulsions are generated. It has been demonstrated to have high internal consistency and inter-rater reliability. It has been well validated and commended for use as an outcome measure in studies of pharmacological treatments for OCD.

The Leyton Obsessional Inventory

(LOI; Cooper, 1970)
This inventory has been described as lengthy and time consuming to administer, but has been shown to have test–retest reliability and application when administered as a written questionnaire (Snowdon, 1980).

The Obsessive–Compulsive Inventory

(OCI-R; Foa *et al.*, 2002)
The OCI-R is an 18-item self-report questionnaire that measures distress associated with obsessional symptoms. Each item is rated from 0 (nil) to 4 (extremely), giving a maximum score of 72. It consists of six, three-item subscales, which broadly correspond to OCD symptoms' dimensions, hoarding being one. It has good test–retest reliability, good discriminant validity and high consistency. A cut-off score of 21 on the total scale marks the threshold between subjects with and without OCD.

Other potentially useful OCD scales in this population include the Maudsley Obsessive–Compulsion Inventory (Hodgson and Rachman, 1977), the Vancouver Obsessive–Compulsive Inventory (VOCI) (Thordarson *et al.*, 2004) and the Symmetry Ordering and Arranging Questionnaire (SOAQ) (Radomsky and Rachman, 2004). These are self-report measures with good psychometric properties that some find useful in assessing a wide variety of symptoms and features of hoarding and OCD (Valente, 2009).

Other psychiatric rating scales

Use of other instruments or questionnaires may be indicated, depending on initial considerations about whether the person living in squalor could have physical, psychological or psychiatric problems. They may appear depressed, in which case a depression screening instrument might be used (for example, the 15-item version of the Geriatric Depression Scale; Almeida and Almeida, 1999). They may appear unduly anxious or paranoid. Mental health professionals may want to use the Brief Psychiatric Rating Scale (Overall and Gorham, 1962), which covers 16 relatively independent symptom areas, including psychosis. Appropriate questions need to be asked about the individual's history and problems, if the person or an informant is willing to provide the information.

Cognitive scales

Because of the substantial proportion of cases where severe domestic squalor appears to be associated with cognitive impairment and its various causes, including dementia due to Alzheimer's disease, vascular dementia, frontotemporal dementia and alcohol-related brain damage, a formal assessment of cognition is a high priority. If assessors are trained in the use of cognitive scales, these can be used to screen for specific cognitive syndromes or disorders, are helpful in monitoring progress or outcome, and are potentially useful in research. Many tools have been developed for the purpose of assessing cognition and an exhaustive review of these is well beyond the purpose of this chapter. Burns *et al.* (2004) have prepared a detailed compendium of cognitive scale and other instruments used in clinical practice and research in contemporary old age psychiatry for readers requiring a more extensive account of these. In this section, examples will be presented of cognitive scales that have already been used in the study of people found to be living in severe domestic squalor.

Executive function: the Executive Interview

(EXIT; Royall *et al.*, 1992)

The EXIT is a 25-item scale that was developed as a consequence of it frequently being difficult or impossible to impose extensive formal neuropsychological test batteries on people with impaired executive function. Clinically based bedside 'frontal lobe' testing can be used to detect impaired executive function, and the EXIT items were selected from a pool of such tests based upon their utility and good correlation with formal tests, including the Wisconsin Card Sorting Task, Trail Making Tests A and B, and Serial Attention Test. The test items include: word fluency, Luria tests, Go/No–Go Task, and snout and grasp reflexes. Each is scored on a three point scale: 0 (intact), 1 (equivocal), 2 (present). A total score of ten or more suggests frontal dysfunction. Experienced interviewers are able to complete the test in 15 minutes with a cooperative subject. Apart from brevity, this test of executive function may be particularly useful in the assessment of those living in squalor because the majority live alone and do not have caregivers or informants. EXIT scores have been shown clinically and on single-photon emission computed tomography (SPECT) and magnetic resonance imaging (MRI) to have a specific relationship with the left mesiofrontal system and may be particularly well suited to detecting clinical conditions such as early Alzheimer's disease, schizophrenia with negative symptoms and apathy (Royall, 2001). Raised scores are often recorded in cases of severe domestic squalor.

The Frontal Behavioural Inventory

(FBI; Kertesz *et al.*, 2000)

The FBI is a 24-item questionnaire where a trained interviewer, together with a caregiver, rate an inventory of behaviours that have been observed to be present in frontal lobe dementia. The questions address both deficit and active behaviours and are rated according to frequency ranging from 0 (none) to 3 (severe and present most of the time). While none of the items specifically refer to living conditions, one question concerns incontinence and another concerns personal hygiene. A total score of 30 or more is suggested to successfully discriminate frontal lobe dementia from other types of dementia, though high scores are elicited in cases of vascular dementia. This instrument has been reported to have high inter-rater reliability and content validity and is easy to use when an informed caregiver is available to interview.

Disgust

The relevance of capacity of people living in squalor to perceive or feel disgust relates to the observation that they are apparently oblivious or unperturbed by their living conditions, and do not appear to see others reacting with disgust. The hypothesis that the capacity of people living in very unclean dwellings to process emotions and detect the facial expression of disgust is, however, relatively untested. Ekman and Friesen (1976) created the best known set of facial stimuli available for testing emotional processing, consisting of photographs of faces expressing one of six emotions (happiness, sadness, surprise, fear, anger and disgust). These are shown randomly to subjects, who are asked to identify which emotion is shown in each photograph. At least one computer battery of three-dimensional colour faces is available to test emotional recognition and the perception of disgust, and could be considered for use in neuropsychological studies of squalor.

General cognition: Mini-Mental State Examination

(MMSE, Folstein *et al.*, 1975)
This is a frequently used general cognitive screening test of cognitive function. It includes items that test attention, new learning, orientation, visuo-spatial function, praxis and language but does not test executive function. A cut off of $\leq$24 suggests significant cognitive impairment. It is fairly brief and simple to administer, though inter-rater reliability and validity are better when administered by trained staff and using the standardised instrument. Because of its widespread usage it can often be used for monitoring in individuals already identified as being cognitively impaired. People with high levels of education from English-speaking backgrounds perform better.

Rowland Universal Dementia Assessment Scale

(RUDAS; Storey *et al.*, 2004)
This brief cognitive screening instrument was designed for use among people with limited education from a non-English speaking background. It has been demonstrated to have good inter-rater reliability and validity. A score of 23 or less indicates possible cognitive impairment and the need for further assessment. Unlike the MMSE, the RUDAS does include some items that test executive function such as word generation, motor sequencing and a test of judgement.

General cognition: Mental Status Questionnaire

(MSQ; Kahn *et al.* 1960)
This and the Abbreviated Mental Test Score (AMTS) are even briefer screening tests used to reveal cognitive difficulties. The MSQ consists of ten questions, most of which are simple. It correlates well with the MMSE. Three or more errors point to impairment, but only if education, intelligence and place of upbringing are taken into account (as for the MMSE).

Clinical assessment of capacity

Issues relating to capacity and the ethics of intervening in cases of severe domestic squalor are discussed in Chapters 7 and 8. There are tools available to assist in the assessment of an individual's capacity, focusing particularly on capacity to consent to medical treatment. We are not aware of any formal measures that have been developed to determine an individual's decision-making capacity with regards to choosing to live at home. Although decision-making capacity is related to cognitive function, this is not the only determinant of whether an individual can make an informed decision regarding whether they are adequately capable of looking after themselves in their own home. Recent publications

(Cooney *et al.*, 2004; Schillerstrom *et al.*, 2009), have highlighted the important relationship between executive function and capacity. Impaired executive function may have a more marked adverse effect on capacity than memory and other cognitive processes, and requires particular attention in the assessment of people in the community found to be living in severe domestic squalor. The final decision as to whether an individual can continue to live independently or not, and whether a substitute decision maker is required, is a legal one.

Readers of this book may be called upon by the relevant legal body to provide advice about an individual's capacity to maintain shelter, safety, nutrition and medical care, or to direct others to meet those needs. In every case, an underlying principle should be that there is no ready-made test for capacity, but instead capacity should be established on a case by case basis according to the specific situation and choices.

Measures of activities of daily living (ADL)

Ability to keep a dwelling clean and well organised is partly dependent on the occupant's physical health and functional abilities. Tools to help in assessment of the latter may prove useful.

Independent Living Skills Survey

(ILSS; Wallace *et al.* 2000)
The ILSS has been presented as a comprehensive, performance-focused, easy-to-administer measure of the basic functional living skills of people with severe and persistent mental illness. It can be used to record how often a subject engages in 'tasks needed to live a satisfying, independent life in the community'. Thus it is said to be a measure of community adjustment.

Instrumental Activities of Daily Living

(IADL; Lawton and Brody, 1969)
Some of the household management activities measured by this instrument may have an effect on domestic cleanliness. Eleven aspects are assessed by a trained interviewer. The scale has been demonstrated to have good validity and high inter-rater reliability. One item concerns housekeeping and is rated zero if the subject does no housekeeping tasks at all.

Insight and informant measures

Lack of concern about their surroundings has been recognised as a common feature of people in the community found to be living in severe domestic squalor. Indeed, the justification by Clark *et al.* (1975) for use of the term

'Diogenes syndrome' was the perceived parallel to the Greek cynic philosopher's contentment in spite of his living conditions. In a London study of occupants of dwellings visited by a heavy duty cleaning team, 28% of clients regarded their homes as 'clean' or 'very clean' and 19% were 'not at all concerned' by their surroundings (Halliday *et al.*, 2000). Similarly, in compulsive hoarding, it has been observed that (unlike in OCD), those living in squalor often display a striking lack of awareness of the severity of the problem (Tolin *et al.*, 2010a). Recognition by individuals that they have a problem as a result of compulsive hoarding has been estimated to occur at least a decade after the onset.

Family informants' perceptions of insight in compulsive hoarding

(Tolin *et al.*, 2010a)
This illustrates an alternative approach to assessing insight in relation to living conditions, by seeking the opinion of informants. Participants were recruited by sending an email to family and friends (or contacts) of individuals identified as having problems with compulsive hoarding. Data were analysed from 558 of the 8,000 to whom the email was sent, a low response rate, which potentially limits the generalisability of the findings reported. The insight of individuals identified by the informant as being hoarders was assessed using an adaptation of item 11 from the Yale–Brown Obsessive Compulsive Scale (Y-BOCS) (Goodman *et al.*, 1989). Self-report answers on this item have shown adequate inter-rater reliability (Matsunaga *et al.*, 2002) and to differentiate OCD patients with and without 'poor insight' (De Berardis *et al.*, 2005). The informant was required to rate the identified hoarder with a score ranging from 0 (normal or complete insight) to 4 (convinced they do not have a problem with acquisition, clutter or difficulty discarding and will argue there is no problem despite all evidence to the contrary). In addition, the discrepancy between how informants rated five aspects of the severity of hoarding in the identified hoarder's home and their expectations for how the hoarder would have rated the same items was elicited. Over half of the informants rated the hoarders as having either poor or no insight. In addition, informant ratings of hoarding severity were significantly higher than were their estimates of what the hoarder would rate. Limitations include the lack of testing for validity and the availability of an informant who knows the subject well (which is frequently not the case among people who live in severe domestic squalor).

Conclusion

There is considerable variation in the severity and nature of living conditions to which the word 'squalor' may be applied. Rating scales are needed to document degrees of uncleanliness and hoarding, and in the assessment and management of persons found to be living in a state of substantial disorganisation and mess.

Full, meaningful assessment of why a person is living in domestic squalor requires documentation not just of the uncleanliness but of factors that might have contributed to its development. In Tables 6.1 and 6.2 we provide lists of potentially useful tools, but recognise that whether they *can* or *should* be used will be determined by circumstances of individual cases and studies.

Table 6.1 Domains of interest and rating scales available.

Clinical or research issue	Suggested tool(s)
Domestic uncleanliness	ECCS
Functionality	ECCS supplementary nine questions
	ADL-H
Hoarding	SI-R
	CIR
	HRS-I
OCD/obsessionality	Y-BOCS/OCI-R
Cognition – brief screen of cognitive function	MMSE
	RUDAS
	MSQ
Cognition – brief screen of frontal and executive function	EXIT
	FBI
Capacity	Capacity evaluation checklists
Self-neglect	SSS
Insight	Item 11 of the Y-BOCS

Note: ECCS, Environmental Cleanliness and Clutter Scale; ADL-H, Activities of Daily Living for Hoarding; SI-R, Savings Inventory-Revised; CIR, Clutter Image Rating; HRS-I, Hoarding Rating Scale-Interview; Y-BOCS, Yale–Brown Obsessive Compulsive Scale; OCI-R, Obsessive–Compulsive Inventory; MMSE, Mini-Mental State Examination; RUDAS, Rowland Universal Dementia Assessment Scale; MSQ, Mental Status Questionnaire; EXIT, Executive Interview; FBI, Frontal Behavioural Inventory; SSS, Self-neglect Severity Scale.

Table 6.2 Instruments relevant to assessment of cases of squalor and/or hoarding.

Instrument	Authors	Abbreviation	Rates	Interpretation
Environmental Cleanliness and Clutter Scale	Halliday and Snowdon (2009)	ECCS	Interior domestic uncleanliness and clutter	Ten items, maximum score =30. Total score >12 indicates moderate to severe squalor. High scores on item A (accessibility) and item C (accumulation of possessions of little value) indicate squalor + hoarding. High scores on other items (including accumulation of refuse) indicate squalor and uncleanliness.
Clutter Image Rating	Frost *et al.* (2008)	CIR	Hoarding and/or clutter	Subject or observer selects one of nine photos of a kitchen, living room and bedroom most like their own home; >3 is 'clinically significant'.
Severity of Self-neglect Scale	Kelly *et al.* (2008)	SSS	Self-neglect	
Activities of Daily Living for Hoarding	Frost *et al.* (2004)	ADL-H		29 items, each scored on a five-point scale ranging from 1 (none) to 5 (severe); three subscales: ADLs; Living Conditions; Safety Issues. Authors suggest subscale mean scores >2.5 warrant priority attention.

7

Law and mess

Michele Slatter

Introduction

Situations of 'squalor' and 'hoarding' pose something of a challenge to the legal system. The terms themselves are not legal terms of art and no traditional action is an exact 'fit'. However, recent years have seen some developments that aim to address the issues behind such cases, so that sustainable outcomes, not just a 'quick fix', can be achieved as a result of going to law. They reflect our better understanding of the incidence and causes of severe domestic squalor[1] and they complement the shift towards a multidiscipline collaborative approach. This chapter reviews the legal options and examines examples of change. In doing so, it attempts to sketch the gradual articulation of robust criteria for intervention, a process that is by no means complete or consistent in this area of professional practice.[2]

Several general points may be made at the outset. First, legal intervention in hoarding or squalor cases is not initiated by the resident[3] themselves; it is invariably the result of an external third party's initiative. It may be a neighbour, a relative or a more incidental connection (meter reader, postman, domiciliary help) who becomes concerned. Their motivation may be quite complex, possibly melding altruistic concerns (the wellbeing of the resident) with a public interest dimension (protection of public health) or an element of self-interest (property

[1] Consistently with other chapters, the phrase 'severe domestic squalor' is used here to encompass any of: problem hoarding, squalor and self-neglect.

[2] The chapter draws particularly on Slatter (2009).

[3] The term 'resident' is used throughout this chapter to designate the person whose behaviour is being challenged by others. It avoids any suggestion that the person should be defined by their behaviour.

Severe Domestic Squalor, John Snowdon, Graeme Halliday and Sube Banerjee. Published by Cambridge University Press.

values, local amenity, fire risk). It is important to remember that in all these cases the resident's behaviour and domestic environment come under unsolicited external scrutiny. This can be met by responses ranging from active justification to complete disengagement. The dynamic of the situation is unpredictable. Its external momentum can pose significant procedural and ethical challenges.

Second, formal legal action is rare in these cases. We can find case reports that clearly concern situations of squalor or hoarding and these contribute largely to the discussion that follows. However, such reports invariably include histories of extended conversations, investigations and negotiations undertaken in order to make progress without needing the formality, stress and expense of a legal hearing. It is clear that this area (perhaps more than most) is one in which compliance is prioritised over enforcement. Generally, cases of severe domestic squalor are addressed 'in the shadow of the law', not in its full glare. Negotiated outcomes are the aim; resident engagement with the process is desired; formal legal action is the least preferred route to change.

This reflects a range of concerns. All parties find legal action expensive, time consuming, unpredictable and stressful. Its impact may be only temporary at best (the 'quick fix' that doesn't last). Negotiated change may be more sustainable, even if less immediate. Away from the law, inter-agency arrangements may be agreed with the resident, securing support for them to achieve change and remain independent. None of these responses will be 'visible' to those seeking a public record, although they may be glimpsed in some reports. The marked preference for compliance explains the timescale of many cases: months and years can elapse while negotiations continue in an attempt to secure improvement before formal legal action is begun. The search for compliance may also be thought the best way to balance the competing interests to which councils and social landlords,[4] for example, are subject. Councils are answerable to *all* ratepayers and cannot preference either the neighbours or the resident. Social landlords need to balance their fiscal responsibilities with their supportive 'social' role and their duties to other tenants and neighbouring occupiers. There are situations where the force of a court order may serve a necessary or strategic purpose. It may encourage resident action;[5] bolster resident resolve;[6] legitimate external intervention in

[4] 'Social landlords' include local authorities and not-for-profit landlords such as Housing Associations, Co-operatives and other non-government rental housing providers supported at least in part by public funds. All these landlords are likely to have a 'social welfare/homelessness avoidance' policy, either by disposition or as a requirement of their funding. They include many seen as landlords of last resort for vulnerable or fragile individuals and have tended to adopt tenancy management practices designed to help sustain precarious tenancies. 'Social landlords' be may be distinguished from private rental landlords who operate free of any similar constraints.

[5] Where the threat of contempt can encourage a clean-up by the resident.

[6] For example conditional possession orders where the condition is to accept and work with supportive agencies or face eviction: *South Australian Housing Trust v G* (RT 06/6181) 10 January 2007.

the property;[7] or directly protect the interests of the resident.[8] These are the cases we can draw on to map the current landscape.

Finally, notice that, although private individuals could initiate legal action themselves, most will alert a public authority to their concerns and expect action to ensue.[9] Consequently, councils, health authorities and social landlords have much the greatest experience of managing cases of severe domestic squalor at present. In future we may see other agencies, such as strata managers, needing similar capabilities: changes in tenure and demographics suggest this is likely.[10] Even though current practice is evolving within the framework of legal powers specific to certain bodies (such as councils or landlords) the patterns of response are eminently transferable and the relevant experience increasingly available.

Legal options

Legal interventions available in squalor and/or hoarding cases may be grouped broadly into two categories: those *focused on the property*, the state of the premises, and those *focused on the person*, the wellbeing of the resident.

Interventions that focus on the state of the *premises* are designed to rehabilitate the property by controlling the impact of the resident's behaviour (the hoarding, the squalor). They highlight the resident's legal responsibilities as an occupier, a tenant, a citizen. The associated remedies aim to achieve a change in the use or state of the property. Such actions include the action of private nuisance; actions to enforce leasehold conditions (whether in long leaseholds or residential tenancies); and some actions brought by local authorities under public health or development legislation. The remedies most frequently resulting from these actions are mandatory orders to clean up the premises. In many cases if the resident does not comply, the local authority or landlord may be entitled to have the work done at the resident's expense. None of the actions were originally designed with a therapeutic agenda.

As our understanding of squalor and hoarding deepens, so does our concern about traditional legal 'remedies' and the range of orders usually available in the 'property' actions. Involuntary relocation (temporary or permanent); eviction; comprehensive forensic cleans; forced de-cluttering by strangers; the sudden removal of goods and animals; restrictions on the use of one's home: such outcomes increasingly seem unsatisfactory from several perspectives, philosophical and practical. They are coercive. They are traumatic. They may apparently override the autonomy and human rights of the resident. Their

[7] Such as a forced clean-up and removal of the resident on conditions; see *Hawkesbury City Council v Dundler* [2005] NSWLEC 662.

[8] For example, guardianship applications.

[9] Use of the guardianship and protection jurisdiction may be the one exception.

[10] See below; evolving tenures to meet affordability and an ageing but independent population.

effects are unsustainable. We now appreciate that, without support, the situation of severe domestic squalor is likely to recur because the resident's behaviour will continue or resume. Fortunately, this more complex understanding is complemented by some changes in agency practice and legal process. Even within the framework of traditional property actions, more subtle responses are emerging that aim to acknowledge a therapeutic dimension, recognising the resident's needs. This approach is expected to achieve more sustainable results and a better balance of the diverse interests involved. The increased role now played by mediation in legal process greatly facilitates the preparation of agreed orders. Increased awareness of the mental and personal context of domestic squalor normalises acknowledgement of the resident's circumstances. Orders can be shaped, at least in part, by medical insight and by the gradual emergence of skilled specialist support providers (although the availability of such support is far from universally accessible). Nevertheless, in the property-focused actions we can still see that dynamic so neatly described by Windeyer J of law 'marching with medicine but in the rear and limping a little'.[11]

The second group of legal interventions focus on the *person*, the resident, and their wellbeing. They may be primarily concerned with issues of legal competency or, more simply, with the conditions in which the resident lives. Their aim is to protect or promote the best interests of the resident. They may include coercive options that can be deployed without the resident's consent and may be actively resisted.

A focus on property: the state of the premises

No clear spectrum of acceptability

In principle there is a range of actions that could be used to challenge the state of premises. They include: the action of private nuisance; actions brought by landlords and others[12] to enforce lease covenants; and actions brought by public authorities to enforce byelaws, amenity standards, development restrictions and public health requirements.

A conspicuous feature of all these actions is the nebulous language used to describe deviant or unacceptable use. Actions can challenge use or condition that is 'a nuisance'; 'unreasonable'; 'not ordinary domestic use'; 'unsightly'; 'untidy'; 'untenantlike'; 'an interference with the peace, comfort and privacy' of others; 'insanitary'; 'unhealthy'; 'offensive, injurious or prejudicial to health'; not 'in a safe or healthy condition'. While some of these terms have been discussed in case

[11] Windeyer J in *Mount Isa Mines v Pusey* (1970) 125 CLR 383 at 395.

[12] And others: in South Australia third parties can seek eviction for breach of tenancy conditions (s 90 *Residential Tenancies Act* 1995); other tenures may also contain restrictive conditions for example strata title types of development (enforced by bodies corporate, homeowners association, etc.); even possibly reverse mortgages; shared equity; rent to purchase.

law[13] or defined in statute,[14] many are used without any elaboration, which suggests an assumption that their meaning is self-evident (and universally agreed). This confidence seems misplaced, especially with criteria such as 'untidy', 'unsightly'[15] and 'untenantlike'. It does not provide robust intervention criteria. Most cases that reach court are at the extremity of the spectrum – the preference for compliance over enforcement ensures this – and likely to provoke widespread disgust. However, the absence of more nuanced legal debate has so far deprived us of a clear threshold for intervention and a touchstone in less extreme cases.

Understandings from nuisance

The jurisprudence of the action of nuisance undoubtedly influences the law's expectations relating to use and condition. The word 'nuisance' itself is used in tenancy agreements, traditional public health legislation, bylaws and local laws, and courts have been inclined to give it its technical meaning, for example: '"nuisance" in... the Act is confined to its legal and technical meaning. It does not mean that someone is a "nuisance" in the ordinary sense of annoying, although annoying conduct may fall within... the Act.'[16]

The action of nuisance is the consummate legal vehicle for balancing competing interests. It can be used against owner-occupiers or tenants and is used to challenge a use of property that causes an 'unreasonable interference with the use

[13] For example, there is an extensive jurisprudence on common law 'nuisance': see below; there are also numerous cases on Order 21 of s 124 *Local Government Act* 1993 (NSW); 'land not in a safe or healthy' condition; see *Wollongong City Council v McLean* [2005] NSWLEC 662.

[14] For example s79(7) *Environmental Protection Act* 1990 (UK) states: '"prejudicial to health" means injurious, or likely to cause injury, to health'.

[15] Community expectations change too: for an example of change in action see the defence to the allegation of 'unsightly' in *Allen v Campbelltown City Council* [2008] NSWLEC 1496. Mr Allen contended that his biodynamic garden 'is not unsightly, instead it is a healthy carbon neutral eco-friendly exhibition garden that has been featured on various documentaries. The garden includes bird attracting, low water use garden plants, flora and nuts and fruits including prickly pears, South American fruits, native spinaches, parsleys and a self-sustaining herb garden.' Nevertheless he was ordered to reduce all weeds and dead and overgrown grasses to a height of 100 mm and 'remove or store away from public view all scrap timber, scrap metal, unused building materials, rubbish, refuse and waste... likely to create a shelter or harborage for cockroaches, vermin and mosquitoes'.

[16] *Ringwood v Noblett & Nancarrow* [1996] SARTT1 S Raymond, Presiding Member, who continued, in a tenancy dispute: '... The Tribunal is called on to consider whether the conduct of Mr Nancarrow amounts to "interference with personal pleasure, comfort and enjoyment normally derived from the use of land, such as through noise, smell, dust, etc." The interference should be substantial and unreasonable. Although the matter is not free from doubt, I am of the view that there must be some connection between the use of premises and the conduct of the tenant. In any urban community and especially in a block of units inevitably there may be aspects of other tenants' behaviour which do not accord with another's taste or standards... it is a matter of balancing these competing interests.'

and enjoyment of another's land'.[17] The interference may be physical interference[18] or an intrusion into 'comfort and amenity'[19] for example by sound or smell. Examples that might apply in squalor or hoarding cases include: dust blowing from neighbouring land and damaging goods,[20] smells emanating from the defendant's premises[21] and vermin attracted to the defendant's property and then spreading further afield.[22] There has also been speculation that a nuisance action could succeed against 'unsightliness'.[23]

The courts will not recognise as a 'nuisance' interference that is merely trivial[24] or transient[25] or would only upset an abnormally sensitive plaintiff.[26] Unless physical damage is caused, the matter will be assessed against the standards of 'reasonable people'[27] in the relevant locality.[28]

'Residential' use is recognised as needing a degree of give and take between neighbours, acknowledging the reciprocal tolerance demanded by urban and suburban life: 'The use of a dwelling house in a street of dwelling houses, in an ordinary and accustomed manner, is not a nuisance though it may produce more or less noise and inconvenience to a neighbour.'[29]

In *Baxter v Camden LBC*[30] Lord Millett stated that 'the ordinary use of residential premises without more is not capable of amounting to a nuisance' but:

17 See Trindade *et al.*, (2007), *The Law of Torts in Australia*, 4th edn, Oxford University Press, pp. 167–93.

18 For example the deposit of dirty black oil smuts on neighbouring windows, laundry and outdoor furniture: *Halsey v Esso Petroleum Co. Ltd. [1961] 2 All ER 145.*

19 *St Helen's Smelting Works v Tipping* (1865) 11 HL Cas 642; damage to items on the property: *Harris v Carnegies Pty Ltd* [1917] VLR 95; *Halsey v Esso Petroleum Co. Ltd. [1961] 2 All ER 145.*

20 *Harris v Carnegies Pty Ltd* [1917] VLR 95.

21 *Bamford v Turley* (1862) 3 B&S 62 (Ex Ch); *Halsey v Esso Petroleum Co. Ltd [1961] 2 All ER 145, [1961] 1 WLR 683, 178 EG 193.* Proving 'unreasonableness' may be difficult: *Baulkham Hills Shire Council v AV Walsh Pty Ltd [1968] 3 NSWLR 138.*

22 *Cartwright v McLaine & Long Pty Ltd* (1979) 24 ALR 97.

23 *Kent v Kavanagh* (1973) 1 ACTR 43; c.f. Young J in *Bathurst City Council v Saban (No 2)* (1986) 58 LGRA 201 at 206.

24 *Stormer v Segram* (1978) 21 SASR 93.

25 *Crown River Cruises Ltd v Kimbolton Fireworks Ltd* [1996] 2 Lloyd's Rep 533.Temporary renovation of adjacent premises must also be endured: *Andreae v Selfridge & Co. Ltd.* [1938] Ch 1 but may be subject to controls that significantly benefit the plaintiff without compromising the project: *Daily Telegraph Co Ltd v Stuart* (1928) 28 SR (NSW) 291.

26 *Robinson v Kilvert* (1889) 41 Ch D 88.

27 *Per* Knight Bruce VC in *Walker v Selfe* (1851) 4 De G and Sm315, 64 ER 849 at 852, using 'plain and sober and simple notions, not merely according to elegant and dainty modes and habits of living'.

28 *Sturges v Bridgman* (1879) 11 Ch D 852.

29 Per Williams ACJ, Webb, Kitto and Taylor JJ in *Clarey v The Principal and Council of the Women's College* (1953) 90 CLR 170 at 173.

30 *Southwark London Borough Council v Mills and others; Baxter v Camden London Borough Council [2001] 1 AC 1.* In these cases tenants brought claims in nuisance when an absence of sound insulation between flats resulted in their being able to hear all the everyday sounds of their neighbours' lives: 'not only the neighbours' televisions and their babies crying but their coming and going, their cooking and cleaning, their quarrels and their lovemaking': Ld Hoffman. There

> Two conditions must be satisfied: the acts complained of must (i) 'be necessary for the common and ordinary use and occupation of land and houses' and (ii) must be 'conveniently done', that is to say done with proper consideration for the interests of neighbouring occupiers. Where these two conditions are satisfied, no action will lie for that substantial interference with the use and enjoyment of his neighbour's land that would otherwise have been an actionable nuisance.[31]

Although this appears to accommodate some latitude, the 'ordinary use of residential premises' still remains a phrase pregnant with uncertainty: 'ordinary' is especially contestable. What is 'ordinary', or 'normal', use? Many cases of hoarding or squalor (of whatever intensity) are unlikely to be 'conveniently done', rendering them potentially actionable through nuisance.

In reality, the importance of the action of nuisance for us is its contribution to the expectations of the law. Cases of squalor or hoarding are infinitely more likely to be challenged by the local authority under statute than by neighbours through nuisance actions. However, the balancing of interests and local 'reasonable' perspectives drawn from nuisance infuse the use of statutory powers (and tenancy conditions) too.

'Ordinary residential use'

Public authorities have used the enforcement of development controls to control cases of hoarding, especially where accumulated material is visible to the public. The legislation can be used to restrict the use of land to the uses permitted for the site. In this context, the scope of 'residential use', the permitted site use, becomes crucial.

In his small suburban garden, Mr Butler kept up to eight cars, two trailers, tyres, metal sheets, piping, a roller door, tool boxes, electrical cabling, electrical tools, a work bench, a clothes dryer, three pianos, three stainless steel sinks, a spare washing machine, shelving units, bricks, a concrete mixer, a ride-on mower, equipment from a telephone exchange and a hovercraft. A shed in the garden was also full of machinery and parts. Mr Butler enjoyed working with metal and machinery; he claimed this collection of material supplied his hobby.[32]

Judge Cole considered 'the ordinary use of a dwelling'. She commented:

> Given that a 'hobby' is part of the ordinary use as a residence, it becomes a question of fact and degree as to whether the particular example under consideration is so far out of line with the manner the hobby is normally practised that it should not be considered as being part of the ordinary residential use.[33]

was no question in these cases of 'unusual' domestic behaviour and the court agreed all the neighbours acted completely 'reasonably'.

[31] Ibid at 12, also Bramwell B in *Bamford v Turley* (1862) 3 B&S 62 at 83–84.

[32] *Butler v City of Mitcham* [2008] SAERDC 20.

[33] [1997] SARTT 25.

She found it 'clear' that the volume of items around the house was well beyond that which could reasonably be said to form part of an ordinary residential use of land and the current use was mixed: 'residential and junk yard'. The 'junk' had to go.

In *Holding and Holding v City of Playford*[34] a committed 'car buff' had a typical single-story detached dwelling on a typical small to mid-sized residential allotment. However, the whole of the backyard was 'used for the collecting, dismantling, storage (and) salvaging... of automobiles' and therefore between one third to one half of the subject land 'is obviously used thus'. The Court felt obliged to conclude that the land was used for a residence and a junk yard, in breach of the zoning.

A similar finding was made against Mr Stankovic, a 60-year-old resident of Kellyville NSW, who stored a large number of bricks, (approximately 100,000), 'piles of timber, scrap metal, general rubbish, used cars, two used trucks, old white goods, empty bottles and (100) pigs' on his residential property. Despite his statement that all the items had a use and he was intending to use them, the court found them to be 'junk'. He was allowed to retain the bricks and wood for a period during which he could apply for consent to construct a dwelling, but all other items had to go and the pig keeping had to stop; the numbers involved being held to be beyond 'personal consumption or the enjoyment of an owner'.[35]

Powers under legislation such as the *Local Government Act 1993* (NSW) enable local councils to act against the types of infringements of amenity that at common law could constitute a nuisance. In *Sutherland Shire Council v Sawyer*, for example, the council moved to limit the number of rabbits kept by Mr Sawyer in his suburban garden to two desexed rabbits (rather than the 340 he had kept there). This limit seemed to challenge both nature and Mr Sawyer, but the court emphasised that 'the waste, odour and other consequences of intensive husbandry of rabbits in an urban or semi-urban environment had the potential to cause public health, environmental and "*significant amenity problems*"...' (original emphasis). In *Kyogle Council v Manning* [2001] NSWLEC 9 the same Act was used to address a nuisance from barking and straying dogs from the respondent's premises where he was permitted to keep up to 120 dogs in accordance with a very detailed site management plan. In *Randwick v Fuller* [1993] NSWLEC 203 it was in effect deployed against Mrs Fuller in response to a neighbour's complaint about the 20 stray cats she looked after in her small house. Bignold J declined to grant the relief sought as 'disproportionate'.

In some cases hoarding may constitute a risk to safety and health, in addition to impacting on the local amenity. Randwick Council took action against noted local identity Gregory Blaxland.[36] Mr Blaxland described himself as a 'person out

[34] [1998] SAEDRC 492.

[35] Ibid. In *Burton v City of Port Adelaide Enfield* it was held that keeping and racing 150 pigeons was an activity done for the 'domestic needs or enjoyment of the occupants of a dwelling': animal hobbies, like other hobbies, are a question of 'fact and degree' per Judge Cole in *Butler* above.

[36] *Randwick City Council v Blaxland* [1997] NSWLEC 161.

of step with other members of his community in terms of his living standards'. The yard (and possibly also the interior) of the 'modest cottage', his home for 40 years, was filled with collected paper, timber, plastic bottles and cans gathered from local beaches. He was also a self-confessed hoarder of newspapers. Complaints indicated that the accumulated matter was a fire hazard and a probable harbourage of vermin and the premises were not 'safe or healthy'. A fire in the premises did nothing to assuage these fears. In a decisive but respectful judgment Bignold J commented:

> the Respondent's activities do not reflect the usual way to use residential premises and although the Respondent is to be commended for his community attitude and responsible attitude in that behalf in collecting materials discarded in public places unfortunately there is a sting in the tail in that these materials finish up in the yard area of his residence.
>
> The Respondent is a self confessed hoarder of newspapers ... He has a passion for reading newspapers. Again, he is entitled to pursue that interest and it is not for me to say whether he uses his time usefully or not. However, I am called upon to make a judgment on a consequence of his collecting and hoarding habits, namely the detriment caused in the local community (and especially to his neighbours) by dint of the accumulation of the papers in his yard area, with the consequent concerns for public health and safety. This is the basis upon which the court is asked to intervene in defence of the environment (including residential amenity) and its proper maintenance.

Mr Blaxland was given four months to clear up the yard.

In *Tavitian v Public and Environmental Health Council and City of Playford*[37] council officers relied on a 'risk of infestation' and causing 'justified offence' under the Public Health Act 1987 (SA) to challenge Mr Tavitian's use of his premises. He had accumulated 'numerous items and objects including garden waste, iron, timber, plastic, tyres, dilapidated motor vehicle bodies containing refuse and rubbish, motor parts, mattresses and a variety of metal frames, tubing, fencing materials and general refuse and rubbish'. He submitted that any risk from his property was only hypothetical and the action was an attempt to impose 'individual preferences, imposed as law disregarding the rights of the ratepayer', a 'harsh, unreasonable, unfair, unjust' approach. His procedural challenge succeeded on a technicality but Judge David Smith added the following comments by the way:

> The photographs show premises cluttered with what can only be described as junk. It is piled high around the house, which is in what I understand to be a residential suburb. I consider that the local Council's resolve to require the appellant to tidy up these premises as nothing less than reasonable, given its obligations to all its rate payers. I exhort the appellant to attend to what is plainly an eyesore. It is not enough to point to the fact that there is a high fence obscuring the view into the premises. Hiding the clutter does not fully address the problem, but perhaps creates another.

[37] [2003] SADC 178.

From hoarding to squalor

While some hoarding and accumulation cases may be treated as 'amenity' problems others, as we have seen, are treated as public health risks. Although Mr Blaxland's case may be an exception, these will generally include some aspect that would be described in lay terms as 'squalor'.[38]

In *Wollongong v McLean*[39] for example, Mrs McLean's suburban house had a yard that was 'unkempt and full of rubbish'. Preston CJ explained:

> No maintenance of any note has been done. Even worse is the accumulation of rubbish. Clothing, shopping trolleys, packaging, building materials, old carpet, discarded kitchen pots and utensils, garden tools, and cleaning utensils, plastic bags and plastic bins among other materials, as well as food waste and animal faeces have been allowed to accumulate on the premises.

A variety of animals, including chickens and ducks, lived in the yard. Gas and electricity were no longer connected to the house. A neighbour described the 'disgusting' smells emanating from the property in hot weather; the snakes and rats that spread from it and his concern about the fire risk that it posed to his home – a concern endorsed by the state fire service. Attempts by her brothers to manage this mess were frustrated by Mrs McLean retrieving items they had placed in skips for removal. The local council issued orders under s 124 *Local Government Act* 1993 (NSW) followed in due course by a successful application to the Court.

In *Hawkesbury City Council v Dundler*[40] the garden was overgrown, scattered with rubbish and was used by the resident as a toilet. Inspection of the interior of the house disclosed sheep, cat and dog excrement in the kitchen and faecal waste throughout the house. Household rubbish, decaying food, papers and miscellaneous detritus covered every space. The RSPCA had removed one dog and 21 cats from the premises in 2004, when the resident was in prison. There was no usable sewerage and the water supply had been cut off. Cowdroy J described the premises as 'clearly unfit for habitation'.

The statutory procedures may not achieve a lasting improvement to the premises. The history of Waverley City Council's actions against Mrs Bobolas[41] and her daughters lasted for almost 20 years, during which time there were several court-ordered council cleans, incurring significant expense to all parties (see Plate 6.1). In the last litigation to date, the council officer concerned:

> observed that rubbish covered most of the front yard, the entire driveway at the side of the house to the fence lines to a depth of approximately one metre and was also being stored on the front verandah behind a shade cloth and that it extended into the back

[38] And would register as such on any proposed 'squalor scale'.

[39] [2006] NSWLEC 295. [40] [2005] NSWLEC 662.

[41] 2005, 2007. The slow and relatively unsuccessful history has led to moves in New South Wales to introduce stronger powers for councils allowing immediate entry to clean up within five years of an order being made.

> yard. He formed the opinion that the accumulation of rubbish was unsightly, a health risk to residents of the property and surrounding residents, a potential harbourage for insects, a potential harbourage for vermin and a potential fire hazard.

The order sought by the Council was granted but enforced with considerable difficulty.

In South Australia, s 15 of the *Public and Environmental Health Act 1987*, to be replaced by the *Public Health Act* 2011, provided for orders requiring 'insanitary premises' to be improved by the person causing or allowing the condition. 'Insanitary' was given a broad statutory meaning, including 'a risk to health'; 'so filthy or neglected that there is a risk of infestation'; being such as to cause 'justified offence to the owner of any land in the vicinity' or emitting 'offensive material or odours'.

In *City of Marion v Lepoidevin*:[42]

> Most of the rooms were stacked with boxes, books, newspapers, stationery and clothing. The kitchen contained decaying food scraps. Some of the rooms contained blown and rusted tins of food and packets of food in poor condition. Rat droppings were on the floor of a bedroom and in drawers and cupboards in the kitchen... The interior of the refrigerator was soiled and bloodstained. Meat in the refrigerator was unfit for consumption. Mouse droppings were on and in benches, shelves and cupboards. Mice were seen to emerge from a mattress as it was being removed. There were signs of food pest activity in the kitchen.

After a report from police, environmental health officers visited the property and observed its condition. For six months they unsuccessfully pursued negotiation, further inspections and eventually a notice. Then, having obtained a warrant, they arranged for the contents to be sorted, stored or discarded and the premises to be cleaned and fumigated.

The premises were held to be a risk to health, creating a risk of infestation. When sued for the costs of the clean-up

> the evidence which the defendant gave... was seriously undermined by his outright and repeated denials that his premises were unclean, let alone in an insanitary condition, in any respect at all... The defendant's capacity for rational thought, and therefore his capacity to give reliable evidence, is rendered suspect by assaults which he committed in the presence of police... and by his ludicrous suggestion in the course of his evidence that the police were responsible for the mice in his premises.

Mr Lepoidevin was ordered to pay the Council's clean-up costs.

Adding in animals

In several of the cases mentioned above[43] animals kept on the property caused particular concern. Their unrestricted presence can certainly intensify the foul

[42] [1997] SADC 3593.

[43] For example in the cases of Ms McLean, Mr Dundler, Ms Fuller and Mr Stankovic describer earlier.

condition of premises. It may reflect problems experienced by the resident in managing daily life. Where 'animal hoarding' occurs, large numbers of animals will be found accumulated without appropriate care or facilities. The resident may be oblivious to their suffering or may actively construe the arrangement as one of animal 'rescue'. Where such conditions exist, not only the local council but also animal welfare organisations will have an interest in the matter. The circumstances may well include offences under local animal cruelty legislation.[44] The animals may be removed to a place of safety[45] and criminal action taken against the resident, for the state of the premises[46] or for the state of the animals.[47] Like other cases under consideration, these cases are not quickly resolved, nor does court action successfully deter future problems.[48] A vet, Helen Hein, kept over 120 German shepherd dogs on her semi-rural property in Surrey, England despite more than 16 enforcement actions and criminal prosecutions over 20 years.[49] She ignored most of these, neither defending the cases nor paying the fines. Her applications to be reinstated on the roll of licensed veterinarians were rejected by the professional governing body because:

> she has... repeatedly refused to admit that she did anything significantly wrong, irrespective of... the (guilty) pleas made at the time. This gives us considerable concern that her offences may be repeated in the future.[50]

In federal jurisdictions such as Australia or the USA, where animal welfare legislation is a state matter, animal hoarders may regularly move back and forward across state borders in attempts to evade prosecution and the confiscation of their animals.[51]

Tenants in trouble

All the cases mentioned so far have involved owner-occupiers. Where the resident is a tenant an alternative, or additional, challenge to the state of their premises can come from their landlord who may take action to enforce tenancy

[44] For example, s 13 *Animal Welfare Act* 1985 (SA).

[45] In *Dundler*, over 20 animals had been removed from the property by the state RSPCA a year before the local council case reached court.

[46] *Dundler, Sawyer.* [47] *Hein.*

[48] Mr Sawyer was found to be 'defiant' of the court, in contumacious contempt, and was fined accordingly.

[49] *Guildford Borough Council v Hein* [2005] EWCA Civ 979, discussed in Slatter, M., 2007, Treasures, trash and tenure: hoarding and housing risk, *People, Place & Policy Online*, 2 (1) 28–36. See also Lawrie, M. Animal hoarders in Australia – shining light through darkness, *Urban Land Management Conference Proceedings* 2005 at www.uam.net.au/PDFs/PUB_Pro05_MarkLawrie_AnimalHoarders.pdf.

[50] *Decisions of the Royal College of Veterinary Surgeons re Helen Elisabeth Hein* 12 September 2003; 20 July 2004 at www.rcvs.org.uk.

[51] For example Margaret Higham was convicted in absentia in relation to cruelty in relation to keeping 170 cross-breed dogs in South Australia during 2006–7, she was found in Victoria with 120 dogs and pleaded guilty in Geelong (Victoria) to charges in relation to those animals in 2008; cases prosecuted by RSPCA.

covenants. Standard covenants include 'condition' covenants, such as keeping the premises reasonably clean and in tenantable repair and 'behaviour' covenants: to refrain from activity that is a 'nuisance' or interferes with the 'peace, comfort and privacy' of neighbours. Any tenure other than freehold renders the resident vulnerable to some degree, as the law must balance the various property interests involved.[52] The tenant's immediate interest must be balanced against the landlord/freeholder's interest in the longer term.

Although most cases relate to residential tenancies this relative vulnerability extends to those with long leaseholds, which have traditionally been assumed to be the equivalent of freehold. The case of *Castle de Joncaire v Harben*[53] in 2007 provides an unusual example of a pure property approach to a serious situation with indications of hoarding, self-neglect and squalor in a long leasehold flat. Ms Harben owned the long leasehold of a flat where she had lived for over 40 years; Ms Castle de Joncaire was the freeholder. Evidence was presented of accumulations of material in the flat, previous council cleans, a fire, pervasive odours and inaccessible bathroom and kitchen facilities, resulting in Ms Harben's use of the garden as a toilet. Ms Castle de Joncaire sought a declaration that Ms Harben was in breach of covenants in her lease relating to condition and repair. Ms Harben declined to engage with the legal process and the Tribunal granted the declaration. This would have enabled an application to forfeit Ms Harben's lease, resulting in her eviction and the loss to her of a major asset, which was also her home.

Changes in law and practice in 'property' cases

The cases already discussed reveal some interesting similarities. The property conditions they address are generally longstanding. All reflect extensive effort on the part of the local authority (often urged on by increasingly anxious neighbours) to resolve the matter through all necessary process before instituting litigation. Most have been the focus of several court actions. The time between initial complaint and ultimate orders is long. There is a low incidence of professional representation among the residents and a relatively high frequency of self-representation or refusal to engage.

The older judgments also demonstrate an exclusive focus on the property issues without any further exploration by counsel or court. For example, in his decision in *Holding v Playford* (the 'car buff' case mentioned earlier, 1997), Commissioner Hitchens commented:

52 So the growing trend to strata-type developments provides bylaws endowing strata corporations (or managers) and homeowners associations with similar responsibilities to balance interests in their planned communities.

53 At www.rpts.gov.uk/Files/2007/February/00102CF1.pdf.

> [Mr Holding] seems to have a number of personal circumstances that would need to be addressed. However, a hearing such as this is not one in which personal circumstances can be addressed and resolved... It is solely one of determining the validity of the Council's notice in law and I must deal with it accordingly.[54]

The resident's mental state was not made an issue. Similarly the 'irrational' quality of Mr Lepoidevin's arguments was highlighted but no link seems to have been made between this and the state of his premises.[55] In similar vein, no reference was made at all to Mr Dundler's mental state when the order to remove him from his filthy residence was made.[56]

However, by the time Ms McLean's case[57] and Mr Butler's case came for decision, in 2006 and 2008, respectively, a change had occurred. Ms McLean's brother assisted her in presenting her case and had also clearly helped in prior negotiations with the council. He was able to identify the problem as linked to her mental condition and with him as her advocate, this perspective shaped the final outcome.[58] The parties together proposed a draft agreed order that was specific and detailed in its requirements. The court was content to adopt this and, in recognition of the assistance given to the council by Mr McLean, directed that each party should bear their own costs. Similarly, Mr Butler presented a draft order that would have required the attendance of his primary care physician and treating psychiatrist at the clear-out of his yard. It also proposed financial assistance and a detailed set timetable for the work. Judge Cole commented:

> I do not have the power in these proceedings to order that Mr Butler be provided with financial assistance. Nor do I have the power to order that he would benefit from a clean-up of his property... It is not the purpose of the orders to dictate the fate of the items now stored on the property. That is a matter for the appellant upon complying with the orders. The focus of the orders is the use and appearance of the property itself... In making the orders, I have had regard to the difficulty Mr Butler experiences in approaching a substantial task. Accordingly, the order is detailed and provides for the clean up to occur in manageable stages.[59]

In a tenancy case, *South Australian Housing Trust v G*,[60] the Tribunal went to the root of the matter. A condition of the order (agreed at the hearing) was that the tenant *must* accept ongoing support through a tenancy and living skills programme to address problems including hoarding and cluttering behaviour. Failure to observe this 'support' condition, like any other condition in the order, could result in an eviction.[61]

54 [1998] SAEDRC 492.
55 *Lepoidevin*, above n 42.
56 *Dundler*, above n 40.
57 Above, n 39 and n 32.
58 The court acknowledged: 'The respondent... is in breach for a reason concerned with her state of mental health.'
59 *Butler v City of Mitcham* [2008] SAERDC 20.
60 (RT 06/6181) 10 January 2007.
61 Showing the strategic use of formal orders to reinforce agreed undertakings. Twelve months after the order was made the tenant was still successfully maintaining her tenancy with the support of the agreed agency.

The Court or Tribunal focuses on the issue as presented to it. These cases show that, in recent years, councils and social landlords have been adapting their presentation of issues. Clearly this is a consequence of changes to their own process designed to reflect the learnings from research[62] and international practice.[63] By reframing the issue before the Court, the discussion and the resultant order can approach the heart of the matter, acknowledging the resident's situation. This should lead to sustainable and cost-effective outcomes. Social landlords have been under a policy imperative to sustain tenancies, avoid eviction and reduce homelessness, which similarly encourages strategies that can support rather than end the tenancy.

Cost effectiveness is a priority for all agencies. Similarly, the need to avoid discrimination[64] and to minimise reputation risk[65] is shared across the field. Current approaches to squalor may reduce the number of 'property' cases requiring court intervention; they should certainly affect the way in which orders are designed.

Inspired by research and the example of hoarding taskforces in the USA,[66] as well as local collaborative experience, many guidelines and protocols now encourage a multidiscipline approach to cases of hoarding and squalor from an early stage. They recognise that there is no single cause or 'template order' in these cases; that the involvement of other services may be necessary for a solution; that regular formal or informal liaison across the team of agencies will be advantageous; and that a holistic approach is most likely to bring about an

[62] Reports such as *Hoarding: A Dangerous Secret* at www.mwcog.org/uploads/pub-documents/zllWXQ20061121162353.pdf; the work of the International OCD Hoarding Centre and Professors Steketee and Frost at www.ocfoundation.org/hoarding/; and local initiatives such as Julia Merkel, 2007, *The Role of Agencies in Response to Clients with Obsessive Compulsive Hoarding Disorder, and the Development of an Agreed Interagency Protocol*, Master of Psychology (Clinical) Thesis, Adelaide University.

[63] The internet has helped disseminate practical knowledge through the generosity of organisations such as: MassHousing, whose hoarding resources are comprehensive at www.masshousing.com; the Fairfax County Hoarding Taskforce at www.fairfaxcounty.gov/code/hoarding/hoarding-task-force.htm; the Chartered Institute of Environmental Health (UK), *Professional Practice Note: Hoarding and How to approach it* (May 2011) at www.cieh.org/uploadedFiles/Core/Policy/Publications_and_information_services/Policy_publications/Publications/Hoarding_PPN_May09.pdf; the New South Wales Partnership against Homelessness (2007) *Guidelines* at www.nsforum.org.au/files/HACC-Misc/HACC-Resources/Guidelinesforfieldstafftoassistpeoplelivinginseveredomesticsqualor.pdf; and Catholic Social Services Sydney, *Squalor and Hoarding Toolkit* published on the internet at http://catholiccommunityservices.com.au/squalorandhoarding/

[64] Hoarding has been recognised as a disability by the (Australian) Human Rights and Equal Opportunity Commission (HREOC) 2004 at www.hreoc.gov.au/disability_rights/decisions/conciliation/accommodation_conciliation.html.

[65] For example, from an apparent abuse of vulnerable citizens or, on the other hand, an apparent indifference to the very real experience of neighbours.

[66] For example Fairfax County VA and the international exchange on hoarding at www.hoardingtaskforce.org/

improvement in the premises. Agencies are developing specialist teams in house whose remit includes hoarding and squalor cases and who undertake liaison responsibilities. Some social landlords and councils are now providing counselling support to the resident. The brief experiment in the UK of using punitive strategies to 'deter' further 'offending' by imposing Anti-Social Behaviour Orders (ASBOs) and Criminal Anti-Social Behaviour Orders (CRASBOs) for hoarding and squalor seems now to be over.[67]

More changes anticipated

It is worth highlighting some further changes that may affect these types of 'property' case.

First, Australian jurisdictions have recently reviewed and renewed their public health legislation, with most now adopting a modern risk-based approach. This provides a more flexible and responsive framework thought to be more appropriate to current and future risks. It supersedes the traditional more specific approach controlling 'insanitary condition' provisions. For example, the new South Australian Act includes a general duty to 'to prevent or minimise any harm to public health caused by, or likely to be caused by, anything done or omitted to be done by the person' S 56 *Public Health Act* 2011 (SA). 'Public health' means the health of individuals in the context of the wider health of the community: s 3. It remains to be seen how this will shape responses to severe domestic squalor.

Second, it may be anticipated over time that hoarding and squalor will need to be addressed in the context of some currently evolving tenures. The increasing densification of cities and the increase in strata title developments and developments with homeowner associations introduce a tenancy-like dimension into 'owned' housing. Since many of the bylaws that regulate such developments include 'condition' covenants requiring 'tidiness' the management companies, managing agents or homeowner associations charged with bylaw supervision will need to decide how they will address any cases that arise. This could include liaison with established task forces or the support of new task forces where none exists.

Third, although expertise in supporting residents in hoarding and squalor situations is developing, it is still very localised, very specialised and stretched

[67] William Atkinson, a 45-year-old with a history of hoarding 'rubbish and putrid waste' was arrested for breaching his CRASBO, which forbade him from doing so. In an interview Mr Atkinson said Uncle Bulgaria, a character from the children's series *The Wombles*, had told him to collect the rubbish. In court his lawyer said: 'This is a very difficult situation, there has been a clinical diagnosis of severe personality disorder and obsessive compulsive disorder and recently he has started hearing voices in his head'. He also said these diagnoses were made in 1983: *Atkinson v Barking and Dagenham* (2004) *Environmental Health News*, v.48, 10 December, p. 1. Mr Atkinson's was the first but not the only (CR)ASBO for hoarding and squalor; see also for example 'Billy from Dagenham' at http://alexsturrock.com/asbos.html.

beyond capacity. There are many sensitivities around the work, including uncertain results, a slow/long timescale and the need to manage the expectations of other interested parties, such as neighbours, and assuage their concerns. It is not clear that these more sophisticated approaches will be cheaper, even if they achieve more sustainable results and are therefore arguably more cost effective. There is always the risk that short-term planning may stifle their development.

In 2007, in an attempt to address the cause of animal hoarding and to reduce recidivism, the RSPCA called on the Victorian State government to recognise animal hoarding as a mental illness. The organisation, which has the primary responsibility for animal cruelty investigations in the state, had become frustrated that animal cruelty prosecutions failed to deal with any mental health issues and therefore did not prevent repeated offences. Although no clear progress has been seen on this proposal, it may herald a new approach to animal hoarding cases and their consequences in the future.

Finally, in a recent English case, a limited Court of Protection order was granted in respect of a tenant facing eviction. The case is discussed further below[68] but the aspect of interest here is that the threat of possession proceedings was triggered by the tenant's refusal to engage with his local authority landlord, including refusals to allow entry for annual inspections of the gas service, thus placing the premises, himself and his neighbours at risk. The order allowed the risk to be managed while minimising distress to the tenant and preventing his eviction from his home of 40 years. This approach effectively links concerns with the *premises* with concerns for the *person*, reflecting more fully current understanding of the causes of many hoarding, squalor and non-engagement cases. It provides a convenient segue to the remainder of this chapter, which considers legal interventions in the interest of the resident.[69]

Focus on the person

Degrees of engagement

As we have seen, even where the primary aim of intervention is to improve the state of the premises, strategies increasingly recognise the importance of identifying and addressing the issues of the resident that underlie the problem. There is no universal response template. Cases differ in crucial respects; variable factors include the predisposing conditions experienced by the resident, their degree of engagement with the process, their degree of insight and their own capacity to respond to their situation.

[68] *AT's Case*, noted by Robert Eckford: When protection matters (2011) 161 *New Law Journal*, 537–9.

[69] For example, living skills programmes, mental health support, parenting projects.

In some less extreme cases, an early escalation of negotiations to a threat of legal action, such as eviction or liability for the cost of a clean-up by authorities, may be sufficient to prompt the resident into action, in their own interest.

More directively, a formal court order mandating actions and timelines, drafted with the cooperation of the resident and supportive family members or agencies, may be successful in achieving gradual but sustainable improvement. It may also serve as an effective encouragement to (re)connect with professional support, thereby improving resident wellbeing as well as the state of the property.[70]

Similarly, conditional possession orders can be linked to a resident tenant's acceptance of help and support designed to enhance their independence.[71] Such orders avoid eviction and may enhance the resident's independent living capabilities.

However, any of these orders is contingent on several variables. First, they reflect an awareness of current understandings of squalor and problem hoarding among frontline staff, managers, advocates and the courts. This is clearly increasing – *vide* the spread of multidiscipline teams and task forces[72] – but is not yet universal. Second, their success often depends on the availability of suitably skilled support and assistance for residents, probably over an extended period and often at no, or low, cost. In this emerging field of expertise, such support may be hard to secure. In an environment of short funding terms and fiscal stringency, the commitment to long-term affordable services may be a significant challenge. Third, these holistic responses need a degree of public acceptance, given that they are unlikely to produce prompt visible outcomes.[73] Last, and perhaps most crucially, they depend on the active involvement and engagement of the resident. This may be secured through family members or other close confidants but in many cases it will not be forthcoming.

Situations in which the resident refuses, declines or is unable to engage present a completely different challenge for all parties. The resulting difficulties are well understood by local authorities and other frontline agencies; not surprisingly there is now an increasing emphasis on techniques to establish contact where at all possible.[74]

[70] See *Wollongong v McLean* [2006] NSWLEC 295 and *Butler v City of Mitcham* [2008] SAERDC 20.

[71] *SAHT v G* (RT 06/6181) 10 January 2007.

[72] Discussed above.

[73] Increasing numbers of complaints about hoarding, unsightly premises and other threats to amenity may indicate a decreased tolerance in the community, although they could also reflect an increasing incidence of hoarding and squalor cases: see Andrew Brown, Michaela Hobby (2009) 'A foot in the door', paper presented at the National Squalor Conference, Sydney at www.nationalsqualorconference.com.au/files/presentations/

[74] For example, see New South Wales Partnership against Homelessness (2007) *Guidelines* p. 11 at www.nsforum.org.au/files/HACC-Misc/HACC-Resources/Guidelinesforfieldstafftoassistpeoplelivinginseveredomesticsqualor.pdf.

When the resident doesn't engage with the process

As can be seen in cases such as *Joncaire de Castle v Harben*[75] and *Hawkesbury City Council v Dundler*[76] discussed above, in a 'property' case the refusal of a resident to engage with their landlord, the local authority, social services and/or the court or tribunal will not of itself impede the legal process. However, where a resident is living in conditions that cause concern,[77] their refusal to engage, accept help or even open the door to an inquiry can pose a threshold problem. It is also likely to reinforce concerns about their health and wellbeing, turning the focus more evidently to the person as well as the premises.

It is useful here to (re)state two fundamental points. First, neither 'severe domestic squalor' nor 'problem hoarding' is a technical legal term used as a criterion for intervention. Where concerns arise about the resident's wellbeing, legal intervention will only be possible if the appropriate statutory conditions are met, and they will be generic, rather than specific to these conditions.[78]

Second, the experience of field officers and agency workers is that people living in severe squalor are

> frequently opposed to assessment and assistance, and may be unaware there is a problem. [They] may be suspicious or evasive, perceiving the assessment as a potential threat to their independence. Reasons for this vary. In some cases it results from apathy associated with an underlying mental disorder. In others, longstanding habits and the individual's personality traits, including rigidity, unfriendliness, suspiciousness, anxiety or avoidance could be the cause... there may also be a history of unsatisfactory dealing with service providers. Cultural and language barriers may also contribute to opposition to assessment and assistance.[79]

However, it is commonly understood[80] that between one third and one half of residents living in conditions of squalor or problem hoarding have no discernible

[75] www.rpts.gov.uk/Files/2007/February/00102CF1.pdf. [76] [2005] NSWLEC 662.

[77] Because of risks to the welfare of the resident or to third parties. A common and consistent vocabulary to describe and assess 'severe domestic squalor' and 'problem hoarding' is yet to evolve. However, tools such as the Environmental Cleanliness and Clutter Scale (Halliday and Snowdon, 2009) and the Clutter Image Rating (Steketee and Frost, 2007c; Frost *et al.*, 2008) are helping to build a shared language to evaluate scenes and determine those cases presenting immediate risks, those presenting imminent risks and those presenting potential risks, either to the resident or others.

[78] As interventions to remedy the state of premises must also satisfy the relevant generic statutory requirements; discussed in the first part of this chapter.

[79] New South Wales Partnership Against Homelessness (2007) *Guidelines* p. 6 at www.nsforum.org.au/files/HACC-Misc/HACC-Resources/Guidelinesforfieldstafftoassistpeoplelivinginsevere domesticsqualor.pdf.

[80] '35 to 50% of people with Diogenes syndrome... have no discernable psychiatric disorder' Chartered Institute of Environmental Health (UK), *Professional Practice Note: Hoarding and How to Approach it* (May 2011) p. 4 www.cieh.org/uploadedFiles/Core/Policy/Publications_and_information_services/Policy_publications/Publications/Hoarding_PPN_May09.pdf; 'half to two thirds of all persons living in severe domestic squalor suffer from dementia or alcohol-related brain damage, or mental

psychiatric disorder. Equally, a regular proportion of residents are not compromised by decision-making disability. Their choice to decline services and engagement is made as an exercise of full legal decision-making capacity. No assumptions should be made that the state of their home 'must' indicate a resident's mental illness or lack of legal competence. These issues must be explored case by case.

Full capacity

Where a resident is fully competent their decision to decline services and assistance is valid. Legal opportunities to override it are limited. As discussed above, opportunities may exist to improve the premises' condition without the resident's consent after appropriate legal process by the local authority. In some jurisdictions animal protection authorities have rights of entry for inspection and action to protect any animals at risk or experiencing harm. Children in the household may be removed by child protection authorities. In other respects the autonomy and privacy of the resident will prevail and any engagement will depend on their voluntary cooperation, secured by negotiation and discussion.

Powers to override the decision of a competent resident in connection with their welfare are now unusual and vulnerable to challenge on human rights grounds.[81] In England, Wales and Scotland, section 47 of the *National Assistance Act* 1948,[82] continues to authorise the involuntary removal from home of individuals, whether or not they have legal capacity, for a maximum of six months if they are:

(a) suffering from grave chronic disease or, being aged, infirm or physically incapacitated, are living in insanitary conditions and
(b) are unable to devote to themselves, and are not receiving from other persons, proper care and attention.

The section is designed to secure 'necessary care and attention' in such cases. However, it may be noted that s 47(2) provides that the medical officer whose certification is needed must be satisfied *either* that removal is in the interests of the person *or* that it is necessary 'for preventing injury to the health of, or serious nuisance to, other persons'. Unlike the Mental Health Act jurisdiction (below) there is no distinct appeal structure that applies to s 47 orders.[83] Data

disorders such as schizophrenia and depression' New South Wales Partnership against Homelessness (2007) *Guidelines* p.6 www.nsforum.org.au/files/HACC-Misc/HACC-Resources/Guidelinesforfieldstafftoassistpeoplelivinginseveredomesticsqualor.pdf.

81 Most obviously, their right to privacy; to family life, to freedom from detention.

82 Substantially echoed by s 126 of the *Health Act* 1956 (NZ): John Holmes, 'New Zealand experience with section 126 of Health Act 1956', paper presented at the National Squalor Conference Sydney 2009.

83 Although once the order has been in force for six weeks an application may be made to the court by or on behalf of the person concerned for the order to be revoked.

on the use of the provision has apparently never been consistently collected and its use is believed to be exceptional. Locality studies reveal major concerns about its impact and potentially broad scope.[84] Since the coming into force of the *Human Rights Act* 1998 there has been even more reason to question its role[85] and its previously infrequent use seems likely to decline further.[86]

Involuntary removal and detention under mental health legislation

Many jurisdictions include legislation that allows for both voluntary and involuntary detention in certain circumstances for a person suffering a mental disorder. Legislation varies but tends to follow a broadly common pattern, based on perceived risk to the patient or to others stemming from his or her mental state. For example, the UK's Mental Health Act 1983 provides that a patient may be compulsorily and involuntarily detained for a limited time for assessment[87] on the grounds that:

(a) he is suffering from mental disorder of a nature or degree which warrants the detention of the patient in a hospital for assessment (or for assessment followed by medical treatment) for at least a limited period; and
(b) he ought to be so detained in the interests of his own health or safety or with a view to the protection of other persons.[88]

An application for assessment needs to be signed by two medical practitioners[89] except in cases of urgent emergency.

'Mental disorder' in the UK Act is defined as 'any disorder or disability of the mind; and "mentally disordered" shall be construed accordingly'.[90] The

[84] Nair and Mayberry (1995); Hobson (1998); Greaves (1991); Forster and Tiplady (1980); Murray and Jacoby (2002).

[85] See the note distributed by the UK Department of Health in August 2000 at www.dh.gov.uk/prod_consum_dh/groups/dh_digitalassets/@dh/@en/documents/digitalasset/dh_4013786.pdf. Comparable issues surround the New Zealand section whose use, similarly, has never been documented and which sits uneasily with the New Zealand Bill of Rights Act 1990. Nevertheless a reformed Public Health Bill in 2007 included a substantially similar provision: s 128.

[86] However, for a cogent plea to maintain such a power as a last resort and as an expression of community values see Holmes, supra, n 72.

[87] 28 days is common. [88] Mental Health Act 1983 (UK) s 2(2). A.

[89] In an 'urgent emergency' support from one practitioner or the patient's nearest relative will suffice to secure 72 hours' detention: s 4(2).

[90] Ibid, s 1(2). Note that definitions can vary. In New South Wales for example, 'mental illness' is defined as: 'a condition that seriously impairs, either temporarily or permanently, the mental functioning of a person and is characterised by the presence in the person of any one or more of the following symptoms: (a) delusions, (b) hallucinations, (c) serious disorder of thought form, (d) a severe disturbance of mood, (e) sustained or repeated irrational behaviour indicating the presence of any one or more of the symptoms referred to in paragraphs (a)–(d)': s4, *Mental Health Act* 2007 (NSW).

power extends to detention for a limited time only and appeal structures preserve the rights of the patient to challenge compulsory orders, whether for treatment or assessment.[91] No assumption is made about the patient's legal capacity; these powers only address the separate and distinct matter of risk to the patient or others due to mental disorder. A patient may further be compulsorily detained for treatment if 'it is necessary for the health or safety of the patient or for the protection of other persons that he should receive such treatment and it cannot be provided unless he is detained under this section'[92] and this is confirmed by two physicians. Provisions generally require that in cases of involuntary procedure or detention the certifying officer(s) must also be satisfied that 'no other care of a less restrictive kind, that is consistent with safe and effective care, is appropriate and reasonably available to the person'.[93]

Such short-term orders may provide an opportunity to clean or clear the premises while the patient's mental health is being assessed,[94] although the impact of any such intervention on the patient's general wellbeing should be carefully evaluated. The assessment period may also provide a chance to ascertain the patient's decision-making capacity.

Although many jurisdictions provide for appeals against detention to a Mental Health Tribunal or Board or to the courts, the increasing prominence of human rights acts, charters and conventions reflects changing legal and community expectations as to the appropriate process required. Challenges will of course depend on the particular circumstances of the jurisdiction: the form of its legislation and the commitments to which it is bound. However, a need to notify patients of their rights to appeal their detention, to ensure 'prompt presentment', to provide a fair hearing, which may require (free) legal advice to patients, and an oral hearing with the parties present are among the more obvious features that are now seen as fundamental to expected process.[95] It has also been cogently argued that if patient rights are to be truly protected, rather than the process merely being 'audited', an interdisciplinary, multimember panel is necessary for all hearings 'to engage the underlying "health" essence of hearings'.[96]

Issues of capacity

If a resident living in severe domestic squalor is found to have a decision-making disability, to lack the cognitive capacity to make relevant decisions about their circumstances, such as accommodation, health and/or financial management,

[91] For example 02–011 [2001] VMHRB 3. [92] Ibid s 3(2).
[93] For example Mental Health Act 2007 (NSW), s 12 (1) (b).
[94] For a recent example discussed in context see *EB & Ors v Guardianship Tribunal* & *Ors* [2011] NSWSC 767.
[95] See for example the discussion by Carney and Beaupert (2008). [96] Ibid 205.

then decisions may need to be made on their behalf. In some cases a substitute decision maker will need to be formally appointed. These situations are inevitably very sensitive.[97]

The assessment of decision-making capacity itself must be undertaken with considerable care. Unwise decisions do not necessarily denote incapacity: it is the decision making that is in issue, not the decision, and a presumption of capacity always applies until rebutted. Capacity is understood to be decision specific. It may fluctuate. One guide for advisors highlights five features to consider: the person must be able to understand the facts involved; understand the main choices; weigh up the consequences of the choices; understand how the consequences affect them and communicate their decision.[98] Capacity should be considered over the 'reasonably foreseeable future'.[99] In the context of financial affairs, considerations may include a capacity to plan for the future and the insight to know when to seek professional advice.[100] Substitute decision making is a last resort: if practicable the resident should be supported and assisted in making their own decisions.

Enduring power of attorney

If the resident has already instituted a valid enduring power of attorney,[101] enduring power of guardianship[102] or medical attorney,[103] the attorney can act within the power conferred if the resident loses capacity. Clearly this provides established substitute decision makers with some confidence that they embody the choice of the resident themself. If mismanagement or abuse is suspected, however (and continuing residence in a situation of squalor would certainly raise a question on this point), such powers and their exercise may be challenged. If necessary, the protective jurisdiction (exercised by courts or tribunals) may be used to appoint an effective guardian or financial administrator.

97 No more so than where members of the close family are divided over an older relative's welfare; see for example *P v D1 & Ors* [2011] NSWSC: 89-year-old mother living with daughter in squalor unacknowledged by either woman. Application for guardianship made by social worker; brothers appointed guardians and one also appointed financial manager. Over five years this situation was exposed to six Guardianship Tribunal hearings and two court hearings largely to address difficulties experienced by the daughter in accepting the situation.

98 NSW Diversity Services (Attorney General's Department) Capacity Toolkit at www.lawlink.nsw.gov.au/lawlink/diversityservices/LL_DiversitySrvces.nsf/pages/diversity_services_capacity_toolkit.

99 *McD v McD* (1983) 3 NSWLR 81,86.

100 *Re GHI (a protected person)* [2005] NSWSC 581.

101 For example under the *Powers of Attorney and Agency Act* 1984.

102 For example under the under the *Guardianship and Administration Act* 1993.

103 For example under Schedule 1 – *Consent to Medical Treatment and Palliative Care Act 1995.*

The protective jurisdiction

Where no enduring powers have been created, informal support from family and friends is sufficient in many cases to provide a practical and effective means of ensuring a person's affairs and daily life are satisfactorily managed, even if they have some level of decision-making disability. However, where the resident is living in conditions of severe domestic squalor third parties, concerned about either the premises or the resident, are likely to raise the question of capacity and the management of the resident's affairs. Resolution may require an application to a guardianship jurisdiction, such as a Guardianship Tribunal, the Court of Protection or equivalent to appoint a substitute decision maker.[104] These jurisdictions intervene in the interests of the resident, on the 'least restrictive' approach, seeking to maximise and maintain autonomy wherever possible,[105] as was stated in *Re ACJ* [2007] NSWGT 15, [46].

Historically, guardianship and financial management jurisdictions had a predominant purpose of protection. However, modern guardianship and financial management legislation tends to strike a balance between providing necessary protection while also promoting empowerment of people with disabilities and minimum intrusion on their rights and liberties.

On the other hand, the priority given to maintaining the autonomy of the person and paying regard to their opinions and wishes as far as possible does *not* mean that a Tribunal or appointing body must make decisions that reflect those wishes: *EB & Ors v Guardianship Tribunal & Ors* [2011] NSWSC 767.

In accordance with the 'least restrictive' approach, Guardianship Orders in many jurisdictions are limited both in scope and in duration.[106] In most cases they are also open to review by the awarding tribunal and an appeal against the award of an order may be made to a superior court.

The role of guardian is concerned with decision making in areas of personal or lifestyle decisions. Their powers may be comprehensive or may be limited to a specific area of decision making, such as where the person will live, what services they will receive or decisions about their health care and medical and dental treatment. As guardian they are not the resident's case manager or carer. It is unusual that a guardian will be granted full decision-making powers or 'coercive' powers, although in appropriate cases they may be empowered to consent to limitations on the resident that would otherwise be unlawful. Financial management orders, usually available through a separate process, similarly operate on the 'least restrictive' approach and provide for a substitute decision maker

[104] Status to apply will be determined according to local legislation. In New South Wales for example any person 'who has a genuine concern for the welfare of the person' may apply for a guardianship order or a financial management order to be granted (*Guardianship Act* 1987, s 9(1)), whereas applications apart from by those most directly involved are only with consent of the court under the UK's *Mental Capacity Act* 2005.

[105] For example see s 4 *Guardianship Act* 1987 (NSW).

[106] This will vary, however. Even between states there are considerable differences.

(a financial manager) who has control of the resident's legal and financial affairs. This could include, for example, control of the sale of their property; provision for the cost of services and the management of related legal matters.[107] In appropriate cases the same person may exercise both lifestyle and financial decisions for the resident under the separate requisite authorities.

Relatives or family friends may be appointed guardians or financial managers although it must be clear that they have the necessary experience and would not have any conflict of interest in the role. Where there are problems in a personal appointment of this kind, the Public Guardian or equivalent may be appointed and staff from that office will exercise the powers in the relevant order.

Scope for future development

Where orders from the protective jurisdiction can be fine tuned to meet the exact needs of the resident, they may be invaluable in some cases when the resident declines to engage with others. However, it must be emphasised that they are only available where there is a decision-making disability and the comments that follow also assume the availability of limited guardianship, where orders can be tailored in scope and duration very precisely to the needs of the case.

In the case of AT, an 80-year-old resident had lived in his rented flat for over 40 years and managed his affairs independently and mostly successfully. However, he suffered from a paranoid delusional disorder whereby he believed that the local authority (his landlord) was in a conspiracy to harm him. He refused to engage with them at any level. This included a refusal to let local authority staff into his home to undertake annual gas inspections, which placed him, his neighbours and the property potentially at risk. The local authority obtained a possession order against him. AT was assessed as lacking capacity to litigate, so the Official Solicitor was appointed as his litigation friend. As an alternative to eviction the local authority proposed removing the gas supply from his home and converting the property to electric heating so that the inspections would no longer be necessary. AT refused to allow this. The Official Solicitor suggested the authority apply to the Court of Protection to obtain the necessary authority. It declined to do this, so the Official Solicitor made the application on behalf of AT instead. In collaboration with the local authority social services staff, the application sought orders that allowed a carefully structured process to ensure the works were done and AT's best interests were protected throughout. It was estimated that the work would take five to six days and that it would not be safe for him to remain at the property during that period.

The order authorised contractors to enter the property (using forced entry if necessary), change the locks and undertake the work. It required AT to reside in a

[107] See for example *Petronaitis v Petronaitis* [2008] NSWSC 798.

specified care home for seven days and permitted the authority to use reasonable and proportionate force if necessary to effect his removal. It also provided for AT to have daily supervised visits to his home and for the use of reasonable and proportionate force if he refused to leave after a visit. No other limitations were imposed on him during the seven-day period.

Evidence was carefully assembled of lack of capacity, risk from his decision and the need for the work to be done. Careful plans were drawn up of how the powers would be implemented, how AT's interests would be protected, how his distress would be minimised, how his move would be effected (including liaison with the police) and what amounted to 'reasonable and proportionate force'.

The overriding argument on which the application relied was that the proposed course of action served the best interests of AT because it avoided his eviction from his long-term home. It was also planned in a way that minimised the short-term risks to his wellbeing (which would have been much greater from a bailiff eviction).

The careful and detailed preparation allowed the court to agree the plan and grant the order at the first hearing. This provided a prompt, economical and tailored resolution to the situation, seen as highly effective and a 'win–win' outcome.

It has been suggested that a similar approach in some cases of squalor and hoarding could be useful to allow cleaning, repair or other works, even possibly periodic works to maintain the state of the premises at a minimum acceptable level. AT's case shows the need for careful and collaborative preparation of such applications.

Collaborative approaches are increasingly encouraged in working with extreme squalor. Increased awareness of the issues around squalor and hoarding are encouraging a greater emphasis on the issues of the person even where agencies' primary concern is to improve the state of the premises. It is understood not only that the resident may have real needs but that any sustainable change will depend on these underlying circumstances being addressed. As this chapter has described, legal interventions are evolving to better address the substantial issues, in traditional 'property' cases as well as those that focus on the person and interests of the resident.

A comparison of powers

Table 7.1 lists some of the legal options available to help intervene in squalor situations in three jurisdictions. Availability of powers differs across the world and even within countries. In their efforts to help those affected by severe domestic squalor, services around the world will encounter varying possibilities for using laws and regulations. It is desirable that guidelines be developed within each of the hundreds of jurisdictions so that services are easily able to find out what is applicable in their own catchment areas.

Table 7.1 A broad comparison of powers.

England	New South Wales	South Australia	Comment
National Assistance Act 1948 (s 47)	No equivalent	No equivalent	Also New Zealand: Health Act 1936 (s 126)
Mental Health Act 2007	Mental Health Act 2007	Mental Health Act 2009	Powers of involuntary detention
Mental Capacity Act 2005	Guardianship Act 1987	Guardianship and Administration Act 1993	Appointment of substitute decision makers
Public Health Act 1936;	Local Government Act 1993 (s 124)	Local Government Act 1999 (s 254)	Powers to issue notices to control nuisances, etc.
Environmental Protection Act 1990			
Prevention of Damage by Pests Act 1949	Equivalent in Local Government Act 1993 (s 124)	Equivalent in Local Government Act 1999 (s 254)	
Town and Country Planning Act 1990	Environmental Planning and Assessment Act 1979	Development Act 1993	

8

The ethics of intervening in cases of severe domestic squalor

Christopher Ryan

> I crossed the staircase landing, and entered the room she indicated. From that room, too, the daylight was completely excluded, and it had an airless smell that was oppressive. A fire had been lately kindled in the damp old-fashioned grate, and it was more disposed to go out than to burn up, and the reluctant smoke which hung in the room seemed colder than the clearer air, – like our own marsh mist. Certain wintry branches of candles on the high chimney-piece faintly lighted the chamber; or it would be more expressive to say, faintly troubled its darkness. It was spacious, and I dare say had once been handsome, but every discernible thing in it was covered with dust and mould, and dropping to pieces. The most prominent object was a long table with a tablecloth spread on it, as if a feast had been in preparation when the house and the clocks all stopped together. An epergne or centre-piece of some kind was in the middle of this cloth; it was so heavily overhung with cobwebs that its form was quite undistinguishable; and, as I looked along the yellow expanse out of which I remember its seeming to grow, like a black fungus, I saw speckle-legged spiders with blotchy bodies running home to it, and running out from it, as if some circumstances of the greatest public importance had just transpired in the spider community.

This chapter examines the ethical issues raised by intervention in cases of severe domestic squalor. In contrast to the chapter on legal issues, which focused primarily on what *could* be done in such cases, this chapter will look at what *should* be done. When is it right, morally and ethically (I will use the words interchangeably) to intervene in such cases? When, even if legally permissible, would it be wrong to do so?

To enliven the ethical discussion, I will refer periodically to the case described in the vignette above. Astute readers will have already recognised this as Pip's first view of Miss Havisham's dining room in Charles Dickens's *Great Expectations*. Miss Havisham's circumstances will provide us with an illustrative example that we can refer back to as needed, but, since any sort of intervention would have

Plate 1.1 John Waterhouse *Diogenes, 1882* oil on canvas 208.3×134.6cm Art Gallery of New South Wales Purchased 1886.

Plate 1.2 A 78-year-old male had bicycles occupying most areas of his dwelling.

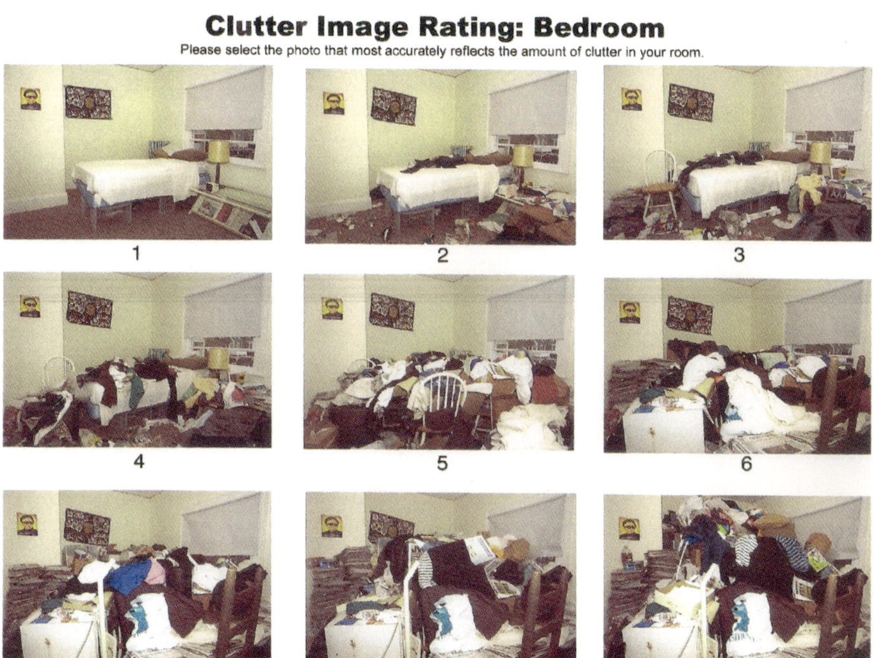

Plate 1.3 Clutter Image Rating Scale (bedroom).

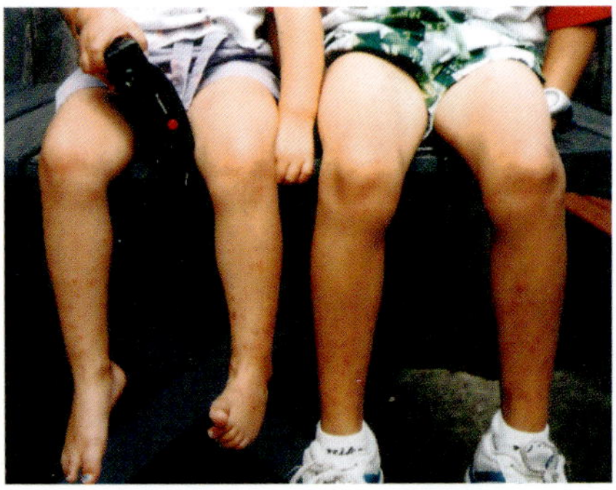

Plate 2.1 Photograph showing bites from insects in overgrown garden.

Plate 2.2 Unclean bathtub with probable faecal contamination.

Plate 2.3 Accumulation of rubbish outside of house.

Plate 2.4 Disorganisation and hoarding in the garden.

Plate 3.1 Refrigerator with maggots.

Plate 3.2 Dirty but dry and cluttered kitchen.

Plate 3.3 Overflowing garbage disposal in kitchen.

Plate 3.4 Cluttered kitchen with inaccessible bench and appliances.

Plate 4.1 Toilet made almost inaccessible by surrounding clutter and accumulated waste.

Plate 4.2 Dirty bathroom with faeces on the floor and exterior of the toilet bowl.

Plate 4.3 Dirty toilet cubicle seen from passageway outside.

Plate 4.4 Toilet showing wet, neglectful squalor.

Plate 5.1 Exterior of a house of a 75-year-old male, which had been inaccessible for one year because of hoarded contents completely filling the dwelling and obstructing entry. He had been sleeping and sheltering under an umbrella erected at the back door.

Plate 5.2 Cluttered living room.

Plate 5.3 Animal hoarding: 7 of 50 animals on this property.

Plate 5.4 'House ruined by squatters', asking: 'How many animals does it take to turn a home into a farm yard?' (*Herald Sun*, 15 June 2011).

Plate 6.1 'A disgrace' (*The Sunday Telegraph*, 9 October 2005). Photographer: Angelo Soulas

Plate 6.2 'Trapped in squalor' (*The Mosman Daily*, 29 November 2001).

Plate 6.3 Health & Science feature 'The collectors' by Kate Benson (*The Sydney Morning Herald*, 8 April 2010).

Plate 7.1 Bed showing stains from faecal incontinence.

Plate 7.2 Bedroom showing 'wet squalor' with floor soiled with faeces and urine.

Plate 7.3 Completely obstructed passageway/hallway.

Plate 7.4 Inaccessible bed due to accumulation of rubbish and items of little value.

Plate 8.1 Dirty hallway and front door (free of clutter).

Plate 8.2 Dirty hallway and walls.

Plate 8.3 Dirty floor, furniture and visible surfaces.

Plate 8.4 Narrow walkways between stacks of paper and items of little obvious value.

been extremely unlikely in Dickensian England, we will update our scenario slightly and place our contemporary *Ms* Havisham in the same general circumstances, but in a modern suburban flat, in a medium-sized housing complex, which we will call Satis Mews.

According to the rating schemes cited in Chapter 1, Ms Havisham's dark, decaying apartment, with 'mice rattling behind the panels', exhibits third-degree, dry, neglectful squalor. We will assume that Ms Havisham has been approached by a local authority to clean up her home and that she has refused to comply. This assumption is not unreasonable since numerous authors have noted that a reluctance or at least an unwillingness to wholeheartedly accept treatment and services is so common as to almost be seen as a defining feature of the syndrome (Cooney and Hamid, 1995; Lauder *et al.*, 2005, 2009).

We will assume too, that all efforts to negotiate with her to agree to a voluntary clean-up have failed. This assumption is very important, because there is a strong ethical obligation to attempt to negotiate with people before using any powers one might have to force them to comply and many authors have stressed that it is often possible over time to build some relationship with the person and thereby convince him or her to cooperate with an intervention (Gannon and O'Boyle, 1992; Cooney and Hamid, 1995).

With these assumptions made, however, the main question we must address in this chapter, and the biggest ethical dilemma that arises in cases of severe domestic squalor is this: under what circumstances is it ethically permissible to override a person's express refusal to allow an authority to clean up his or her home? Perhaps, surprisingly, very little has been written about this dilemma. When authors have broached the subject, their discussions have been brief, inconclusive and often focus more on legal issues than strictly ethical ones (Sherry, 1990; Gannon and O'Boyle, 1992; Jackson, 1997; Strang *et al.*, 1998; Lauder *et al.*, 2005; Ballard, 2010).

The answer to this question is, superficially at least, relatively easy. It involves a relatively straightforward algorithm that involves asking up to three questions and then proceeding on the basis of each answer (see Figure 8.1). While the algorithm is straightforward in itself, determining the answers to its questions will often be extremely difficult.

Question one is: 'Does the person have the decisional capacity to refuse the offer of assistance to clean up his or her home?' If the answer is no, then the next question is: 'Would cleaning up the home, despite their objections, be in the person's best interests?' If it would be, then one should proceed with the clean-up.

If the answer to question one is yes, then one should ask question two: 'Has the person made any sort of promise (explicit or implicit) to keep his or her home in a reasonable state?' I will explain what I mean by this below, but if the answer is yes, then it is again likely that a forced clean-up will be ethically justified.

If the answer to this question is no, one should go on to question three: 'Is the state of the person's home significantly adversely affecting the lives of other people to the extent where forced intervention is justified?' If the answer is yes the clean-up may ethically proceed, if no it should not.

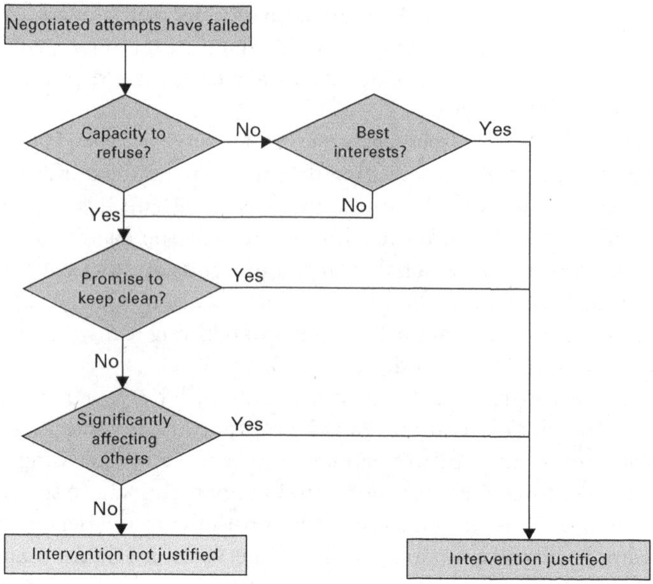

Figure 8.1 Ethical intervention in severe domestic squalor.

We will look at each of these questions in detail below. We will also look, at the end of the chapter, at some other ethical issues that arise in the context of squalor. Before we do, though, we should pause briefly to review what we mean by an ethical dilemma and the ways that such a dilemma may be approached.

Ethics

An ethical dilemma arises when people disagree about, or an individual is unsure about, how to proceed in a particular circumstance. The source of disagreement or uncertainty is not, however, based on disagreement or uncertainty about the facts of the situation, nor is it apparently about some issue that could be clarified with greater application of technical knowledge. Instead the source of disagreement or uncertainty lies in dispute about what would be the *right* thing to do in this circumstance – 'right' in the ethical or moral sense.

There are a number of ways of approaching a problem of what may or may not be right. Here I will focus on only three of these approaches. These three are probably the approaches most commonly used in the ethics literature. Two of the approaches described represent schools of thought on approaches to ethical dilemmas. The third is more by way of a technique. We will be employing all three when we set out to tackle the three questions in our algorithm.

The first school, and that which will be most familiar to most readers, is the deontological approach. Deontology is an approach that looks to the rights or obligations or duties that surround a particular situation and suggests that the right course of action is that which best engages these rights, obligations or duties. The focus here is upon what acts must or must not be done, regardless, to some extent, of the consequences of those actions. In fact the word 'deontology' is derived from the Greek *dei*, meaning 'one must'.

There is no one deontological school. There are many of them, varying, not surprisingly, according to the various rights or obligations or duties that each subscribes to. A familiar example of such a list of musts and must-nots is the Bible's Ten Commandments, but the elements of a deontological catalogue need not be God-given and need not contain a set number of elements. Other deontological imperatives frequently cited are 'do unto others as you would have them do unto you', or 'all innocent human beings have a right to life', or 'do not lie', or 'all torture is wrong'. Whatever the right or obligation or duty cited, the deontologist holds that the acts associated with them are either right or wrong in and of themselves, and that their moral worth does not depend upon their consequences.

Consequentialist schools, not surprisingly, take the opposing view. Consequentialists argue that if one is uncertain about how to proceed, in an ethically contentious situation, one should look, not at the actions themselves, but rather examine the consequences of the proposed actions. Utilitarianism, the major consequentialist school, suggests that the right course of action is that course which results in the most non-moral good. What constitutes 'non-moral good' varies among utilitarians, but usually it is something akin to happiness or general wellbeing.

Although a deontological approach and a consequentialist approach will sometimes lead in different directions, more commonly the application of one approach is simply reinforced by the application of the other. Moreover, since neither approach is without its problems when trying to tackle an ethical dilemma, most people draw on both when presented with one. Those familiar with the widely promulgated four-principles approach (Beauchamp and Childress, 2009) will note that this is something of a hybrid of the two schools described. Respect for autonomy and justice seem to have much in common with a deontological approach; while beneficence and non-maleficence seem more utilitarian in their orientation.

The third approach to solving an ethical dilemma that I want to describe, before returning to squalor, is casuistry. Casuistry is not a school of ethical thinking, but rather a technique that may be useful when trying to find a way through an ethical dilemma. It involves comparing the circumstances surrounding the case where one is faced with an ethical quandary on how to proceed, with the circumstances surrounding similar but different cases where one is more certain of the right thing to do. If one is unsure whether to take course A or B in a certain situation, X, but is sure that B is right in a similar situation, Y, then a careful comparison of the circumstances of X and Y might assist in deciding whether or not B might be the right course in situation X as well.

Of course this is just a précis of some of the more prominent ethical approaches. There are myriad other schools that approach ethics in different ways, and even the deontological and utilitarian schools described may be further split into myriad subschools. Nonetheless this book is primarily about squalor not ethics, and this most basic of introductions will suffice. With it under our belt, let's return to our algorithm for solving the dilemma around unwanted intervention in squalor.

Autonomy and capacity

Recall that question one was: 'Does the person have the decisional capacity to refuse the offer of assistance to clean up his or her home?'

Respect for autonomy, familiar from the four-principles approach, demands that, all things being equal, we should allow people to chart their own course in life. This is often set out in deontological terms as a good thing in itself, but even in utilitarian terms, it is easy to argue that the best way of maximising wellbeing in a community is to allow people to pursue their own ideas of happiness. Of course there are limits on what we should allow people to do, and we will return to these when we come to address our algorithm's third question, but for the most part our society places a high value on allowing people to do as they wish as long as they are not harming others or interfering with others' autonomy. It is respect for autonomy that underlies the importance we place on gaining valid consent before someone undergoes an operation, and it is respect for autonomy that, in many ways, underlies our preference for democracy as a means of organising power.

If Ms Havisham chooses to live in squalor, then, all things being equal, surely our default response should be to allow her to do just that. Leaving aside for a moment the effect that the squalor might have on other people, surely, if Ms Havisham is capable of making her own decisions, it is irrelevant that we might feel that living in cleaner circumstances might be better for her. It is her life, she may live it as she chooses.

As strong as the force of respect for autonomy is, however, its existence as an influence in any individual set of circumstances depends crucially on ascertaining that the person's apparent choice represents a real and valid choice. Whether or not an apparent choice in any particular decision is valid will crucially depend upon whether or not the person has the capacity to make that decision.

Decision-making capacity (or competence, the terms are usually used interchangeably) refers to whether or not the person can do three things with respect to the decision in front of them.

First, he or she must be able to understand, comprehend and believe any information relevant to the decision. Note that the information must be presented in a form that the person is capable of understanding. One does not lack decision-making capacity simply because one is a native English speaker and all the information presented has been in Icelandic. Note too that when we say that the person must be able to 'believe' the information presented, this does not imply that one lacks decision-making capacity simply if one chooses not to believe something told to them. It refers instead to the *ability* to believe the information. A person who is profoundly depressed, for example, may simply be unable to believe that they are worthy of any sort of treatment that might relieve their depression, and that lack of ability to believe may be a direct consequence of their depression.

Second, to have decision-making capacity, one must be able to use the information presented and weigh it in the balance to come to a decision. Someone with a profoundly impaired short-term memory, for example, may be able to comprehend and believe information as it is presented but then may not be able to retain it long enough to use it to come to a decision.

Third, the person must be able to communicate whatever decision they have come to. Again the difficulty here must be more than a simple language barrier. The sort of situation usually envisaged here is one, unlikely to be relevant in cases of squalor, where a person suffers locked-in syndrome and though able to understand and process information perfectly normally, they are then unable to speak or move to communicate their thoughts.

When considering the dilemma confronting us then, we must first discover whether Ms Havisham understands the benefits of accepting help to clean up her house and the disadvantages of continuing to live in squalor. If we are convinced that she does understand this information, the next question is whether or not she can use that information, whether she can weigh it in the balance, in such a way as to make a valid decision to refuse assistance. Notice that in making these judgements it is important to focus on Ms Havisham's abilities and not upon the desirability or otherwise of her final choice. One cannot be said to lack decision-making capacity merely because the choice that one comes to seems irrational or stupid or contrary to one's best interests. Respect for autonomy means respect for people's right to make all the irrational, stupid or contrary to one's best interests decisions one wants to make. If I am a Jehovah's Witness and have made a considered decision to refuse blood products, even though I know this will result in my death, then that is up to me. To take some more banal, but perhaps familiar, examples: I am at liberty (generally speaking) to regularly spend a percentage of my income on poker machines despite the fact that in the long run I cannot gain monetarily from this; or to go skydiving despite it being a relatively dangerous pursuit.

While the presence or absence of capacity must be the key to determining the rights and wrongs of coercive treatment when a person refuses intervention, most case reports, including those most strident about the need to intervene, do not mention capacity at all (Anderson and Bach-Norz, 1991).

The only way of testing capacity in cases of severe domestic squalor is to patiently go through the benefits of cleaning up with the person and asking him or her of their understanding of these to try to gauge that understanding. That done, it is necessary to ask them to describe why exactly they have decided, given the circumstances, that they will refuse assistance with a clean-up, and try to ascertain whether or not their descriptions reveal an ability to weigh the information in context. Note that this ability to weigh does not imply that the final decision will be rational. Ms Havisham, for example, may be perfectly able to understand all the information presented and to weigh it up, but might still, competently refuse clean-up assistance on the grounds, important to her, that she prefers to maintain her house as a shrine to her lost chance at happiness, and that she prefers to be continually reminded of her tragedy.

Some researchers have attempted to devise a screening tool to help identify those persons who, having been identified as self-neglecting, might also lack capacity (Naik *et al.*, 2006). The authors of the tool acknowledge, however, that it cannot replace careful clinical assessment of capacity. While in other clinical situations such a tool might uncover a possible problem with capacity, it seems reasonable to say that in the case of severe domestic squalor, the simple fact that the person is living in squalor seems sufficient, at least, to raise reasonable doubt about a person's capacity, so a screening tool for this population seems superfluous.

If a person living in severe domestic squalor retains decisional capacity then they may only be forced to clean up their house if there are reasons for overriding their autonomous choice for living as they do. We will address these reasons in the two remaining questions of our algorithm.

If the person living in squalor does not have decisional capacity around the issue of refusal of clean-up, then we will say that their voiced objections to assistance do not reflect an autonomous choice and therefore need not be adhered to. This, however, does not automatically mean that we can morally move in to clean up their home. The next question is whether or not the intended course of action is in the incompetent person's best interests.

Generally speaking a best interests determination will not be too difficult in cases of domestic squalor. Even though there is a paucity of studies showing the efficacy of intervention in severe domestic squalor (Snowdon *et al.*, 2007), there will be few cases where it can be successfully argued that it is in a person's best interests to live in filth. Nonetheless, in cases where the degree of squalor is relatively low, and where one can assume that the person will be extremely distressed by an action to remove it, or in cases where even significant squalor is corrected only to re-appear within weeks or months, one might be justified in asking whether a clean-up is really going to bring benefit to the person concerned. Even in cases of incapacity one would not be justified in cleaning up a domicile if that action were going to cause more harm to the individual than good. Not at least without further justification as might arise in asking the remaining questions in the algorithm.

A prior undertaking of reasonable cleanliness

The algorithm's second question is: 'Has the person made any sort of promise (explicit or implicit) to keep his or her home in a reasonable state?'

There is an ethical duty on all of us to keep our binding promises. Again support for this notion comes both from deontological and consequentialist perspectives. From the former perspective, keeping a promise seems like the sort of thing that is a moral good in itself. From the latter perspective, if there were no presumption that we would, generally speaking, make good on our word, promises, with all their current social worth, would soon become bankrupt currency.

In the context of severe domestic squalor, promise keeping will usually arise when the person of interest is living in accommodation that is not his or her own. Generally speaking, rented, leased or borrowed accommodation is only made with a (usually explicit, but sometimes simply implied) promise that the occupant will keep the residence reasonably tidy. If Statis Mews were a public housing facility, or if Ms Havisham were living in private rental accommodation, then it would be relatively easy to argue that when she signed the lease she took on, as part of the conditions of the rental agreement, that she would keep her home reasonably clean and tidy. In failing to do so, she has therefore breached that agreement and having done so, it is reasonable that the agreement as a whole be subject to re-negotiation – presumably a demand that she cannot continue to live there if she does not comply with a clean-up order.

If, however, Ms Havisham owns her own accommodation in Statis Mews, and if the purchasing agreement contained no such pledge, then it cannot be argued that Ms Havisham is in breach of such a pledge and, if we want her to comply with a clean-up order, we will need to ask the final question of our algorithm.

Harm to others

'Is the state of the person's home significantly adversely affecting the lives of other people to the extent where forced intervention is justified?'

Recall from our discussion on autonomy that while we should generally allow people to chart their own course in life, there are some limits on what we should allow people to do. We do not generally allow others to exercise their autonomy if they are causing, or are likely to cause, significant harm to others. Even if Ms Havisham is both competent to decide to live as she does, and if she is breaking no prior undertaking to do so, we are likely to be justified in overriding her competent objections if it is clear that the squalor with which she has surrounded herself presents a *significant* threat to the welfare of those around her.

A lot will hang on the word 'significant' in these situations and there will often be plenty of room for disagreement as to what threats are worthy of inclusion in such a calculus. Threats to others' lives and limbs, for example, will always be included, but what about a threat to a neighbourhood's property prices? It is arguable, for example, that the state of Ms Havisham's domicile leaves her home and adjacent homes vulnerable to fire risk. Those familiar with *Great Expectations* will know that just this risk eventually came to pass. However, the exact extent of the fire risk is difficult to calculate and the risk to the homes of others will crucially depend on the physical layout of the buildings concerned. It might be tempting to argue that any sort of fire risk might justify a forced intervention to remove the source of risk, but before leaping to that conclusion it is worth considering how much risk would need to be posed by a tidy person who habitually smokes in bed, before one would feel justified in forcibly preventing such an action. Similarly, Ms Havisham's home is infested with rodents, but so are many other people's homes and we do not feel justified in taking out clean-up orders against them.

Every person might reasonably have some expectation of respect for the notion that 'their home is their castle'. Our home is a private space where we might expect special protection of our right to autonomy. Most people would agree that while many behaviours might be unacceptable in a public space, most behaviours should be permitted 'in the privacy of one's home'. People are free to wander the corridors of their own home stark naked, but very few public locations allow such immodesty.

The more private a person's squalid circumstances, the more we are likely to accept their continuance and the more significant a harm, or potential harm, must be to override their right to own-home autonomy. Squalor in the front yard is not as private as squalor in the front room, and the significance bar for squalor in the public–private place of the front yard is likely to be set lower than that set for squalor confined to the inside of a home.

Only if the harm (or potential harm) to others is significantly great enough to overcome the competent person's reasonable expectation to freedom to do as they will in their own home, will we be free to forcibly intervene to reverse their squalid circumstances.

Mental illness

Many authors and protocols suggest that if a person living in squalor also has a mental illness that puts them at risk of harm then these circumstances alone justify coercive intervention (Gannon and O'Boyle, 1992; Cooney and Hamid, 1995; Weiss, 2010). However, while many people who live in severe domestic squalor will be mentally ill (Halliday *et al.*, 2000; Snowdon *et al.*, 2007), and while many mentally ill people will lack the capacity to validly refuse offers to clean up their premises, it is decisional capacity that is the crucial first element that needs be taken into account when considering the rights and wrongs of intervention. The mere presence of mental illness cannot be equated with an absence of decisional capacity, and there is no ethical basis for coercive intervention solely because a person has a mental illness.

It is not surprising that many authors wrongly assume that the presence of a serious mental illness would allow a forced intervention, since the mental health legislation of most countries currently allows forced treatment of mentally ill people if they are regarded as a danger to themselves or others, regardless of considerations of capacity. Mental health legislation that might allow forced intervention in squalor on the same grounds, highlights the difference between legal and ethical approaches to a particular problem. While it may well be legal to forcibly clean up a mentally ill person's home in those jurisdictions without consideration of their capacity, it could not be said that such an action would be ethically permissible (Ryan, 2011).

Confidentiality and shared squalor

Two other ethical considerations are worthy of brief mention before concluding.

While particular answers to the questions posed in the algorithm may allow, or even impose a duty upon, clinicians to organise intervention when a person lives in squalor, nothing in the algorithm relieves the clinician of their assumed duty of confidentiality. It is inevitable that organising such an intervention will involve breaching confidentiality to some degree, and such breaches are justified for reasons similar to those justifying intervention in the first place. Nonetheless, it is extremely important that clinicians make every attempt to minimise any breach. This duty may extend to not sharing certain information with family members if the person of concern objects to this (Ballard, 2010). Any breach of confidentiality must be limited to that absolutely required to carry out the necessary intervention.

It is not uncommon for people to live in squalor as a couple and in these cases account needs to be taken of the ethical considerations applying to each when intervention is entertained (Halliday *et al.*, 2005). Depending on the circumstances, one or other of the co-habitants might figure in the algorithm in different ways. For example, when deciding whether or not each person is truly consenting to live in the squalid circumstances we must consider whether one is being coerced by the other. A choice made under the forceful influence of another may not truly be a free choice. Similarly while one person may competently decide to live in squalor, some co-habitants may lack the capacity to make that decision due to their young age (children cannot be said to have capacity to make such a decision) or cognitive impairment.

In these circumstances the best interests of the incompetent person are likely to out-weigh even a competent refusal by a person with capacity, as their proximity to the squalor will significantly decrease the harm threshold required when considering question three. Even if Ms Havisham were competent, lived in her own home and posed no real threat to anyone else in the community, the squalid circumstances of her domicile would undoubtedly justify an ultimatum that she either comply with a clean-up order or face losing custody of her adopted daughter Estella.

9

Media portrayals of squalor and hoarding

Changing the media changes everything: all politics, all literature, all society.
(Sardar and van Loon, 2010)

Introduction

The media (newspapers, magazines, radio, television and newer agencies of mass communication) are powerful. They influence people. Media outlets differ in their approach, depending on their prime objectives. In non-state funded services it is common that their main aim is to maximise shareholder value (i.e. to make money, most commonly via advertising). It will therefore be important to them that the material they provide is what people want to read or see or hear.

People have varying tastes, interests, likes and dislikes. It would be difficult for the media to please all of them, even if each page, segment or programme were aimed at a different group within the community. But those who run newspapers, television channels or other organs of mass communication may respond to market research that shows that more of the public is attracted to one topic or type of presentation than to another. A high proportion of the members of certain groups may be attracted to items they can read (or watch or hear) about sport – and commonly one or two sports in particular. The media outlet that best covers the topic may gain the biggest audience or readership. The bigger the audience, the more the owners (be they tycoons, shareholders, the government or an interest group) will be pleased. The more that people read/hear/watch an item, the bigger the potential for getting a message across. Communicators (whether regarding soap powder, political viewpoints or educational material) will be pleased, and the owners gain financially or in other ways.

Because it can be fascinating to their audience or readership, the media have taken an interest in people whose lives can be regarded as extraordinary or a striking aberration from normal, whether that be because of their status, wealth, position, achievement, genius, appearance, afflictions or indeed, lifestyle and behaviour. That people who live isolated, odd and lonely lives, such as hermits, monks, anchorites, the infirm, the aged and the reclusive, make good subject matter for writers is unquestionable. The added dimension of failing to wash or maintain personal hygiene, neglecting domestic comfort and social niceties (where these are available), or living amid waste and rubbish, particularly when one has the means and capacity to do otherwise, has long been regarded as worthy of documentation, and in some cases, is ancient history.

What is perhaps more remarkable is the recent increase in media portrayal of (and presumably public interest in) such matters, particularly in developed countries such as Australia, the UK and the USA. The clearest and most obvious example of this is the increasing number of newspaper publications, television news bulletins or segments of current affairs programmes regarding people who are found to be living in severe domestic squalor. By the time such stories reach the attention of the media and become newsworthy, the severity of the problem is commonly such that someone's safety is at risk. An accompanying picture, graphic or film segment seems to be regarded as essential. Self-neglect, being trapped as a consequence of the volume of one's hoarded possessions, and alleged abuse of dependant relatives living in the same dwelling, are relatively commonly presented. Reclusiveness, isolation and impact upon neighbours are common themes as well. Reports of animal hoarding (and its consistent relationship with domestic uncleanliness) are also on the increase. Further evidence of expanding media attention in this area is the advent and popularity of entire television series, part documentary, part reality TV, focused upon the themes of squalor and hoarding, such as *Life of Grime* and *Hoarders*.

The ramifications of the evolving increase and the nature in which squalor is portrayed in the media are likely to be far reaching. The object here is not to carry out an academic analysis of media portrayals of squalor or hoarding. Such studies are certainly needed and should form part of the research agenda into squalor. In this chapter we will consider the relevance of media portrayals of squalor and consider the ways in which these portrayals may shape public opinion about interventions aimed at managing such problems.

We will begin by presenting historic and contemporary examples of squalor and hoarding as featured by the media, and in books, films and on stage. We will consider to what extent the intensity of recent media coverage is beneficial or counter-productive in relation to provision of resources, and shaping public opinion. We will finish with a consideration of the ethics of media organisations and journalists and the agendas behind publication or airing of a squalor case.

Historic descriptions of squalor and hoarding

On a page titled 'Diogenes without a barrel' in *English Eccentrics* (1958), Sitwell reproduced a report from the *Wolverhampton Chronicle* published in about 1880, describing a man living alone in state of gross self-neglect. Literary portraits of lonely, self-neglectful fictional characters, such as Gogol's Plyushkin in *Dead Souls* (1842) or Dickens's Miss Havisham in *Great Expectations* (1861) were published earlier.

The case of the Collyer brothers, who came to be known as 'the Hermits of Harlem' remains as remarkable and fascinating as it was when the *New York Times* began publishing stories about the enigmatic pair in 1939. In the absence of finding cooperative occupants of the four-story Brownstone mansion to speak to, the newspaper published local gossip that the brothers had vast piles of cash they were afraid to bank and lived in a state of 'orientalist splendor' (Wikipedia). Homer and Langley Collyer were well educated sons of a local surgeon, who became increasingly reclusive after the death of their mother. They lived in almost total isolation from 1938 until 1947, when they were found dead. One is said to have died in a booby trap they set against intruders. After their deaths, the house was found to be filthy and so severely cluttered that a crane was required to remove some 50 tons of possessions, including the chassis of a motor vehicle and early X-ray equipment. In addition to countless bundles of papers and newspapers, the house was described as containing 'a great deal of garbage' and had been so poorly maintained it had to be torn down.

Without intended irony, after their deaths, the *New York Times* (March 26, 1947) stated that there was 'something unattractive about the avidity with which society now pores over every detail of the Collyer brothers. . . it is almost as though society were taking revenge upon the brothers for daring to cut the thread that binds man to his fellows'. Their unwanted notoriety was such that an obituary was published in *Time* (April 7, 1947) entitled 'The Shy Men'. One of the earliest newspaper reporters to have exposed the Collyers, Helen Worden Erskine, also wrote about the brothers in her book *Out of this World* (1953), a collection of stories about recluses and hermits.

Granick and Zeman (1960) conducted one of the few scientific studies of newspaper publications concerning such cases. In seven New York newspapers covering most of the years from 1942 to 1959 they identified stories that concerned 105 people who they determined were 'aged recluses'. Their description of 40% of the series as living in homes that were a 'shambles, piled with trash, unkempt and dingy' compared with only 8% whose homes were neat, suggests that many of the subjects were people who lived in squalor and/or hoarded things. In most of the remaining cases there was no information about the way in which the recluses had kept their homes. They noted that most lived alone and had never married. It was reported in these newspapers that, far from being impoverished, many were discovered to have had considerable wealth. The authors suspected many were likely to have a psychiatric illness and emphasised the need for further research.

No analysis of media portrayals of squalor can be complete without mentioning *Grey Gardens*. From its genesis as a documentary in 1975 it has been adapted into a Broadway musical (2006), a feature film starring Jessica Lange and Drew Barrymore (2009), and at least two plays, *A Few Small Repairs* and *Little Edie and the Marble Faun*. *Grey Gardens* came about because of newspaper stories concerning two women living in an increasingly dilapidated mansion in the New Hamptons in squalor. That they were the aunt and first cousin of a former first lady of the USA, Jacqueline Kennedy Onassis, heightened the newsworthiness. However, their story is compelling in any case and not dissimilar to other cases. Why they let their living conditions decline to such a degree without seeking or accepting help and without appearing to the outsider to be unhappy or even troubled by their situation, resonates with modern equivalents. How did they allow themselves to become so isolated?

Phelan Beale left his wife and left the house to her. Edith (senior) had little income and insufficient means to maintain the house. Over the years, *Grey Gardens* (named because of the colour of sea dunes and the sea mist) fell into disrepair. By 1972, the Beales were occupying just one room of a mansion that was increasingly home to numerous cats and raccoons, was infested with fleas, full of garbage, heavily overgrown and had no running water. A front page story in the *New York Magazine* and an article in the *National Enquirer* resulted in inspections by the Suffolk County Health Department and sufficient intervention and repairs (paid for by Ms Kennedy Onassis) to at least meet the local building and health codes.

Albert and David Maysles visited the house in 1975 and obtained permission from both women to make a documentary utilising a technique that is now referred to as 'direct cinema'. This involves asking few or no questions, and the camera following a subject, leaving them to tell their own story. The documentary received wide critical acclaim (Searight, 2007) and says much about the powerlessness endured by women, even from affluent backgrounds, during that era; their dependence upon men for status, income and security; and the damaging effects of marital breakdown.

Howard Hughes was no stranger to the media, having been a producer of films in his early life, including one nominated for an Oscar in 1931, *The Front Page*, which was about newspapers. With age, possible addiction to drugs and alcohol, and having had several head injuries and neurosyphilis over the ten years preceding his death in 1976, this very wealthy man became increasingly reclusive, suspicious and obsessive. He feared germs, and lived in hotel rooms surrounded by piles of newspapers, television guides, discarded paper tissues and towels, empty boxes and medicine bottles, never allowing the use of a vacuum cleaner. As a celebrity and someone whose behaviour seemed quite bizarre, he was subjected to a number of media exposés including the cover story of *Time Magazine*; 'Howard Hughes Exclusive: His Secret Life' (December 13, 1976).

Newspapers

So how is squalor presented in contemporary news? What sort of headlines do we see leading stories that concern severe domestic squalor in current news? Google alerts using the word 'squalor' to identify relevant material posted on the World Wide Web in the preceding week can be used to identify the common types of news headlines, particularly those involving police or violation of a legal code. While these alerts to stories are not exclusively the domain of newspapers (some, for example, are from television news broadcasts or radio), they are indicative of the types of newspaper stories that concern squalor and hoarding. In the week preceding Sunday 23 October 2011, selected at the time of preparing this chapter, relevant headlines and vignettes included:

Police: man took elderly woman's money, left her to live in squalor (Evansville Courier)

After a 10 month investigation by Police in Evansville (US) the carer of an 88 year old female with dementia was arrested. The elderly woman had been discovered by Police in a freezing house with a filth encrusted sink, thick cobwebs hanging from the ceilings and a refrigerator full of expired food. She was dishevelled and had been defaecating and urinating in a hole next to the toilet which wasn't working. Her carer, who she had known for at least 15 years, had paid her rates but was taking most of her income, including rent obtained from two other properties she owned.

Young children found in squalor (Jersey Evening Post)

A pregnant, heroin addicted mother of 2 children, aged 11 months and 4 years, was found guilty of child neglect by the Royal Court but spared from going to gaol. The children were found living in 'filthy and dangerous conditions' in a St Hellier (Jersey Islands, UK) flat that was littered with more than 100 syringes, mouldy baby bottles, dirty dishes, smelly bed linen and dirty nappies.

Burnsville suspends license of problem-plagued complex (Minneapolis Star Tribune)

The rental license of owners of a 138 dwelling complex in Minneapolis was suspended after inspectors found the occupants were 'living in squalid conditions with rampant insects, moldy carpet, crumbling drywall, faulty plumbing and dozens of fire code violations.

Cats found living in squalor continue to be rescued: some put down (Syracuse, NewsChannel 9 WSYR)

The New York Society for Prevention of Cruelty to Animals (SPCA) were removing 70 cats from a house described as filthy and having faeces everywhere after Police discovered the situation when checking upon the homeowner, who had since been hospitalized. Some of the cats and a dog (also found living there) had already been put down because of their physical condition.

Police: victims held in squalor in theft scheme (NPR)

Four severely developmentally disabled adults with signs of starvation and gross physical abuse were found chained up lying in their own excrement in a small boiler room of an apartment building in Philadelphia by the landlord and neighbours. Police charged 3 people with assault, kidnapping, conspiracy and theft.

Hills District Mother arrested for raising children in squalor (Pittsburgh Tribune-Review)

A 26 year old mother of 4 children, ages ranging from 2 to 8 years, was arrested in Pittsburgh Hills District, having been charged with 'child-endangerment'. Police found garbage, flies, fleas, gnats and animal droppings where they were living. Although the family would have been eligible for family support services and the mother told Police she had previously requested these, the family were unknown to local area services before the arrest.

During the same week, a Google alert for 'hoarding' noted that service representatives from a local hoarding task force were interviewed by journalists about the challenges in dealing with severe hoarding. They stated that in about one third of the cases it was necessary to 'condemn' the dwelling – presumably due to structural deterioration.

So what kinds of issues or subjects do these stories reveal as being newsworthy and of concern to the media (and by extension, to ourselves)? The common themes were:

- neglect or abuse of children
- neglect or abuse of adults or elderly without capacity (because of developmental disability or dementia)
- neglect by landlords and property managers
- violations of building, fire, or public health laws (including failure to act on notifications and warnings)
- animal hoarding
- hoarding
- substance abuse
- allegations of lack of community or family support services
- role of neighbours in identifying problems and/or the impact of the problem upon them
- challenges for services when required to intervene (such as police, health, council and social services).

Why were these reports written? We will later discuss what it is about squalor and hoarding that appears to make it so newsworthy. Many of the headlines (and stories) are sensationalist, prepared specifically to shock, alarm, frighten, anger and most of all, attract the attention of as large a number of readers as possible. The most vitriolic and hostile are reserved for cases where severe harm appears to have been inflicted and/or where there has been flagrant defiance of community expectations and conventions. For example, making front-page news was the following headline:

A DISGRACE. The battle in a top Sydney suburb to clean up the dirtiest house in NSW

Elsewhere in the same issue could be found:

EXCLUSIVE: Mountain of garbage in Sydney yard. A stinking mess (*The Sunday Telegraph*, 9 October 2005)

A photograph of a property described as being worth over a million dollars, near Bondi Beach, was published on the front page (Plate 6.1), and a similar photo, but including the owner, accompanied the story on page 9. The article described a garden filled three-metres high with rubbish collected from garbage bins and from piles of items left outside houses on council clean-up days. It was described as the 'largest pile of waste ever collected by a single household in Australia'. Spillage onto other properties and the street, the unsightliness, smell, infestation with rats and effect upon immediate neighbours were described. The money and time spent by the local council trying to redress the problem, and their need to argue their case in the Land and Environment Court before they could clear the property, were given coverage. Note that the inside of the house was never seen. The court order only applied to exterior areas.

Four years later, when the rubbish had piled up again, *The Daily Telegraph* published an aerial view of the house with another attention-grabbing headline:

Rubbish pile you can see in space (16 September 2009)

Very often, stories like this one are presented from the point of the view of the long-suffering neighbours and immediate local community, with an emphasis on their rights having been overlooked and complaints ignored.

Like child abuse in other forms, situations where there is neglect (particularly, maternal) of children who are discovered to be living in squalid and uninhabitable living conditions, also garner condemnation by the press. These stories, also from Australian newspapers, concern three similar but different cases:

Mum needed a holiday. Why eight kids were abandoned in a squalid home (*Daily Telegraph, Australia, 27 May 27 2009*)

The article stated that eight children were left in the supervision of the eldest, aged 15. The house was described as 'squalid, putrid and uninhabitable' and a 'rubbish-strewn cesspit'.

Children had no food. Weeping pregnant mum refused bail (*The Daily Telegraph*, Australia, 25 June 2008)

A mother was charged with failing to provide food and shelter for her 5 children after an Ambulance was called to the rubbish strewn home.

Or a more introspective:

> **Children of the damned. Shocking images of poverty and neglect have left us ashamed of our indifference (*The Daily Telegraph,* 28 June 2008)**
>
> Four children were allegedly abandoned by their 35 year old mother and found hungry, cold and alone in public housing surrounded by an accumulation of possessions, rubbish, dog faeces, urine, dirty clothing and rotten and smelly food.

An editorial comment in one of the papers was titled 'Children suffer in land of plenty' (*The Daily Telegraph*, Australia, 28 June 2008) and asked: 'Why, in contemporary Australian society, are so many children being raised in conditions the RSPCA has previously decreed not fit for household pets?'

Such problems are not exclusive to Australia. A newspaper article reported that in Austria, three daughters, aged 7, 11 and 13, were imprisoned in their home by their mother, a 53-year-old lawyer, after their parents' divorce. Their home, in an up-market suburb, was reported to be in 'indescribable filth' with excrement that was piled a metre high and a floor that had been eaten away by urine and rodents.

In some cases, an investigative journalistic approach is taken, where the public 'right to know' is the backdrop against which the story has been written. Sometimes editorials have discussed society's failure to address such problems in a meaningful way, often for exceedingly long periods, thereby prolonging suffering for the various individuals involved in such cases. For example, under the headline 'Trapped in squalor', *The Mosman Daily* in Sydney (29 November 2001) related that:

> Neighbours of an elderly couple living in an upmarket Sydney suburb reported that their flat was like a 'rubbish dump', malodorous and filled with empty bottles, plastic bags, rotten fruit, rats and cockroaches. Neighbours had lodged a petition with the council and contacted local health services and the community centre but believed that because the problem was 'too hard' one organization was passing responsibility for doing anything about it, to the next.

In many instances, the driving concern and newsworthy aspect of the case is seen to be the *neglect* that commonly underlies cases of squalor: self-neglect, neglect of dependent children or the elderly, neglect by landlords and property managers, neglect of responsibilities, and neglect to intervene by people in positions of authority, such as councils, community and health services.

One tragic type of news story concerning squalor or hoarding is that of the occupant who is not discovered until after their death, trapped or killed (e.g. crushed, starved or burnt), as a direct consequence of their living conditions. More of these describe evidence of hoarding in contrast to the above cases of neglect:

> **Loner who built network of tunnels out of rubbish in his home dies after getting lost in labyrinth (Mail Online, UK, 7 January 2009).**

Crushed to death by 16 years' worth of shopping (*International Express*, 13 January 2009).

Each room in the house was so packed there was just a 2 foot wide path between her things with which to move around the dwelling and initially she could not be found.

Hoarders buried, bitten by rats in house full of rubbish (*The Daily Telegraph*, 27 May 2010)

Being discovered at home dead as a consequence of squalor or hoarding may be happening less than it did previously. In Granick and Zeman's (1960) study of New York newspaper stories concerning aged recluses, mentioned above, many of them living in dwellings that were described as a 'shambles', 'unkempt', or 'piled with trash', a third had died or were near death when they came to journalists' attention.

In contrast to many of the stories that are primarily aimed at selling newspapers or maximising ratings, and are obviously sensationalist and inflammatory in their pitch, there is a small number of publications where the prime purpose appears to be educational and directed at provision of information. While these also generally include a relevant photograph and case history, the information is clearly de-identified or the consent of the person described has been obtained and the headline and article are sympathetic and informative rather than devaluing or pejorative. These articles are characterised by consultation with relevant experts or experienced professionals. Sometimes these are published in association with events such as publication of relevant academic research or the provision of funding to develop a related service.

Examples include:

'The collectors' (Health & Science section of the *Sydney Morning Herald*, 8 April 2010; Plate 6.3)

and

'Rotten truth about our forgotten old folk' (Adele Horin, *Sydney Morning Herald*, 5 May 2008)

Almost all such stories are written with the sense that living in squalor or being surrounded by a dangerous or uncomfortable excess of possessions is 'strange and peculiar', particularly when it affects someone well known. The *Sydney Morning Herald* in 1998 used the headline 'Strange but true: celebrating Sydney's resident eccentrics' when describing a man known as the Fridgeman of Glebe. He was pictured with some of his 3,000 broken refrigerators, which he was reported as repairing in order to distribute to the needy from his home.

Television

On television, media portrayals of squalor and hoarding mainly appear either as short stories (a two- to five-minute item) on a current affairs-type programme, or in the form of a documentary, or as the focus of a reality television and/or lifestyle television series.

Current affairs programmes

A Current Affair and *Today Tonight* are 30-minute weekday evening commercial current affairs programmes shown in Australia. They are high rating programmes, and in terms of numbers of people exposed to any media form concerning squalor, more Australians are likely to have come across problems of squalor or hoarding in the context of *A Current Affair* or *Today Tonight* than through any other media format. Each of these programmes is recognised by media critics and the public as employing sensationalist journalism, and each commonly features segments concerned with problems related to squalor.

The content of stories concerning squalor and hoarding on both of these programmes is very similar to the types of stories discussed in relation to newspapers. The five-minute segments are generally very simple. The host introduces the story against a graphic, usually showing the living conditions, which is described in extreme, judgemental and subjective language. Someone (maybe the occupant) is identified as a victim. The host crosses to the reporter in the field who then goes inside the dwelling on camera (if permitted) and attempts to interview the occupant, with or without their consent. Often neighbours are interviewed as well. A person is identified as being responsible. The story crosses again to the reporter who may be seen apparently pursuing this person and demanding answers. Sometimes an opinion is sought from an 'expert' on the matter but in the short segment time this conveys little.

Television series

Life of Grime

A series of reality television programmes called *Life of Grime* was shown in Britain in 1999, and a second series appeared in 2000. Council staff, such as environmental health officers, garbage collectors and rat catchers from various cities across England were shown as they tried to ensure compliance with relevant legislation. Wikipedia attributed the popularity of these series to a 'disgust factor' and the 'eccentric but often lucid characters encountered either hoarding rubbish or keeping huge numbers of animals'. The most famous was Edmund Trebus who was described as welcoming the BBC in to film his conflict with Haringey Council (North London).

In 2005, the USA produced its own version of a *Life of Grime* on the Discovery Times Channel. This was reality television following the work of environmental health officers in New York City. Strikingly, it featured problems of infestations with vermin and animal hoarding.

Life Laundry

Three series of *Life Laundry* in 2002 to 2004 were produced by the BBC. These were reality television programmes hosted by Dawna Walter, a professional organiser, and Mark Franks, a house clearance specialist. Each 30-minute episode focused on a volunteer with a serious and chronic cluttering and hoarding problem. Viewers watched as each hoarder was persuaded to make attitudinal shifts, de-sentimentalise, downsize, rationalise, clean, decorate and sell things.

The *Life Laundry* series format was subsequently used for at least five other series in the USA and elsewhere but rebadged as *Clean Sweep*, *Neat*, *NeatTV*, *Clean House* and *Mission: Organization.*

How Clean is Your House?

How Clean is Your House? (a UK Channel 4 series shown in 2003–2009) was an entertainment lifestyle programme. It featured two female hosts, described as expert cleaners. Each 30-minute episode focused on a filthy, squalid house. While cursory inquiries and discussion occurred about how the circumstances had arisen, the main focus of the programme and the hosts was on conducting a major clean-up, and usually required the assistance of a professional cleaning team. The occupants were advised and shown how to clean and expected to pitch in. Swabs of various dirty spots were sent off to the laboratory and reports concerning the bacteria they invariably grew were presented as evidence of dangers to the householder of the unclean lifestyle.

Hoarders

The four series of *Hoarders* (shown on A & E Television in the USA from 2009 onwards) uniquely combined features of reality television and documentary. Each one-hour episode juxtaposed stories from two separate households where hoarding was so severe that a threat of eviction or legal action such as loss of custody of children was at stake and presumably provided motivation to agree to address the problem forthwith and in front of the cameras. Most of the hoarders and their families were shown working with a psychologist and a professional organiser, together with a crew of professional cleaners, to try and deal with the problem. The viewer (and household) were informed at the beginning that the cleaning services and removal trucks would be available for only two days (mostly) maximum.

And there are others. Three series of *Hoarding: Buried Alive* have been shown in the USA on TLC/Discovery, with a format almost identical to that of the *Hoarders* series. *Confessions: Animal Hoarding* is an American documentary series on Animal Planet since 2010, that shows visits to homes of people who have acquired multiple animals and live in what are described as 'toxic conditions'. In some episodes of *Neighbours at War*, a New Zealand reality television series that focused on feuding neighbours, the conflict was specifically related to severe domestic squalor and/or keeping excessive numbers of animals. *Renters* is a New Zealand reality television (TVNZ) programme shown in 2003, 2005 and 2011 to 2012, that follows rental property managers; several episodes have shown severe squalor and hoarding by tenants.

Reality television and *Hoarders*

There is little doubt that the escalation in television depictions of squalor and hoarding is in part attributable to the development of reality television, a genre that lends itself particularly well to this subject matter. *Hoarders* is one of the most relevant and successful examples of these television programmes. Reality television is characterised as showing real events and unscripted situations featuring ordinary people, as opposed to professional actors. In the documentary style subtype of this genre, to which almost all of the televisions series we have listed belong, various types of professional, such as environmental health officers, cleaners and psychologists are shown in their day-to-day work dealing with a series of clients or volunteers who have agreed to appear on film. Dealing with squalor and/or hoarding has been featured in the self-improvement/makeover type of reality television programme and in series focused on dwelling renovation.

Critics are divided as to the merits of reality television in general. A major impetus for its development is that production costs are significantly less than for scripted programmes. While not all reality television shows rate highly, almost all mentioned in this chapter that portray squalor and hoarding have had sufficient audience numbers to ensure that they ran over several series. Others have suggested that a reason for the success of reality television is *schadenfreude* (meaning enjoyment obtained from the troubles of others); it is believed that some viewers derive 'pleasure' by seeing others in shameful or humiliating situations. It has been argued that reality television is successful at present because it is much more lively, diverse and unpredictable than its alternatives.

Hoarders has been a constructive series of programmes, providing helpful lessons about how the media can be useful to professionals working in this area, to educate, communicate public health messages and perhaps even assist with secondary and tertiary prevention of the problem. Feedback suggests that the series has been useful, particularly to the families of hoarders, people often traumatised by living or growing up in such an environment, but lacking knowledge of where to go for help and experiencing substantial pressure to keep the problem a secret, or buried.

What are the positive ingredients of this series? First, all the subjects are compelling and interesting people. Most had accumulated so much 'stuff' that keeping their dwellings clean had become impossible. The footage of their living conditions, together with voice-over narration concerning potential consequences if they were unable to change things, quickly established the severity of the problem and the urgency to find a solution. In other words, these were people we could relate to, and we were interested to know the outcome.

Second, the professionals featured in the series are people we can identify with. They are people who treat their clients gently, and with respect and humanity, even the most frustrating hoarder. That is not to say that they are simply nice to the client. Frequently they are required to do and say things that their clients would probably have preferred them not to. We see them engaging the client, problem solving and undertaking motivational interviewing in an effort to persuade the client to change. Crises that inevitably arise in the context of the clear-up, clean-up and make-over are dealt with sensitively and without ridicule or humiliation.

Third is the diversity. The series reveals the complexity of such cases, and a need for flexibility in seeking solutions. Age, household structure, family members, types of dwellings, educational background, employment status, income and the types of things each person 'hoarded' varied greatly. How 'stuff' came to take up such a large amount of space in each of these people's homes also greatly varied. Some acquired possessions through excessive shopping, some resisted discarding things that they clearly thought might have value, or had sentimental value or might help to trigger important memories, while in other cases the hoarding could be seen as primarily a consequence of disorganisation, amassing rubbish and limited living skills.

While *Hoarders* has many strengths, it also has shortfalls. The main concern is the frame in which the intervention is undertaken and cases are managed. The plan to intensively intervene over a period of just a few days, during which the occupants must decide what to keep and then the cleaners have to remove a very large volume of 'stuff' before leaving the place clean and organised, is a necessary consequence of the cameras with time and funding limits and the desire to create a sense of drama. As discussed in earlier chapters, such an approach, without full attention to personality and situational problems, is likely to fail. 'Reality' may be a misnomer. Programming the intervention to occur in this way heightens the emotions of those involved and creates drama. Whether the interventions usually cause more good than harm is worth researching. Nevertheless, the presentation of such cases for discussion and comment on how best to intervene is beneficial.

Television dramas

Possibilities for knowledge enhancement through television drama concerning health problems or predicaments are well recognised, and producers and writers regularly consult with professionals when developing scripts. *The Simpsons*, *Friends*, *CSI* and *Nurse Jackie* have all featured episodes or characters where hoarding, squalor and neglect were concerns.

Talk shows

The Oprah Winfrey Show (NBC) was one of the most watched daytime television programmes not only in the USA but also elsewhere. On at least two occasions the show addressed the problem of hoarding and extreme clutter, and included interviews with people who hoard and with relevant experts such as psychologist David Tolin and a professional organiser (Peter Walsh). Comparable programmes in other countries have presented segments on hoarding.

Radio

Segments on informative radio programmes in the USA, Australia and elsewhere have allowed discussion of squalor and hoarding situations and what interventions might be helpful. Word pictures and descriptions of the difficulties faced by occupants and by their neighbours have aroused interest in seeking better ways of dealing with such situations.

New media

The internet and the World Wide Web are a wonderful source of information and mis-information. The knowledge and beliefs of those responsible for keeping web material up to date vary. Blogs accessible on the internet provide a range of insights, experiences and opinions from people who live in squalor or hoard, and from their family members. Some websites allow possibilities for self-help. For example, the Squalor Survivors website provides useful ideas on how to reduce the amount of rubbish in a dwelling, and can show people that overcoming their problem is possible. Procrastinators Anonymous and Clutterers Anonymous provide tips for getting started, and by Googling one of the relevant organisations, those concerned to seek change can find links to other sites that may prove useful. The following are relevant sources of information on the internet:

Squalor Survivors www.squalorsurvivors.com
Children of Hoarders www.childrenofhoarders.com
National Association of Professional Organizers www.napo.net
National Study Group on Chronic Disorganization www.nsgcd.org

Films, books and plays

The media can influence public opinion and can convey public health messages. Education and change of attitudes can be achieved through published material (the press, magazines, the internet and books), television documentaries and news items, radio discussions, public talks and seminars, and also through artistic endeavours. The media might therefore be embraced and used to educate the general public and service providers about squalor, hoarding and disorganisation.

There is also a growing literature that discusses the merits and advantages of using films, where good illustrative examples are available, to teach medical students and psychiatrists about clinical problems, phenomena, dilemmas and interventions (Byrne, 2003). The following are likely to be of interest and have scenes that may be helpfully utilised for the purpose of teaching others about squalor and/or hoarding, and in some cases, illustrate frequently associated mental health issues. Some are fictional while others are based on real cases. Our list is deliberately selective and contemporary:

- *Grey Gardens* (see above)
- *Unstrung Heroes* (hoarding associated with schizophrenia, personality disorder and obsessive–compulsive disorder)

- *Iris* (squalor/neglect and dementia)
- *Slumdog Millionaire* (squalor in developing countries)
- *Withnail and I* (squalor associated with students, unemployment, and alcohol and drug abuse)
- *Trainspotting* (squalor and substance abuse)
- *Bad Boy Bubby* (squalor and abuse)
- *Sunshine Cleaning* (forensic cleaners and their clients)

Books and novels may be useful in the same way. Charles Dickens helped transform British culture and society. His stories (many of them based upon real events and situations, personal experiences and people he came across) commonly describe characters plunged into situations that could only be described as squalid. In addition to his philanthropy, Dickens clearly aimed to highlight social problems, such as poverty, social disadvantage, isolation, crowding and lack of education. Works of fiction can prompt politicians, for example, to take action on behalf of those whose difficulties have been previously ignored.

The Collyer brothers have been the subject of a film (*Unstrung Heroes*), three plays and two novels (Weiss, 2010). *The Lady in the Van* is a short story and was later a play, by Alan Bennett. It was first published in 1989 and is a sympathetic presentation of an elderly Miss Shepherd, a lady who had lived in various vehicles in a state of severe squalor for 15 years.

Media ethics

We need to consider the ethics of media who portray disadvantaged people, those who are disabled, outsiders or persons with psychiatric problems (some of whom live in squalor), in a negative way. What do we think about them identifying where they live and even their names? Most countries have laws that constrain the media, and codes of ethics for journalists. These laws protect the public from being exposed to indecent or offensive material and individuals from being unjustly accused, misrepresented or vilified. Are media organisations who publish or broadcast stories of this type complying with their own guidelines regarding standards, or are they violating their own codes of ethics?

The Australian Press Council has received complaints about local newspaper stories concerning the way people have been presented as living in squalid conditions. In 1994, the *Adelaide Advertiser* presented a story headlined 'Is this SA's filthiest house?' together with graphic pictures and a story about the family who had been living in the house for ten years. The article referred to concern about the family and the house and referred to the involvement of local councils and the Department for Family and Community Services, and conflict between the two. Readers disputed whether journalistic standards and ethics were maintained in this case. However, both the newspaper and the Australian Press Council (APC) (Adjudication No. 715) rejected this, stating that the identity of those concerned had been 'scrupulously protected' and the failure of government agencies to effectively deal with this family's situation over such a long period justified its publication. The APC stated that none of its principles had been breached.

The APC was asked on another occasion to deal with complaints from community representatives concerning a large front-page photograph of an Aboriginal man standing in his kitchen, published in *The West Australian* on 16 March 2010. The photograph accompanied a story about a Department of Indigenous Affairs report on conditions in the town of Roebourne, many of whose townsfolk are Aboriginal. The photograph had a caption that named the man in the picture and referred to him as being 'surrounded by squalor' and 'in his filthy kitchen'. The text of the article quoted the man as saying 'no one should have to live in such conditions'. The focus of the story was almost completely on the report's findings and the conditions in general in the town, and was not about any specific individual's home. The photograph was published again the following day together with multiple letters received by the paper in response to the photograph, all of which angrily criticised the man in the photograph for being irresponsible and for not keeping his kitchen clean or tidy. The complaints to the APC were about use of a photograph, the caption and publication of the letters, all ridiculing the man pictured and (the complainants said) reinforcing negative stereotypes about indigenous people. The author of the original story expressed regret about the caption distracting readers from the main issue, which was the appalling state of the town. However, the newspaper stood by its use of the photograph and subsequent correspondence, saying that they drew attention to overcrowding, alcohol and drug abuse in Roebourne, and may have resulted in government services prioritising the need for action there. The newspaper also commented that the man in the photograph (and others in that community) were not unhappy with the publication and were very happy with the attention it had drawn to the situation.

The subsequent findings of the APC (Adjudication 1468, July 2010) highlight the ethical dilemma confronting the media in such cases. The APC regarded the article as frank, accurate and important, but at the same time upheld the complaints about the newspaper publishing the photograph, caption and so many derogatory letters about the pictured individual, thus distracting attention from the substance of the report.

Last, but by no means of least importance, is the question of capacity to give consent. This is rarely addressed in news stories. In at least some of such cases, it is likely that capacity to consent, either to be interviewed or to have photographs taken, is impaired, uncertain or lacking. On occasions, particularly in television current affairs programmes, we have observed that people living in squalor have told the interviewer or cameraman to 'go away'. Some have questioned whether Little Edie (Beale-Bouvier), when she participated in the filming of her and her mother for *Grey Gardens*, was given adequate information and whether she was able to give informed consent.

Why focus on 'hoarding' rather than dirtiness?

In this book we have described domestic squalor and have explored whether there are different subtypes of squalor. Some of the environments we have described have been characterised by an accumulation of items and material, resulting in inaccessibility of facilities and problems getting in and around a dwelling. Some refer to this as clutter or hoarding. In other cases, either in the absence of accumulation of possessions, or in addition to it, the uncleanliness, dirtiness or filth is what strikes the observer.

In relation to media portrayals, there is clearly a preference for the publication of photographs that show accumulation as opposed to uncleanliness and filth. On television, the cameras (or editors) tend to concentrate on heaped-up items that block access, even when the text of the accompanying article or narration given by the journalist also describes filth and dirtiness.

This may be because it is harder to record filth and 'wet squalor' in a picture, whereas piled-up clutter (the cleanliness of which is difficult to gauge) is often astonishing and obvious. It is true that some television reports have focused in on cockroaches, flies and vermin, but they seem to have avoided showing pictures of dirty toilet bowls, maggots or other potentially nausea-inducing findings.

The word 'squalor' is used by journalists for a relatively small minority of cases, even in the most sensationalist media forms (such as the tabloid newspaper and some current affairs programmes). These are often the most severe or extremely dirty cases, but they also seem to incur the greatest degree of condemnation for other reasons – for example, because of occupants' extraordinary resistance to requests to improve the situation or because of severe neglect of children or others. In addition, the dwellings seen in severe animal hoarding cases often and understandably pick up the label of being squalid. Journalists who get inside such homes are likely to feel repulsion at the odour, excreta and mess.

Media reports use the word 'hoarding' in cases where squalor and disorganised mess should be equally or preferentially brought to attention. For example, in several of the eight households shown in the first *Hoarders* series on television, the dwellings were filthy in addition to being crowded with possessions. An overpowering stench commonly received comment, as did the difficulty experienced by visitors in breathing. The presence of vermin was visible in some of the episodes. In several of the cases it was unclear when and how their clutter had been amassed, and how much of it is was an accumulation of rubbish as opposed to things that are more commonly considered collectibles. Why do journalists (and others) refer to these as cases of hoarding?

We suggest that 'hoarding' is considered a less pejorative term and 'hoarding' is seen as a more acceptable problem than being dirty or squalid. It also implies that there has been purposive activity, with energy expended in the development of the situation, whereas to live in filth suggests a more profound lack of social skills, absence of insight, apathy or laziness. For television filming that requires the consent and participation of someone with problems of this nature, and particularly when they are being asked to do more than simply let others have a glimpse of their living conditions, being referred to as a hoarder or disorganised may be acceptable while mention of squalor would not be.

Why are the media so interested?

One reason why the media give attention to squalor and hoarding is the 'human interest factor'. But can we be more precise? As previously mentioned, some would have it that there is a 'disgust factor', which is perhaps particularly relevant to squalor. If not 'disgust' it is that it is 'strange and unusual'. The uncleanliness seems so far removed from what most of us can imagine being able to tolerate, that it fascinates us. Or perplexes us? Or seems bizarre? The words chosen by tabloid newspapers and sensationalist current affair programmes are quite clearly designed to provoke shock and alarm: 'Shameful, scandalous, disgraceful!' In the safety of their own homes, such reports might bring vicarious satisfaction to people who are glad to be different from that.

The basic unit of news is the 'story'. Each of these reported situations can be seen as meeting the requirements of a 'good story', with easily identifiable dynamics or concerns (for example, greed, protection, fear, hunger, vulnerability) and preferably 'closure' or an ending (rescue, protection, arrest, safety, consequences). Depending upon the time at which a particular situation triggers attention, not all may be resolved, in which case the writers would hope for ongoing interest and a desire to know what eventuates.

Commercial pressures mean that both commercial and publicly owned media organisations are under pressure to maximise their audience. Stories that can be described as 'exclusive' get priority. *Media Watch* is an Australian ABC weekly television programme that provides comments on how the media report news (www.abc.net.au/mediawatch/transcipts). In a segment titled 'Reporting rubbish', it criticised use of the label 'exclusive' for a subject that had not only been reported by various newspaper outlets, sometimes on several occasions, but also had been seen repeatedly on different current affairs programmes – at least ten times within a year!

The seriousness of the case (like most news stories) is another determinant of whether the interest of people (and the media) will be aroused. In many stories of people living in squalor, laws have been or are at risk of being broken. Agenda setting by newspaper editors and television producers is potentially important here. For example, the availability of an expert commentator or valued opinion leader, or even the development of a new intervention or research finding that may have implications for dealing with the problem in the future, may trigger publication or heighten the frequency with which it is aired or run.

In their analysis of newspaper stories concerning aged recluses between 1942 and 1959, Granick and Zeman (1960) observed that the possible association with deviant behaviour created interest through its sense of mystery and violence.

They also observed the tantalising possibility of finding items of great value among the hoarded possessions or on the premises of mysterious and deviant reclusive characters. They contrasted this profusion of reports about recluses with the lack of apparent interest or any publication in the field of behavioural sciences at that time.

Tabloid sensationalism?

A majority of the media stories about people who are found to be living in squalor, even when their headlines are sensationalist, do not directly blame or devalue the occupant. That is with the exception of situations where the occupant has neglected the rights of others, such as dependent minors or pets, or ignored the requests of authorities to do something about the situation over a prolonged period of time.

Not all of the dramatic headlines and condemnation, particularly those calling into criticism the lack of action by local authorities or apparent paralysis of public services, can simply be regarded as 'sensationalism'. Sometimes it is only the interest and the involvement of the media that provides the impetus to sufficiently shake up the system to achieve any sort of resolution. In 'Trapped in squalor', the case was covered on several occasions in both the press (Plate 6.2) and on television. Echoing the cries of neighbours and the local council, a reporter on one programme commented: 'If you think the authorities should step in, don't hold your breath. Residents have been trying to get something done for years!'

When something was at last done, there is little doubt that the media spotlight was the stimulus for action. In this case, as in others, the media focused attention on gaps and inefficiencies in services, and at the same time, provided education to the community and to staff of services. Media attention can be very persuasive and assist in lobbying politicians and administrators when seeking improved coordination and services.

A second example is the Bondi house. The story appeared year after year, in the press (Plate 6.1) and on television. Doubtless it helped the ratings, but clearly the publicity was what led to a necessary change to the Local Government Act, which ultimately led to a partial resolution.

A Western perspective

This chapter is only a reflection of what is happening in high-income countries. It may have less relevance in the developing world and outside the urban perimeter. To what extent has there been a change in our cultural acceptance of uncleanliness (and poverty), and is this only a feature of certain developed countries? Have attitudes changed or evolved over decades? We believe they have, and that this is a topic that merits further research.

Conclusions

Media accounts of isolated and often elderly individuals found to be living among an extraordinary volume of possessions (including an accumulation of rubbish and items of little obvious value) or squalor have become commonplace. At their core, these stories share similar concerns about neglect – by the occupants themselves, landlords, local councils, health and community services, failing to act upon calls for help, sometimes over prolonged periods. A newer but increasing trend is to see news reports of squalid living conditions associated with the collection of large numbers of animals. Deaths and near deaths as a consequence of hoarding can still be a cause for media attention. The last decade has seen the emergence of a great many more media portrayals of squalor and hoarding with a plethora of reality television programmes addressing this. The best of the reality television programmes present the material with intelligent sensitivity. Such programmes, together with the increasing appearance of educational material in print, on radio and on the internet, have begun to deliver important public health messages to individuals, families and communities faced with problems of this nature.

Anticipating the future, the internet is a portal through which many, if not most, media resources may eventually be accessed. While this will include extreme views and polarising opinions, misleading accounts, out-of-date information and 'sensationalism', it also can provide access to resources that we can expect to use increasingly in the future. These will allow us to learn from and assist people dealing with or living in unclean or grossly disorganised dwellings. We recommend familiarising ourselves with relevant websites that are easy to search, current and a source of good quality information and opinion.

The media's depiction of squalor and hoarding is important. We may learn a lot from portrayals on news programmes, on reality television and from films and literature. The media can help in recruiting public interest and in securing services or political intervention. Service providers and those familiar with squalor or hoarding situations have a role to play in challenging media portrayals, when necessary. There is value in working with media outlets that can help promote public understanding and scientific investigation.

10

Conclusions

Introduction

We started by asking why one would wish to publish a book on living in severe domestic squalor. We hope that the content of this book is an answer to this question in itself. The major achievement here is a simple one. We have, for the first time, in one place, brought together all the major elements of the conundrum that is living in severe domestic squalor. Looking back over the chapters there seem to be two main results of this that have value. These are:

(1) **A balanced summary of the evidence base** – we can be clear about what we know.

(2) Identification of gaps in the evidence base – we can be clear about what we do not know; **best practice in taking action** – we can act (or defer from intervention) in a way informed by the evidence; and **setting the agenda for research and development** – we can be clear about the agenda for further work needed to improve our knowledge base and so our actions in the world help deal with the problems posed by living in severe domestic squalor.

Here we will summarise the main messages emerging on squalor under these two themes.

A balanced summary of the evidence base

So what do we know? We know 'severe domestic squalor' exists across cultures and has existed across time. We hold that this is the best term to use because *it does not describe the people; it refers to the living conditions.* Starting at the macro level, cities and districts can be squalid as well as individual dwellings. Here the determinants will be at the level of local and national governance and government. However, even in the most un-conducive of personal and political circumstances, people will generally find a way to generate living conditions that are as clear and safe as possible. Equally, it appears that in all cultures it is possible to identify a small group of individuals whose living conditions would be rated as squalid and unacceptable by their peers.

It is clear that accumulation of dirt, refuse, degraded material and vermin can result in living conditions within a dwelling being unhealthy, unsafe and potentially harmful. If the filth and degradation are so foul that they are likely to have unacceptably deleterious effects on the people living there or nearby, we believe 'severe domestic squalor' is an appropriate descriptive term. There is a *universality* to squalor, which is filtered through the social, political, cultural, civic and legal structures in which people live. Our preferred definition of severe domestic squalor is:

> When a person's home is so unclean, messy and unhygienic that people of similar culture and background would consider extensive clearing and cleaning to be essential. Accumulated dirt, grime and waste material extend throughout living areas of the dwelling, along with possible presence or evidence of insects and other vermin. Rotting food, excrement and certain odours may cause feelings of revulsion among visitors. As well as accumulation of waste, there may have been purposeful collection and/or retention of items to such a degree that it interferes with occupants' ability to adequately clean up the dwelling.

Squalor varies. Some people cannot get in or out of their homes because they are packed with items. Others live in relatively bare premises, which are still very unclean. The nature of squalor and the extent of the accumulation of rubbish and/or valued items differ between cases. One useful distinction to make is between *wet squalor* when describing homes where moist or liquid excrement, decayed material, grease, or water spillage or overflow are prominent features of the uncleanliness; and *dry squalor* where there has been a disorganised accumulation of dry goods, often including clothing, papers, material contained in plastic bags and/or electrical devices, in a way that does not allow adequate cleaning. Such items may have been selected and collected purposefully or not; failure to discard unused or unusable items may have been purposeful or not.

A further descriptive typology that may be of help in communicating about squalor is as follows:

(1) Dry, neglectful squalor
(2) Rubbishy, neglectful squalor
(3) Wet, neglectful squalor
(4) Dry clutter
(5) Dry extensive clutter or hoarding, and
(6) Dry, semi-organised hoarding.

In terms of severity of squalor the work of the Squalor Survivors website is of particular value since this was generated by people who found that their living conditions were unacceptable, themselves. They refer to four degrees of squalor:

First degree squalor – The first is where little piles are starting to emerge and disorganisation is starting to cause inconvenience. 'You might be embarrassed for other people to see your mess... but you would still let them in the house.'

Second degree squalor – The piles have expanded to cover items up, and restrict use of facilities. Normal movement is impeded by the piles of stuff. People are discouraged from coming inside.

Third degree squalor – Where 'you have all the above, plus you have rotting food and animal faeces and/or urine in the house... Essential household repairs may not be done, because you are too afraid to let a tradesperson see your house.'

Fourth degree squalor – Where 'you have all of the above, plus you have human faeces and/or urine in your house that is not in the toilet'.

The use of rating scales such as the Environmental Cleanliness and Clutter Scale (ECCS) or the Living Conditions Rating Sale (LCRS) is at an early stage in terms of gold standard psychometric development, but they are now available and can be used to quantify degree of squalor. This can be useful to communicate empirical evidence about the case clinically, and to be able to monitor progress over time. Such instruments can also be used practically in research. Personal uncleanliness may not go hand-in-hand with environmental squalor.

Living in severe domestic squalor is a rare condition. Our best estimates are that it affects around 1 per 1,000 (0.1%) of those over 65 and less in younger age groups. Research into why people come to live in squalor reveals heterogeneity of aetiology. All research and published reports to date are hampered to a significant extent by selection bias. This occurs when the cases referred to a particular service are aggregated into a case series. Such cases do not capture all cases of squalor in a population; they only identify those who were referred to a particular agency (and then generally only report on those who consent to be interviewed). This results in a group selected for the indication (or the contra-indication) in making such a referral. This means that referrals to older people services will have few younger people living in squalor included within; that referrals to mental health services will have a high level of mental disorder; and that referrals to geriatric medicine services will have a high level of physical disorder. This is exactly the pattern we see from the published literature to date. However, it would be very difficult to locate a true population sample of people living in squalor because of the low absolute rate of such living circumstances in the general population and because these individuals would be likely not to cooperate with classical forms of case finding (e.g. postal questionnaires or door knocking).

Two groups seem to emerge: a group where the living in squalor appears to be attributable (at least in part) to a health problem (usually a mental disorder but sometimes a physical issue); and a group where there is no identifiable underlying disorder, other than of personality. In terms of mental disorder, those affecting frontal function seem particularly implicated (e.g. dementia and schizophrenia). However, as relatively few of those with such mental disorder end up living in squalor, the reasons why need to be uncovered. Early commentators identified a particular pattern, one of a domineering, quarrelsome and independent individual, with gradually developing rejection of the community, resentment of any outside interference and an abandonment of the accepted standards of behaviour of the neighbourhood. Co-morbidity with alcohol abuse has also been reported often. It may be that mental disorder, physical disorder, personality type and substance misuse interact in specific cases to generate a set of circumstances where living in squalor becomes more likely.

The term Diogenes syndrome has been useful in enabling a focus on this area but also has some conceptual difficulties that lead us to the conclusion that the use of the descriptive term 'severe domestic squalor' is likely to be of greater utility going forward. The research to date is clear that living in severe domestic squalor is not a sole province of older people. There are many younger people who do so. Equally, some who live in squalor do so with others; this may present both complications and possibilities in terms of intervention.

Hoarding is common in those who live in squalor, but most people who hoard do not live in squalor. Those with primary hoarding problems seem different from those living in squalor. Those who hoard excessively commonly recognise that they have a problem and may seek treatment. Such insight is rare in those living in squalor as is the desire for intervention and compliance with any management plan suggested. The literature on hoarding has evolved separately from that on squalor, and there would be value in seeing what might be learned from each other and what happens when there is overlap.

Identification of gaps in the evidence base, best practice in taking action, and setting the agenda for research and development

The previous section makes clear how little we know and how much there is to learn. We need to understand the full range of the distribution, determinants and control of the syndromes that result in people living in squalor. We therefore need research that spans from the descriptive to the epidemiological to the evaluation of interventions. We need qualitative studies that will help us to understand the ways that people come to live in squalor, how best to engage with people living in squalor and how this might be controlled.

There is a clear need for biological research, focusing on neuropsychological functioning and imaging brain function. Equally important are studies of the psychological and social causative factors. We need to agree a system of classification so that we can go out and find cases to understand just how common are the subtypes of living in squalor. We can then generate strategies to find and quantify the numbers living in squalor. Development of interventions and service response is as vital and these are likely to be more successful if they are based on empirical data on the aetiology and preferred methods of engagement.

We need to understand the outcomes of those living in squalor; what allows for recovery? What happens to people who live in squalor? What is the true risk of mortality and illness associated with living in squalor? This research needs to encompass, not only the obvious medical and social spheres but also the legal, psychological and veterinary aspects, so clearly set out in the preceding chapters.

There is the opportunity for positive read-over of insights from one area of squalor research to another. For example, the literature on hoarding has evolved separately from that on squalor and there would be value in seeing what might be learned from each other and what happens when there is overlap. There are major fundamental questions that remain unanswered. For example, what are the barriers and facilitators for those with mental disorder ending up living in squalor? Some do; many more do not. Why?

There is a world of research on squalor waiting out there to be designed, funded and completed. Those media outlets that profit from the production and airing of shows presenting those in squalor for entertainment purposes might wish to contribute to this.

We have already seen that much can be done, but that effective action very often requires multifaceted, multi-agency, coordinated approaches that may need to be sustained over years. The law is not enough by itself and neither are health services, social services, families or the voluntary sector. Keeping the interests of the person living in squalor central, while balancing public health and the impacts on others, is certainly tricky. But it is possible, with skill, care, commitment and cooperation. Joint understanding and joint action are needed and we hope that this book will help to enable this by providing an insight into the contributions to knowledge and action developed across agencies.

Final thoughts

Squalor is important. Its negative effects make it worth taking action. The Beveridge report was published in the UK in the midst of the Second World War. There were reputedly mile-long queues to buy the book, which set out to wage war on and triumph against 'five giants': want, disease, ignorance, idleness and squalor. The squalor that Beveridge developed a welfare state to conquer was squalor in terms of living conditions. At the time there were slum areas in every British city; overcrowding was a major problem that had only been made worse by bomb damage. The consequent house building of the 1940s and 1950s sought to address this, providing decent homes for the working class. Squalor can exist at this macro level as well as at the level of the individual. Even in high-income countries there remain examples of both. We continue to need strategies to work at both levels.

In this book we have demonstrated that squalor is a universal human phenomenon. It is multifaceted: a cause and a consequence; overt and hidden; personal and societal; a sign, a symptom and a disorder at the same time. We have seen how squalor can be a consequence and a cause of distress, disability and death, not only to the humans affected, but also to animals, where they are unlucky enough to be involved. We have seen that it is a problem at every level and we have seen just how complicated it is to deal with. Equally we have seen that positive action is possible where there is the will.

We hope that this book has provided both a stimulus to creative co-working, and some of the information needed to generate effective action. In severe domestic squalor it often seems that each case is so different, and that the cases are so rare, that there is nothing that can be carried from one case to another in terms of understanding. This can lead to a feeling that there is a need to start from first principles, 'to invent the wheel' each time, to act effectively. This is not the case. The principles presented here are ones that can be used to promote best outcomes for all. Society, by turns, appears titillated and disgusted by squalor. The media attention that squalor has attracted signifies this clearly. Its airtime is disproportionate to its impact; the morality of the programming is often that of the freak show, an activity described by the Disability Social History Group as 'the pornography of disability' (www.disabilityhistory.org/). The growth of the voice of those affected by living in squalor is an immensely important development. It is only by working with people who live in squalor themselves and understanding their experiences, that we will build truly enduring solutions.

References

A & E Networks (2010). *Hoarders: the Complete Season One.* (DVD). Screaming Flea Productions, Inc.

Abrams, R. C., Lachs, M., McAvay, G., Keohane, D. J. and Bruce, M. L. (2002). Predictors of self-neglect in community-dwelling elders. *American Journal of Psychiatry,* **159**, 1724–30.

Ageing, Disability and Home Care website (2012). www.haccohs.adhc.nsw.gov.au/common_risk_areas/domestic_squalor [Accessed 9 April 2012]

Al-Adwani, A. and Nabi, W. (2001). Coexisting Diogenes and Capgras syndrome. *International Journal of Psychiatry in Clinical Practice,* **5**, 75–6.

Allen, C. (2004). Opening the closed door: strategies for coping with animal hoarders. *Animal Sheltering.* July/Aug 2004. The Humane Society of the United States. pp. 15–27.

Almeida, O. P. and Almeida, S. A. (1999). Short versions of the Geriatric Depression Scale: a study of their validity for the diagnosis of a major depressive episode according to ICD-10 and DSM-IV. *International Journal of Geriatric Psychiatry,* **14**, 858–65.

Alper, L. S. (1993). The child–pet bond. In Goldberg, A. (ed.), *The Widening Scope of Self Psychology: Progress in Self Psychology.* Hillsdale, NJ: The Analytic Press, pp. 257–70.

American Psychiatric Association (2000). *Diagnostic and Statistical Manual of Mental Disorders, Fourth Edition, Text Revision (DSM-IV-TR).* Washington, DC: American Psychiatric Press.

Anderson, D. N. and Bach-Norz, D. (1991). Limitations of guardianship. *Psychiatric Bulletin,* **15**, 574.

Anderson, S. W., Damasio, H. and Damasio, A. R. (2005). A neural basis for collecting behavior in humans. *Brain,* **128**, 201–212.

Arluke, A. (1993). Bringing animals into social scientific research. *Society and Animals,* **1**, 5–7.

Arluke, A. and Luke, C. (1997). Physical cruelty toward animals in Massachusetts, 1975–1996. *Society and Animals,* **5**, 195–204.

Ballard, J. (2010). Legal implications regarding self-neglecting community dwelling adults: a practical approach for the community nurse in Ireland. *Public Health Nursing,* **27**, 181–7.

Barocka, A., Seehuber, D. and Schone, D. (2004). Messy house syndrome. *MMW Fortschritte der Medizin,* **146**, 36–9.

BBC Press Office (2007). Fiona Bruce to take over Antiques Road Show [Press release] www.bbc.co.uk/pressoffice/pressreleases/stories/2007/06_june/22/bruce.shtml [Accessed 9 April 2012]

Beauchamp, T. L. and Childress, J. F. (2009). *Principles of Biomedical Ethics.* New York: Oxford University Press.

Beauchet, O., Imler, D., Cadet, L. *et al.* (2002). Diogenes syndrome in the elderly:clinical form of a frontal dysfunction? Four case reports. *Revue de Medicine Interne*, **23**, 122–31.

Berry, C., Patronek, G. and Lockwood, R. (2005). Long-term outcomes in animal hoarding cases. *Animal Law*, **11**, 167–94.

Bratiotis, C., Schmalisch, C. S. and Steketee, G. (2011). *The Hoarding Handbook*. Oxford: Oxford University Press.

Brown, S-E. (2004). The human–animal bond and self psychology: toward a new understanding. *Society and Animals*, **12**, 67–86.

Brown, S. E. and Katcher, A. H. (2001). Pet attachment and dissociation. *Society & Animals Journal of Human–Animal Studies*, **9**, 25–41.

Burns, A., Lawlor, B. and Craig, S. (2004). *Assessment Scales in Old Age Psychiatry*, 2nd edn. London: Martin Dunitz.

Byrne, P. (2003). Psychiatry and the media. *Advances in Psychiatric Treatment*, **9**, 135–43.

Carney, T. and Beaupert, F. (2008). Mental health tribunals: rights drowning in 'unchartered' health waters? *Australian Human Rights Review*, **3**, 181–208.

Castrodale, L., Bellay, Y. M., Brown, C. M. *et al.* (2010). General public health considerations for responding to animal hoarding cases. *Journal of Environmental Health*, **72**, 14–18.

Chakraborty, V., Cherian, A. V., Math, S. B. *et al.* (2012). Clinically significant hoarding in OCD: results from an Indian study. *Comprehensive Psychiatry*. In press.

Chan, S. M. S., Leung, P. Y. V. and Chiu, F. K. H. (2007). Late-onset Diogenes syndrome in Chinese – an elderly case series in Hong Kong. *Neuropsychiatric Disease and Treatment*, **3**, 589–96.

Chiu, S. N., Chong, H. C. and Lau S. P. F. (2003). Exploratory study of hoarding behaviour in Hong Kong. *Hong Kong Journal of Psychiatry*, **13**, 23–30.

Clark, A. N. G., Mankikar, G. D. and Gray, I. (1975). Diogenes Syndrome: a clinical study of gross neglect in old age. *Lancet*, **1**, 366–8.

Cohen, L., Angladette, L., Benoit, N., and Pierrot-Deseilligny, C. (1999). A man who borrowed cars. *Lancet*, **353** (9146), 34.

Cohen, A. S., Brown, L. A. and Minor, K. S. (2010). The psychiatric symptomatology of deficit schizophrenia: a meta-analysis. *Schizophrenia Research*, **118**, 122–7.

Cole, A. J., Gillett, T. P. and Fairbairn, A. (1992). A case of senile self-neglect in a married couple: 'Diogenes à deux'? *International Journal of Geriatric Psychiatry*, **7**, 839–41.

Collis, G. M. and McNicholas, J. (1998). A theoretical basis for health benefits of pet ownership; attachment versus psychological support. In C. C. Wilson and D. C. Turner (eds), *Companion Animals in Human Health*. Thousand Oaks, CA: Sage Publications, pp. 105–22.

Cooney, C. and Hamid, W. (1995). Review: Diogenes syndrome. *Age and Ageing*, **24**, 451–3.

Cooney, L. M., Kennedy, G. J., Hawkins, K. A. and Hurme, S. B. (2004) Who can stay at home? Assessing the capacity to choose to live in the community. *Archives of Internal Medicine*, **164**, 357–60.

Cooper, J. (1970). The Leyton obsessional inventory. *Psychological Medicine*, **1**, 48–64.

Cybulska, E. (1986). Gross self-neglect in old age. *British Journal of Hospital Medicine*, July, 21–5.

Cybulska, E. (1998). Senile squalor: Plyushkin's not Diogenes' syndrome. *Psychiatric Bulletin*, **22**, 319–20.

Damecour, C. L. and Charron, M. (1998). Hoarding: a symptom, not a syndrome. *Journal of Clinical Psychiatry*, **59** (5), 267–72.

Darzins, P., Molloy, D. W. and Strang, D. (2000). *Who Can Decide? The Six Step Capacity Assessment Process.* Adelaide: Memory Australia Press, Alzheimer's Association (SA) Inc.

De Berardis, D., Camapanella, D., Gambi, F. *et al.* (2005). Insight and alexithymia in adult outpatients with obsessive–compulsive disorder. *European Archives of Psychiatry and Clinical Neuroscience*, **255**, 350–8.

Department of Primary Industries (2012). Responsible Pet Ownership Program, www.pets.info.vic.gov.au/02/scp_whypet.htm [Accessed 9 April 2012]

Dong, X., Simon, M. A. and Evans, D. A. (2011). Prevalence of self-neglect across gender, race, and socioeconomic status: findings from the Chicago Health and Aging Project. *Gerontology.* Online, December 21.

Dong, X., Simon, M. A., Wilson, R. S. *et al.* (2010). Decline in cognitive function and risk of elder self-neglect: findings from the Chicago Health Aging Project. *Journal of the American Geriatrics Society*, **58**, 2292–9.

Drummond, L. M., Turner, J. and Reid, S. (1997). Diogenes' syndrome – a load of old rubbish? *Irish Journal of Psychological Medicine*, **14**, 99–102.

Drummond, L. M., Hameed, A. K. and Ion, R. (2011). Physical complications of severe enduring obsessive–compulsive disorder. *World Psychiatry*, **10**, 154.

Ekman, P. and Friesen, W. (1976) *Pictures of Facial Affect.* Palo Alto, CA: Consulting Psychologists Press.

Erskine, H. W. (1953). *Out of This World.* New York: Putnam.

Esposito, D., Rouillon, F. and Limosin, F. (2003). Diogenes syndrome in a pair of siblings. *Canadian Journal of Psychiatry*, **48**, 571–72.

Evans, D. W., Leckman, J. F., Carter, A. *et al.* (1997). Ritual, habit, and perfectionism: the prevalence and development of compulsive-like behavior in normal young children. *Child Development*, **68** (1), 58–68.

Fish, D. G. (2008). Collyer hoarding cases: mental health, fire, health, team needed. *New York Law Journal*, 31/12/08, 3.

Flores, P. J. (2004). *Addiction as an Attachment Disorder.* Lanham, MD:Jason Aronson.

Foa, E. B., Huppert, J. D., Leiberg, S. *et al.* (2002). The obsessive–compulsive inventory. *Psychological Assessment*, **14**, 485–96.

Folstein, M. F., Folstein, S. E. and McHugh, P. R. (1975). 'Mini-mental state': a practical method of grading the cognitive state of patients for the clinician. *Journal of Psychiatric Research*, **12**, 189–98.

Fond, G., Jollant, F. and Abbar, M. (2011). The need to consider mood disorders, and especially chronic mania, in cases of Diogenes syndrome (squalor syndrome). *International Psychogeriatrics*, **23**, 505–7.

Forster, D. P. and Tiplady, P. (1980). Doctors and compulsory procedures: S 47 of the National Assistance Act 1947. *British Medical Journal, i*, 739.

Frost, R. O. and Gross, R. C. (1993). The hoarding of possessions. *Behavior Research and Therapy*, **31**, 367–81.

Frost, R. O. and Hartl, T. L. (1996). A cognitive-behavioral model of compulsive hoarding. *Behaviour Research and Therapy*, **34**(4), 341–50.

Frost, R. O. and Steketee, G. (2010) *Stuff. Compulsive Hoarding and the Meaning of Things.* Boston: Houghton Mifflin Harcourt.

Frost, R. O., Steketee, G., and Williams, L. (2000). Hoarding: a community health problem. *Health & Social Care in the Community*, **8** (4), 229–34.

Frost, R. O., Steketee, G. and Grisham, J. (2004). Measurement of compulsive hoarding: saving inventory-revised. *Behavior Research and Therapy*, **42** (10), 1163–82.

Frost, R. O., Steketee, G., Tolin, D. F. and Renaud, S. (2008). Development and validation of the Clutter Image Rating. *Journal of Psychopathology*, **30**, 193–203.

Frost, R. O., Tolin, D. F., Steketee, G., Fitch, K. E. and Selbo-Bruns, A. (2009). Excessive acquisition in hoarding. *Journal of Anxiety Disorders*, **23** (5), 632–9.

Frost, R. O., Patronek, G. and Rosenfield, E. (2011a). A comparison of object and animal hoarding. *Depression and Anxiety*, **28**, 885–91.

Frost, R. O., Steketee, G. and Tolin, D. F. (2011b). Comorbidity in hoarding disorder. *Depression and Anxiety*, **28** (10), 876–84.

Fry, D. R. (2000). Non-senile squalor. *Journal of the Royal Society of Medicine*, **93**, 107.

Fullana, M. A., Vilagut, G., Rojas-Farreras, S. *et al.* (2010). Obsessive–compulsive symptom dimensions in the general population: results from an epidemiological study in six European countries. *Journal of Affective Disorders*, **124** (3), 291–9.

Gannon, M. and O'Boyle, J. (1992). Diogenes syndrome. *Irish Medical Journal*, **85**, 124.

Gaston, R. L., Kiran-Imran, F., Hassiem, F. and Vaughan, J. (2009). Hoarding behavior: building up the 'R factor'. *Advances in Psychiatric Treatment*, **15**, 344–53.

Gibbons, S., Lauder, W. and Ludwick, R. (2006). Self-neglect: a proposed new NANDA diagnosis. *International Journal of Nursing Terminologies and Classifications*, **17**, 10–18.

Goodman, W. K., Price, L. H., Rasmussen, S. A. *et al.* (1989). The Yale–Brown Obsessive Compulsive Scale. 1. Development, use, and reliability. *Archives of General Psychiatry*, **46**, 1006–11.

Granick, R. and Zeman, F. D. (1960). The aged recluse – an exploratory study with particular reference to community responsibility. *Journal of Chronic Diseases*, **12**, 639–53.

Greaves, D. A. (1991). Can compulsory removal ever be justified for adults who are mentally competent? *Journal of Medical Ethics*, **17**, 189–94.

Gregory, C. A. and Hodges, J. R. (1993). Dementia of frontal type and the focal lobar atrophies. *International Review of Psychiatry*, **5**, 397–406.

Greve, K. W., Curtis, K. L., Bianchini, K. J. and Collins, B. T. (2004). Personality disorder masquerading as dementia: a case of apparent Diogenes syndrome. *International Journal of Geriatric Psychiatry*, **19**, 701–5.

Grisham, J. R. and Barlow, D. H. (2005). Compulsive hoarding: current research and theory. *Journal of Psychopathology and Behavioral Assessment*, **27**, 45–52.

Grisham, J. R., Frost, R. O., Steketee, G., Kim, H. J. and Hood, S. (2006). Age of onset of compulsive hoarding. *Journal of Anxiety Disorders*, **20** (5), 675–86.

Hahm, D. S., Kang, Y., Cheong, S. S. and Na, D. L. (2001). A compulsive collecting behavior following an A-com aneurysmal rupture. *Neurology*, **56**, 398–400.

Halliday, G. and Snowdon, J. (2009). The Environmental Cleanliness and Clutter Scale (ECCS). *International Psychogeriatrics*, **21**, 1041–50.

Halliday, G., Banerjee, S., Philpot, M. and Macdonald, A. (2000). Community study of people who live in squalor. *Lancet*, **355**, 882–6.

Halliday, G., Snowdon, J. and Simpson, B. (2005). Diogenes syndrome in a pair of siblings. *Canadian Journal of Psychiatry*, **50**, 567.

Hamilton, M. (1967). Development of a rating scale for primary depressive illness. *British Journal of Social and Clinical Psychology*, **6**, 278–96.

Handy, G. (1994). Handling animal collectors, Part 1: interventions that work. *Shelter Sense*. The Humane Society of the United States.

Herrán, A. and Vázquez-Barquero, J. L. (1999). Treatment of Diogenes Syndrome with risperidone. *Aging, Neuropsychology, and Cognition*, **6**, 96–8.

Hoarding of Animals Research Consortium (2000). People who hoard animals. *Psychiatric Times*, **17**, 25–9.

Hoarding of Animals Research Consortium (2002). Health implications of animal hoarding. *Health and Social Work*, **27**, 125–32.

Hoarding of Animals Research Consortium (2004). Report of a forum on 3 April 3 2004, Boston. Originally obtained from the HARC website. (See Patronek *et al.* (2006) below.)

Hoarding of Animals Research Consortium (2011). Website. www.tufts.edu/vet/hoarding/ [Accessed 9 April 2012]

Hobson, S. J. (1998). The ethics of compulsory removal under Section 47 of the National Assistance Act 1948. *Journal of Medical Ethics*, **24**, 38–43.

Hodgson, R. J. and Rachman, S. (1977). Obsessional–compulsive complaints. *Behavior Research and Therapy*, **15**, 389–95.

Homma, A., Ishii, T. and Niina, R. (1994). Relationship of behavioral complications and severity of dementia in Japanese elderly persons. *Alzheimer Disease and Associated Disorders*, **8** (Supplement 3), 46–53.

Hope, B. (1997). Half of the world lives in 'medieval' squalor. *British Medical Journal*, **315**, 208.

Hwang, J. P., Yang, C. H., Tsai, S. J. and Liu, K. M. (1997). Behavioural disturbances in psychiatric inpatients with dementia of the Alzheimer's type in Taiwan. *International Journal of Geriatric Psychiatry*, **12** (9), 902–6.

Hwang, J.-P., Tsai, S.-J., Yang, C.-H., Liu, K.-M. and Lirng, J.-F. (1998). Hoarding behavior in dementia. A preliminary report. *American Journal of Geriatric Psychiatry*, **6**, 285–9.

Iervolino, A. C., Perroud, N., Fullana, M. A. *et al.* (2009). Prevalence and heritability of compulsive hoarding: a twin study. *American Journal of Psychiatry*, **166** (10), 1156–61.

Illawarra Good Living Conditions Working Group (2009). *Good Living Conditions Protocol*. Wollongong: Uniting Care Ageing.

Institute for Challenging Disorganization (2011). *Clutter Hoarding Scale*. Downloadable from www.challengingdisorganization.org/node/58 [accessed April 2012].

International Code Council (2009). *2009 International Property Maintenance Code*. Washington, DC: International Code Council. Cited in Bratiotis *et al.* (2011).

Jackson, G. A. (1997). Diogenes syndrome – how should we manage it? *Journal of Mental Health*, **6**, 113–16.

Jasper, J. M. and Nelkin, D. (1992).*The Animal Rights Crusade: The Growth of a Moral Protest*. New York: The Free Press.

Jolley, D. and Read, K. (2009). Diogenes syndrome. *International Journal of Geriatric Psychiatry*, **24**, 778–9.

Jurgens, A. (2000). Refuse hoarding syndrome. *Psychiatrische Praxis*, **27**, 42–6.

Kafetz, K. and Cox, M. (1982). Alcohol excess and the senile squalor syndrome. *Journal of the American Geriatrics Society*, **30**, 706.

Kahn, R. L., Goldfarb, A., Pollack, M. and Gerber, I. E. (1960). Brief objective measures for the determination of mental status in the aged. *American Journal of Psychiatry*, **117**, 326–8.

Kaladjian, A., Jeanningros, R., Azorin, J.-M., Anton, J.-L. and Mazzola-Pomietto, P. (2011). Impulsivity and neural correlates of response inhibition in schizophrenia. *Psychological Medicine*, **41**, 291–9.

Kelly, P. A., Dyer, C. B., Pavlik, V., Doody, R. and Jogerst, G. (2008). Exploring self-neglect in older adults: preliminary findings of the self-neglect severity scale and next steps. *Journal of the American Geriatrics Society*, **56**, S253–S260

Kertesz, A., Nadkarni, N., Davidson, W. and Thomas, A. W. (2000). The frontal behavioural inventory in the differential diagnosis of frontotemporal dementia. *Journal of the International Neuropsychological Society*, **6**, 460–8.

Kim, H. J., Steketee, G. and Frost, R. O. (2001). Hoarding by elderly people. *Health and Social Work*, **26** (3), 176–84.

Klosterkötter, J. and Peters, U. H. (1985). Diogenes syndrome. *Fortschritte der Neurologie-Psychiatrie*, **53**, 427–34.

Kohut, H. (1971). *The Analysis of the Self.* New York: International Universities Press.

Kuehn, B. M. (2002). Animal hoarding: a public health problem veterinarians can take a lead role in solving. *Journal of the American Veterinary Medical Association*, **221** (8), 1087–9.

Laërtius (1925) [1972]. *Diogones. [Lives of eminent philosophers].* Volume 2. Translated by Robert Drew Hicks (Loeb Classical Library ed.). Cambridge, MA: Harvard University Press.

Lauder, W., Anderson, I. and Barclay, A. (2005). A framework for good practice in interagency interventions with cases of self-neglect. *Journal of Psychiatric and Mental Health Nursing*, **12**, 192–8.

Lauder, W., Roxburgh, M., Harris, J. and Law, J. (2009). Developing self-neglect theory: analysis of related and atypical cases of people identified as self-neglecting. *Journal of Psychiatric and Mental Health Nursing*, **16**, 447–54.

Lawton, M. P. and Brody, E. M. (1969). Assessment of older people: self maintaining and instrumental activities of daily living. *The Gerontologist*, **9**, 179–86.

Lebert, F. (2005). Diogenes syndrome: a clinical presentation of fronto-temporal dementia or not? *International Journal of Geriatric Psychiatry*, **20**, 1203–4.

Lewandowski, K. E., Cohen, B. M. and Öngur, D. (2011). Evolution of neuropsychological dysfunction during the course of schizophrenia and bipolar disorder. *Psychological Medicine*, **41**, 235–41.

Macmillan, D. (1957). Psychiatric aspects of social breakdown in the elderly. *Royal Society of Health Journal*, **77**, 830–6.

Macmillan, D. (1969). Features of senile breakdown. *Geriatrics*, **24**, 109–18.

Macmillan, D. and Shaw, P. (1966). Senile breakdown in standards of personal and environmental cleanliness. *British Medical Journal*, **2**, 1032–7.

Maier, T. (2004). On phenomenology and classification of hoarding: a review. *Acta Psychiatrica Scandinavica*, **110**, 323–37.

Marcos, M. and Gómez-Pellín. (2008). A tale of a misnamed eponym: Diogenes syndrome. *International Journal of Geriatric Psychiatry*, **23**, 990–1.

Marx, M. S. and Cohen-Mansfield, J. (2003). Hoarding behavior in the elderly: a comparison between community-dwelling persons and nursing home residents. *International Psychogeriatrics*, **15** (3), 289–306.

Mataix-Cols, D., Frost, R. O., Pertusa, A. *et al.* (2010). Hoarding disorder: a new diagnosis for DSM-V? *Depression & Anxiety*, **27** (6), 556–72.

Mataix-Cols, D., Pertusa, A. and Snowdon, J. (2011). Neuropsychological and neural correlates of hoarding: a practice friendly review. *Journal of Clinical Psychology*, **67** (5), 467–76.

Matsunaga, H., Kiriike, N., Matsui, T. *et al.* (2002). Obsessive–compulsive disorder with poor insight. *Comprehensive Psychiatry*, **43**, 150–7.

Mayne, A. J. C. (1982). *Fever, Squalor and Vice. Sanitation and Social Policy in Victorian Sydney.* St Lucia: University of Queensland Press.

McDermott, S. (2008). The devil is in the details: self-neglect in Australia. *Journal of Elder Abuse and Neglect*, **20**, 231–50.

McDermott, S. and Gleeson, R. (2009). *Evaluation of the Severe Domestic Squalor Project: Final Report.* Sydney: Social Policy Research Centre, University of New South Wales.

Mendez, M. F. and Shapira, J. S. (2008). The spectrum of recurrent thoughts and behaviors in frontotemporal dementia. *CNS Spectrums*, **13** (3), 202–8.

Monfort, J. C., Hugonot-Diener, L., Devouche, E., Wong, C. and Péan, I. (2010). Diogenes's syndrome: an observatory study in a Paris district. *Psychologie et Neuropsychiatrie du Vieillissement*, **8**, 141–53.

Mueller, A., Mitchell, J. E., Crosby, R. D., Glaesmer, H. and de Zwaan, M. (2009). The prevalence of compulsive hoarding and its association with compulsive buying in a German population-based sample. *Behaviour Research and Therapy*, **47** (8), 705–9.

Murray, B. and Jacoby, R. (2002). The interface between old age psychiatry and the law. *Advances in Psychiatric Treatment*, **8**, 271–8

Naik, A., Pickens, S., Burnett, J., Lai, J. M. and Dyer, C. B. (2006). Assessing capacity in the setting of self-neglect: development of a novel screening tool for decision-making capacity. *Journal of Elder Abuse & Neglect*, **18**, 79–91.

Naik, A. D., Teal, C. R., Pavlik, V. N., Dyer, C. B. and McCullough, L. B. (2008). Conceptual challenges and practical approaches to screening capacity for self-care and protection in vulnerable older adults. *Journal of the American Geriatrics Society*, **56**, S266–S270.

Nair P. and Mayberry, J. F. (1995). The compulsory removal of elderly people in England and Wales under section 47 of the National Assistance Act and its 1951 Amendment: a survey of its implementation in England and Wales in 1988 and 1989. *Age & Ageing*, **24**, 180–4.

Nakaaki, S., Murata, Y., Sato, J. *et al.* (2007). Impairment of decision-making cognition in a case of frontotemporal lobar degeneration (FTLD) presenting with pathologic gambling and hoarding as the initial symptoms. *Cognitive and Behavioral Neurology*, **20** (2), 121–5.

Nathanson, J. N. (2009). Animal hoarding: slipping into the darkness of comorbid animal and self-neglect. *Journal of Elder Abuse and Neglect.* **21** (4), 307–24.

National Center on Elder Abuse (2006). www.ncea.aoa.gov [Accessed 9 April 2012] Cited in Dong *et al.* (2010).

Nordsletten, A. E. and Mataix-Cols, D. (2012). Hoarding versus collecting. Where does pathology diverge from play? *Clinical Psychological Review*, **32**, 165–76.

Orrell, M. W., Sahakian, B. J. and Bergmann, K. (1989). Self-neglect and frontal lobe dysfunction. *British Journal of Psychiatry*, **155**, 101–5.

Overall, J. E. and Gorham, D. R. (1962). The Brief Psychiatric Rating Scale. *Psychological Reports*, **10**, 799–812.

Patronek, G. J. (1999). Hoarding of animals: an under recognized public health problem in a difficult to study population. *Public Health Reports*, **114**, 82–7.

Patronek, G. J. and Nathanson, J. N. (2009). A theoretical perspective to inform assessment and treatment strategies for animal hoarders. *Clinical Psychology Review*, **29** (3), 274–81.

Patronek, G. J., Loar, L. and Nathanson, J. N. (2006). Animal hoarding: structuring interdisciplinary responses to help people, animals, and communities at risk. Report issued by the Hoarding of Animals Research Consortium (HARC), and formerly available on their website www.tufts.edu/vet/hoarding.

Pavlou, M. P. and Lachs, M. S. (2006). Could self-neglect in older adults be a geriatric syndrome? *Journal of the American Geriatrics Society*, **54**, 831–42.

Paxton, M. K. (2011). *The Secret Lives of Hoarders*. New York: Perigee (Penguin).

Pearce, S. M. (1998). *Collecting in Contemporary Practice*. London: SAGE Publications.

Pelletier, R. and Pollett, G. (2000). *Task Force on Senile Squalor: Final Report*. London, Ontario: Middlesex-London Health Unit.

Pertusa, A., Fullana, M. A., Singh, S., Alonso, P., Menchon, J. M. (2008). Compulsive hoarding: OCD symptom, distinct clinical syndrome, or both? *American Journal of Psychiatry*, **165** (10), 1289–98.

Pertusa, A., Frost, R. O. and Mataix-Cols, D. (2010a). When hoarding is a symptom of OCD: a case series and implications for DSM-V. *Behaviour Research and Therapy*, **48** (10), 1012–20.

Pertusa, A., Frost, R. O., Fullana, M. A. *et al.* (2010b). Refining the diagnostic boundaries of compulsive hoarding: a critical review. *Clinical Psychology Review*, **30** (4), 371–86.

Phillips, K. A., Stein, D. J., Rauch, S. L. *et al.* (2010). Should an obsessive–compulsive spectrum grouping of disorders be included in DSM-V? *Depression and Anxiety*, **27** (6), 528–55.

Post, F. (1982). Functional disorders: description, incidence and recognition. In F. Post and R. Levy (eds), *The Psychiatry of Later Life*. Oxford: Blackwell, pp. 180–1.

Rachman, S., Elliott, C. M., Shafran, R. and Radomsky, A. S. (2009). Separating hoarding from OCD. *Behaviour Research and Therapy*, **47** (6), 520–2.

Radomsky, A. S. and Rachman, S. (2004). Symmetry, ordering and arranging compulsive behavior. *Behaviour Research and Therapy*, **42**, 893–913.

Rasmussen J. L., Steketee, G. S., Tolin, D. F., Frost, R. O. and Brown, T. A. (2012, submitted). Assessing squalor in hoarding: the Home Environment Index.

Rathbone-McCuan, E. and Bricker-Jenkins, M. (1992). A general framework for elder self-neglect. In E. Rathbone-McCuan and D. R. Fabian (eds), *Self-Neglecting Elders: A Clinical Dilemma*. Westport, CT: Auburn House.

Reifler, B. V. (1996). Diogenes syndrome: of omelettes and soufflés. *Journal of the American Geriatrics Society*, **44**, 1484–5.

Reinisch A. I. (2008). Understanding the human aspects of animal hoarding. *Canadian Veterinary Journal. December*; **49** (12): 1211–14.

Reinisch, A. I. (2009). Characteristics of six recent animal hoarding cases in Manitoba. *Canadian Veterinary Journal*. **50**, 1069–73.

Roe, P. F. (1977). Self-neglect. *Age and Ageing*, **6**, 192–4.

Royall, D. R. (2001) The FAB: a frontal assessment battery at the bedside. *Neurology*, **57**, 565.

Royall, D. R., Mahurin, R. K. and Gray, K. F. (1992). Bedside assessment of executive cognitive impairment: the Executive Interview. *Journal of the American Geriatrics Society*, **40**, 1221–6.

Ryan, C. J. (2011). One flu over the cuckoo's nest: comparing legislated coervice treatment for mental illness and other illness. *Journal of Bioethical Inquiry*, **8**, 87–93.

Samios, K. (1996). *Into the Loathsome Den: the Characteristics of Persons Living in Squalor. Unpublished dissertation.* Sydney: Royal Australian and New Zealand College of Psychiatrists.

Samuels, J. F., Bienvenu, O. J., Grados, M. A. *et al.* (2008). Prevalence and correlates of hoarding behavior in a community-based sample. *Behaviour Research and Therapy,* **46** (7), 836–44.

Sardar, Z. and Van Loon, B. (2010). *Introducing Media Studies.* London: Icon Books.

Saxena, S. (2008). Recent advances in compulsive hoarding. *Current Psychiatry Reports,* **10** (4), 297–303.

Saxena, S. and Maidment, K. M. (2004). Treatment of compulsive hoarding. *Journal of Clinical Psychology,* **60**, 1143–54.

Saxena, S., Brody, A. L., Maidment, K. M. and Baxter, L. R. Jr. (2007). Paroxetine treatment of compulsive hoarding. *Journal of Psychiatric Research,* **41**, 481–7.

Schillerstrom, J. E., Salazar, R., Regwan, H., Bonugli, R. J. and Royall, D. R. (2009). Executive function in self-neglecting adult protective services referrals compared with elder psychiatric outpatients. *American Journal of Geriatric Psychiatry,* **17**, 907–10.

Searight, H. R. (2007) When does the observer become observed? The Maysles meet the Beales. *PsycCRITIQUES,* **52**, 1554–0138.

Sebit, M. B., Acuda, W. and Chibanda, D. (1996). A case of the frontal lobe syndrome following head injury in Harare, Zimbabwe. *Central African Journal of Medicine,* **42**, 51–3.

Segal, D. L., Qualls, S. H. and Smyer, M. A. (2011) *Aging and Mental Health.* Chichester: Wiley Blackwell.

Serpell, J. A. (2002). Anthropomorphism and anthropomorphic selection: beyond the 'cute response'. *Society and Animals,* **10** (4), 437–54.

Shah, A. (1990). Senile squalor syndrome: what to expect and how to treat it. *Geriatric Medicine,* **20**, 10–26.

Shah, A. K. (1992). Senile squalor syndrome: a small case series. *Care of the Elderly,* **4**, 299–300.

Shaw, P. (1957). The evidence of social breakdown in the elderly. *Journal of the Royal Society for the Promotion of Health: Royal Society of Health Journal.* **77**, 823–30.

Sherry, D. (1990). Autonomy versus beneficence: the dilemma and its implications in home care. *Home Healthcare Nurse,* **8**, 13–15.

Simpson, J. A. (1999). Attachment theory in modern evolutionary perspective. In J. Cassidy and P. R. Shaver (eds), *Handbook of Attachment Theory. Research and Clinical Applications.* New York: Guilford Press, pp. 115–40.

Sitwell, E. (1958). *English Eccentrics.* London: Dennis Dobson.

Slatter, M. M., (2009). 'Too much of a good thing': changing legal responses to hoarding. In H. J. Ahrens, C. von Bar, G. Fischer and A. Spickhoff (eds), *Medizin und Haftung.* Berlin: Springer, pp. 597–613.

Snowdon, J. (1980). A comparison of written and postbox forms of the Leyton Obsessional Inventory. *Psychological Medicine,* **10**, 165–70.

Snowdon, J. (1987). Uncleanliness among persons seen by community health workers. *Hospital and Community Psychiatry,* **38**, 491–4.

Snowdon, J. and Halliday, G. (2009). How and when to intervene in cases of severe domestic squalor. *International Psychogeriatrics,* **21**, 996–1002.

Snowdon, J. and Halliday G. (2011). A study of severe domestic squalor: 173 cases referred to an old age psychiatry service. *International Psychogeriatrics*, **23**, 308–14.

Snowdon, J., Shah, A. and Halliday, G. (2007). Severe domestic squalor: a review. *International Psychogeriatrics*, **19**, 37–51.

Snowdon, J., Pertusa, A. and Mataix-Cols, D. (2012). On hoarding and squalor: a few considerations for DSM-5. *Depression and Anxiety*, **29**, 417–24.

Snyder, J. M. (2009). Animal hoarding: a multi-disciplinary approach. RSPCA Australia Scientific Seminar.

Solanto, M. V. (2000a). The predominantly inattentive subtype of attention-deficit/hyperactivity disorder. *CNS Spectrum*, **5**, 45–51.

Solanto, M. V. (2000b). Clinical psychopharmacology of AD/HD: implications for animal models. *Neuroscience & Biobehavioral Reviews*, **24**, 27–30.

Sprengelmeyer, R., Young, W., Pundt, I. *et al.* (1997). Disgust implicated in obsessive–compulsive disorder. *Proceedings of the Royal Society of London*, **264**, 1767–73.

Steketee, G. and Frost, R. (2003). Compulsive hoarding: current status of the research. *Clinical Psychology Review*, **23** (7), 905–27.

Steketee, G. and Frost, R. O. (2007a). *Treatment of Compulsive Hoarding*. New York: Oxford University Press.

Steketee, G. and Frost, R. O. (2007b). *Compulsive Hoarding and Acquiring: Workbook*. Oxford: Oxford University Press.

Steketee, G. and Frost, R. O. (2007c) *Treatments that Work: Compulsive Hoarding and Acquiring. Therapist Guide*. New York. Oxford University Press.

Steketee, G., Frost, R. and Kim, H. (2001). Hoarding by elderly people. *Health & Social Work*, **26**, 176–84.

Steketee, G., Frost, R. O. and Kyrios, M. (2003) Beliefs about possessions among compulsive hoarders. *Cognitive Therapy and Research*, **27**, 467–79.

Steketee, G., Frost, R. O., Tolin, D. F., Rasmussen, J. and Brown, T. A. (2010). Waitlist controlled trial of cognitive behavior therapy for hoarding disorder. *Depression and Anxiety*, **27** (5), 476–84.

Steketee, G., Gibson, A., Frost, R. O. *et al.* (2011). Characteristics and antecedents of people who hoard animals: an exploratory comparative interview study. *Review of General Psychology*, May 16: advance online publication.

Storey, J. E., Rowland, J. T., Conforti, D. A. and Dickson H. G. (2004). The Rowland Universal Dementia Assessment Scale (RUDAS): a multicultural cognitive assessment scale. *International Psychogeriatiatrics*, **16**, 13–31.

Strang, D. G., Molloy, D. W. and Harrison, C. (1998). Capacity to choose place of residence: autonomy vs beneficence. *Journal of Palliative Care*, **14**, 25–9.

Thomas, N. (1997). Hoarding: eccentricity or pathology: when to intervene? *Journal of Gerontological Social Work*, **29**, 45–56.

Thordarson, D. S., Radomsky, A. S., Rachman, S. *et al.* (2004). The Vancouver Obsessive Compulsive Inventory (VOCI). *Behaviour Research and Therapy*, **42**, 1289–314.

Tolin, D. F. and Villavicencio, A. (2011) Inattention, but not OCD, predicts the core features of hoarding disorder. *Behaviour Research and Therapy*, **49** (2),120–5.

Tolin, D. F., Frost, R. O. and Steketee, G. (2007). *Buried in Treasures*. New York: Oxford University Press.

Tolin, D. F., Frost, R. O., Steketee, G., Gray, K. D. and Fitch, K. E. (2008). The economic and social burden of compulsive hoarding. *Psychiatry Research*, **160** (2), 200–11.

Tolin, D. F., Fitch, K. E., Frost, R. O. and Steketee, G. (2010a). Family informants' perceptions of insight in compulsive hoarding. *Cognitive Therapy and Research*, **34** (1), 69–81.

Tolin, D. F., Frost, R. and Steketee, G. (2010b). A brief interview for assessing compulsive hoarding: the Hoarding Rating Scale Interview. *Psychiatry Research*, **178**, 147–52

Tolin, D. F., Meunier, S. A., Frost, R. O. and Steketee, G. (2011). Hoarding among patients seeking treatment for anxiety disorders. *Journal of Anxiety Disorders*, **25** (1), 43–8.

Trindade, F., Cane, P. and Lunney, M. (2007). *The Law of Torts in Australia*, 4th edn. Oxford University Press, pp. 167–93.

Ungvari, G. S. and Hantz, P. M. (1991). Social breakdown in the elderly, I. Case studies and management. *Comprehensive Psychiatry*, **32**, 440–4.

Urdang, L. (1991). *The Oxford Thesaurus*. Oxford: Clarendon Press.

Valente, S. M. (2009). The hoarding syndrome: screening and treatment. *Home Healthcare Nurse*, **27**, 432–40.

Volle, E., Beato, R., Levy, R. and Dubois, B. (2002). Forced collectionism after orbito-frontal damage. *Neurology*, **58**, 488–90.

Vostanis, P. and Dean, C. (1992). Self-neglect in adult life. *British Journal of Psychiatry*, **161**, 265–7.

Wallace. C. J., Liberman, R. P., Tauber, R. and Wallace, J. (2000). The independent living skills survey: a comprehensive measure of the community functioning of severely and persistently mentally ill individuals. *Schizophrenia Bulletin*, **26**, 631–58.

Weiss, K. J. (2010). Hoarding, hermitage and the law: why we love the Collyer brothers. *Journal of the American Academy of Psychiatry and Law*, **38**, 251–7.

Whitehead, T. (1975). Diogenes syndrome. *Lancet*, **1**, 627–8.

Williams, H., Clarke, R., Fashola, Y. and Holt, G. (1998). Diogenes' syndrome in patients with intellectual disability: 'a rose by any other name'? *Journal of Intellectual Disability Research*, **42**, 316–20.

Wilson, E. O. (1984). *Biophilia Hypothesis*. Cambridge, MA: Harvard University Press.

Winsberg, M. E., Cassic, K. S. and Koran, L. M. (1999). Hoarding in obsessive–compulsive disorder: a report of 20 cases. *Journal of Clinical Psychiatry*, **60** (9), 591–7.

Worth, D. and Beck, A. M. (1981). Multiple ownership of animals in New York City. *Transactions & Studies of the College of Physicians of Philadelphia*, **3**, 280–300.

Wrigley, M. and Cooney, C. (1992). Diogenes syndrome – an Irish series. *Irish Journal of Psychological Medicine*, **9**, 37–41.

Wustmann, T. and Brieger, P. (2005). A study of persons living in neglect, filth and squalor or who have a tendency to hoard. *Gesundheitswesen*, **67**, 361–8.

Appendix A: ENVIRONMENTAL CLEANLINESS AND CLUTTER SCALE*

PAGE 1 (of 5)

DEMOGRAPHIC DETAILS

MRN	

(This sheet may be removed if it is desirable to de-identify the client when communicating with other agencies)

NAME OF CLIENT	SURNAME			OTHER NAMES		
Date of birth ***and/or*** **approx age of client**						
Sex ***(please circle)***	MALE			FEMALE		
Marital Status ***(please circle)***	SINGLE	MARRIED/ DEFACTO	WIDOWED	DIVORCED	SEPARATED	UNABLE TO DETERMINE
Address						
Does he/she live alone? ***(please circle)***	YES			NO		
If not, who with?						
Number and type of pets						
Home ownership	OWNER	TENANT-private	TENANT-DOH	OTHER- non-owner (lodger)		
Accommodation type	HOUSE	UNIT	BEDSIT	OTHER (specify)		
How long has he/she been living like this? ***(please circle)***	LESS THAN 1 YEAR	1-3 YEARS	4-10 YEARS	OVER 10 YEARS		
Known medical illnesses and/or disabilities						
Mental disorders now or in the past						

* *Developed by Graeme Halliday and John Snowdon,* EMAIL: jsnowdon@mail.usyd.edu.au

This scale is based on the version devised by Snowdon (1986) which mostly used items listed by Macmillan and Shaw (1966). Accessibility, food and vermin items, together with some descriptions used by Samios (1996) in her adaptation of the scale, have been included.

ENVIRONMENTAL CLEANLINESS AND CLUTTER SCALE

To rate cleanliness of clients' accommodation

PAGE 2 (of 5)

Raters should circle the box or number that best fits their observations in relation to the different items. These descriptions are meant to be indicative but raters may decide between one category and another based on aspects not mentioned in the boxes.

Rater: .... Rater's phone no: .... Date: ..../......../.........

A. ACCESSIBILITY (clutter):

0	1	2	3
EASY TO ENTER AND MOVE ABOUT DWELLING.	SOMEWHAT IMPAIRED access but can get into all rooms.	MODERATELY IMPAIRED access. Difficult or impossible to get into one or two rooms or areas.	SEVERELY IMPAIRED access e.g. obstructed front door. Unable to reach most or all areas in the dwelling.
0–29%	30 to 59%	60 to 89%	90 to 100%
of floor-space inaccessible for use or walking across			

B. ACCUMULATION OF REFUSE or GARBAGE

In general, is there evidence of excessive accumulation of garbage or refuse e.g. food waste, packaging, plastic wrapping, discarded containers (tins, bottles, cartons, bags) or other unwanted material?

0	1	2	3
NONE	A LITTLE Bins overflowing and/or up to 10 emptied containers scattered around.	MODERATE Garbage and refuse littered throughout dwelling. Accumulated bags, boxes and/or piles of garbage that should have been disposed of.	A LOT Garbage and food waste piled knee-high in kitchen and elsewhere. Clearly no recent attempt to remove refuse and garbage

C. ACCUMULATION OF ITEMS OF LITTLE OBVIOUS VALUE:

In general, is there evidence of accumulation of items that most people would consider are useless or should be thrown away?

0	1	2	3
NONE	SOME ACCUMULATION: but collected items are organised in some way and do not much impede movement or prevent cleaning or access to furniture and appliances.	MODERATE EXCESSIVE ACCUMULATION: Items cover furniture in most areas, and have accumulated throughout the dwelling so that it would be very difficult to keep clean.	MARKEDLY EXCESSIVE ACCUMULATION: Items piled at least waist-high in all or most areas. Cleaning would be virtually impossible: most furniture and appliances are inaccessible.

PLEASE INDICATE TYPES OF ITEMS THAT HAVE BEEN ACCUMULATED:

☐ Newspapers, pamphlets, etc. ☐ Clothing ☐ Other items (what?...)

☐ Electrical appliances ☐ Plastic bags full of items (If known, what items? ....)

D. CLEANLINESS of floors and carpets (excluding toilet and bathroom):

0	1	2	3
ACCEPTABLY CLEAN IN ALL ROOMS.	MILDLY DIRTY Floors and carpets look as if not cleaned or swept for days. Scattered rubbish.	VERY DIRTY Floors and carpets very dirty and look as if not cleaned for months. *Rate 1 if only one room or small area affected.*	EXCEEDINGLY FILTHY With rubbish or dirt throughout dwelling. *Excrement usually merits a 3 score.*

E.	CLEANLINESS of walls and visible furniture surfaces and window-sills:			
	0	1	2	3
	ACCEPTABLY CLEAN IN ALL ROOMS.	MILDLY DIRTY Dusty or dirty surfaces. Dirt comes off walls on damp rag or finger.	VERY DIRTY Grime or dirt on walls. Cobwebs and other signs of neglect. Greasy, messy, wet and/or grubby furniture.	EXCEEDINGLY FILTHY Walls, furniture, surfaces are so dirty (e.g. with faeces or urine) that rater wouldn't want to touch them.

F.	BATHROOM and TOILET:			
	0	1	2	3
	REASONABLY CLEAN	MILDLY DIRTY Untidy, uncleaned, grubby floor, basin, toilet, walls, etc. Toilet may be unflushed.	MODERATELY DIRTY Large areas of floor, basin, shower/bath, are dirty, with scattered rubbish, hair, cigarette ends, etc. Faeces and/or urine on outside of toilet bowl.	VERY DIRTY Rubbish and/or excrement on floor and in bath or shower and/or basin. Uncleaned for months or years. Toilet may be blocked and bowl full of excreta.

G.	KITCHEN AND FOOD:			
	0	1	2	3
	CLEAN HYGIENIC	SOMEWHAT DIRTY AND UNHYGIENIC Cooktop, sink untidy and surfaces dirty, maybe with some spilt food. Refuse mainly in garbage bin. Food that could go off (e.g. meat, remains of meal) left uncovered and out of fridge. *Rate 1 if no food but fridge dirty.*	MODERATELY DIRTY AND UNHYGIENIC Oven, sink, surfaces, floor are dirty, with piles of unwashed crockery and utensils etc. Bins overflowing. Some rotten or mouldy food. Fridge unclean.	VERY DIRTY AND UNHYGIENIC Sink, cook-top, insides of all cupboards filthy. Large amount of refuse and garbage over surfaces and floor. Much of the food is putrid, covered with mould and/or rotten, and unsafe to eat. *Rate 3 if maggots seen.*

H.	ODOUR:			
	0	1	2	3
	NIL/PLEASANT	UNPLEASANT e.g. urine smell, unaired.	MODERATELY MALODOROUS Bad but rater can stay in room.	UNBEARABLY MALODOROUS Rater has to leave room very soon because of smell.

I.	VERMIN (***Please circle***: rats, mice, cockroaches, flies, fleas, other):			
	0	1	2	3
	NONE	A FEW (e.g. cockroaches)	MODERATE Visible evidence of vermin in moderate numbers e.g. droppings and chewed newspapers.	INFESTATION Alive and/or dead in large numbers.

J.	SLEEPING AREA:			
	0	1	2	3
	REASONABLY CLEAN AND TIDY.	MILDLY UNCLEAN Untidy. Bed unmade. Sheets unwashed for weeks.	MODERATELY DIRTY Bed sheets unclean and stained, e.g. with faeces or urine. Clothes and/or rubbish over surrounding floor areas.	VERY DIRTY Mattress or sleeping surface unclean or damaged. Either no sheets or (if present) extremely dirty bedding/linen. Surrounding area filthy.

Add up circled numbers to provide a TOTAL SCORE: ☐

DO YOU THINK THIS PERSON IS LIVING IN SQUALOR? (circle one)	NO	YES, mild *Not clutter*	YES, moderate *Not clutter*	YES, severe *Not clutter*
	Clutter (lots), *not squalor*	Yes, mild *+ clutter (lots)*	Yes, moderate *+ clutter (lots)*	Yes, severe *+ clutter (lots)*

SUPPLEMENTARY QUESTIONS (to add to description but not to score) :

Comments or description to clarify/amplify/justify or expand upon above ratings:

PERSONAL CLEANLINESS Describe the clothing worn by the occupant and their general appearance:			
0	1	2	3
CLEAN AND NEAT. Well cared for.	UNTIDY, crumpled. One or two dirty marks and in need of a wash.	MODERATELY DIRTY, with unpleasant odour. Stained clothing.	VERY DIRTY, stained, torn clothes, malodorous.

ACTIVITIES AFFECTED BY CLUTTER/ACCUMULATION

(Please circle the appropriate number for the 8 activities)

	Easily accessible	Accessible but with some difficulty	Access much restricted	Access impossible
KITCHEN:				
1. Use of refrigerator	0	1	2	3
2. Use of stove/cooker	0	1	2	3
3. Use of kitchen sink and adjacent surfaces	0	1	2	3
Average of 1–3 (i.e. total of the three scores divided by 3)				
TOILET/BATHROOM:				
4. Use of toilet	0	1	2	3
5. Use of bath/shower	0	1	2	3
6. Use of bathroom sink	0	1	2	3
Average of 4–6 (i.e. total of the three scores divided by 3)				
BEDROOM:				
7. Bed accessible for sleeping?	0	1	2*	3
LIVING ROOM:				
8. Can seats be reached and sat on?	0	1	2*	3

*Scores of 2 given if the bed/seat can be reached (with difficulty) and can then be cleared of clutter enough to use it for lying/sitting.

Continuation...SUPPLEMENTARY QUESTIONS (to add to description but not to score):

Is there running water in the dwelling ?	YES *or* NO ?
Is electricity connected and working?	YES *or* NO ?
Can the dwelling be locked up and made secure?	YES *or* NO ?

MAINTENANCE, UPKEEP, STRUCTURE

This rates the state of repair and upkeep by owner/landlord. If the accommodation was cleaned up as much as possible, to what extent would the dwelling require painting, refurbishment, structural repairs, etc before it would be reasonably habitable?

0	1	2	3
NONE	A LITTLE Minor repairs and some painting.	A FAIR AMOUNT Some structural repairs plus painting.	LOTS Major structural repairs required, and then painting.

TO WHAT EXTENT DO THE LIVING CONDITIONS MAKE THE DWELLING UNSAFE OR UNHEALTHY FOR VISITORS OR OCCUPANT(S)?

0	1	2	3
NOT AT ALL	POSSIBLE RISK of injury e.g. by falling.	CONSIDERABLE RISK of fire, injury or health problem.	VERY UNSAFE The dwelling is so cluttered and unhealthy that people should not enter it, (except if specialists with appropriate clothing and equipment) and/or there is a high fire risk.

Appendix B: A relative's appeal for guidance

By B. P.

After my wife and I cleaned up her brother's boarding house room for the fourth time, we realised that not only did he have problems, but we did as well. I do not propose to address my brother-in-law's (BIL's) problems here. Nor will I address the multitude of hoarding/squalor issues that beset various other individuals that have emerged among family and friends once we started openly discussing the problem. But I do want to highlight the problems that my wife and I had.

You should not be surprised to know that we were traumatised by the initial experience four years ago. Not even BIL's request to order a rubbish skip and bring a wheelbarrow could have prepared us. But the trauma became angst as we found great difficulty in finding accessible and appropriate advice, guidance and support.

I need to emphasise generally why I think advice, guidance and support for family and friends is so important. It is because this is how you might avoid some of the hoarding/squalor crisis. This is how you might avoid expensive government and NGO intervention at a later stage when the situation may have become intractable. And so this is how it may be possible to empower family and friends to help the susceptible individual early in the piece.

The advice, guidance and support for 'carers' that I hope can one day become a reality needs to cover a range of issues. These should include: recognising the problem; identifying what might lead to successful and ongoing intervention; the mechanics of such intervention; advice about persuading a family member with a hoarding, squalor or similar problem to seek professional help; how to persuade other family members to acknowledge there is a problem and to assist; how to find relevant information and support relating to their local area.

I recognise that well intentioned but misguided family intervention can be disastrous. I am aware of an instance of siblings threatening each other with legal action should one sister attempt to interfere with their parent's living conditions. I understand that many living in squalor may do so through personal choice, of a sort. We saw the distress on BIL's face as we carried away yet another load of soggy putrefying newspapers intermingled with decaying food, loose change, unused birthday and Christmas presents, official correspondence and doubtless items of substantial personal value. But if the alternative is for example eviction, the clean-up is the less worse option. For him and others of his ilk any intervention will be disturbing.

But even more disturbing will be the way forward. We have announced to BIL that we will never again be available for clean-up duties. And that we will instead assist him to learn to manage his rubbish, food and recycling; that we will agree mutually, via a written contract, on the measures necessary; that we will assist him to seek professional counselling; that we will, through the wider family, monitor his progress; that he will have a goal such as inviting his mother over for a cup of tea. But we have reached this point only by extensive enquiries and by fortuitous contact with a number of experts in this field who have kindly made time to provide advice. Which is all very gratifying but is hardly the ideal way to disseminate guidance to the world at large.

Finally, I do remain concerned about the preliminary diagnosis of any underlying condition. Assuming that the nature of any intervention will be dependent on that diagnosis, it would seem self-evident that diagnosis should ideally precede that intervention. That would obviously require the full cooperation of the individual, which may not be forthcoming. Even should there be cooperation, how accessible is appropriate professional help to such individuals? This will be our next voyage of discovery. Will BIL continue to cooperate now that the crisis has passed? Can BIL, on a pension and paying substantial rent, find a local primary care physician who bulk-bills? Will the primary care physician see the need to give BIL a referral and will the primary care physician be aware of an appropriate specialist for this condition? Will the specialist visits be fully covered by Medicare? Presumably any counselling is better than none, or will the wrong treatment exacerbate BIL's condition?

I want to finish by returning to our own personal trauma. Health professionals who deal with hoarding and squalor on a routine basis presumably have appropriate training and access to counselling if necessary. Family and friends willing to commit themselves to assisting an individual needing help have no such advantage. Guidance and advice to family and friends therefore needs to spell out clearly what to expect, and to indicate where direct intervention by professionals is the preferred course of action instead. And how to access action from those professionals.

Index

Note: page numbers in *italics* refer to figures and tables, those in **bold** refer to boxes and those with suffix 'n' refer to footnotes. Plate numbers are given where appropriate.